Praise for *Smashing the Tablets*

"*Smashing the Tablets* unscrolls the ancient into a congregation of brilliant, strange, and necessary voices. A glorious reminder of how marvelously undead the bible is—after all."

— Sabrina Orah Mark, author of *Happily: A Personal History—with Fairy Tales*

"Filled with smart, funny, transgressive, thoughtful essays and stories by many of my very favorite Jewish writers, *Smashing the Tablets* is the best kind of anthology—the one you hold dear, pass around, and read again and again."

— Lauren Grodstein, author of *We Must Not Think of Ourselves: A Novel*

"*Smashing the Tablets* is irreverent and rowdy, furious and funny, inventive and learned. It reminds us that the old texts don't have to be read in the old ways—and, indeed, that revisiting them can help us see the present through new eyes."

— Lily Meyer, author of *Short War*

"This book is the kind of art we need in this moment: radical, imaginative, and most of all unafraid. Shattering a thing can be an act of faith: we make space for that thing to reform. *Smashing the Tablets* teaches us this lesson twenty-four times, in twenty-four ways."

— Shelly Oria, editor of *I Know What's Best for You: Stories on Reproductive Freedom*

Smashing the Tablets

SUNY SERIES IN CONTEMPORARY JEWISH LITERATURE AND CULTURE

EZRA CAPPELL, EDITOR

Dan Shiffman, *College Bound:*
The Pursuit of Education in Jewish American Literature, 1896–1944

Eric J. Sundquist, editor, *Writing in Witness: A Holocaust Reader*

Noam Pines, *The Infrahuman: Animality in Modern Jewish Literature*

Oded Nir, *Signatures of Struggle:*
The Figuration of Collectivity in Israeli Fiction

Zohar Weiman-Kelman, *Queer Expectations:*
A Genealogy of Jewish Women's Poetry

Richard J. Fein, translator, *The Full Pomegranate: Poems of Avrom Sutzkever*

Victoria Aarons and Holli Levitsky, editors,
New Directions in Jewish American and
Holocaust Literatures: Reading and Teaching

Jennifer Cazenave, *An Archive of the Catastrophe:*
The Unused Footage of Claude Lanzmann's Shoah

Ruthie Abeliovich, *Possessed Voices:*
Aural Remains from Modernist Hebrew Theater

Victoria Nesfield and Philip Smith, editors,
The Struggle for Understanding: Elie Wiesel's Literary Works

Ezra Cappell and Jessica Lang, editors,
Off the Derech: Leaving Orthodox Judaism

Nancy E. Berg and Naomi B. Sokoloff, editors,
Since 1948: Israeli Literature in the Making

Patrick Chura, *Michael Gold: The People's Writer*

Nahma Sandrow, *Yiddish Plays for Reading and Performance*

Alisha Kaplan and Tobi Aaron Kahn, *Qorbanot*

Sara R. Horowitz, Amira Bojadzija-Dan, and Julia Creet, editors
Shadows in the City of Light: Images of Paris in
Postwar French Jewish Writing

Alana Szobel, *Flesh of My Flesh: Sexual Violence in Modern Hebrew Literature*

Ranen Omer Sherman, *Amos Oz: The Legacy of a Writer in Israel and Beyond*

Adi Mahalel, *The Radical Isaac: I. L. Peretz and the Rise of Jewish Socialism*

Marla Brettschneider, *Jewcy*

Smashing the Tablets
Radical Retellings of the Hebrew Bible

Edited by

Sara Lippmann and Seth Rogoff

AN IMPRINT OF STATE UNIVERSITY OF NEW YORK PRESS
www.sunypress.edu

Photo credit: Shutterstock.

Published by State University of New York Press, Albany

© 2025 State University of New York

All rights reserved

Printed in the United States of America

No part of this book may be used or reproduced in any manner whatsoever without written permission. No part of this book may be stored in a retrieval system or transmitted in any form or by any means including electronic, electrostatic, magnetic tape, mechanical, photocopying, recording, or otherwise without the prior permission in writing of the publisher.

Links to third-party websites are provided as a convenience and for informational purposes only. They do not constitute an endorsement or an approval of any of the products, services, or opinions of the organization, companies, or individuals. SUNY Press bears no responsibility for the accuracy, legality, or content of a URL, the external website, or for that of subsequent websites.

EU GPSR Authorised Representative:
Logos Europe, 9 rue Nicolas Poussin, 17000, La Rochelle, France
contact@logoseurope.eu

Excelsior Editions is an imprint of State University of New York Press

For information, contact State University of New York Press, Albany, NY
www.sunypress.edu

Library of Congress Cataloging-in-Publication Data

Names: Lippmann, Sara, editor. | Rogoff, Seth, 1976– editor. | Auslander,
Shalom, writer of preface.
Title: Smashing the tablets : radical retellings of the Hebrew Bible / edited by
Sara Lippmann, Seth Rogoff.
Description: Albany : State University of New York Press, [2025] | Series:
Excelsior editions | Includes bibliographical references and index.
Identifiers: LCCN 2024027043 | ISBN 9798855801170 (pbk. : alk. paper) | ISBN
9798855801163 (ebook)
Subjects: LCSH: Bible. Old Testament—Criticism, interpretation, etc. | American
literature—Jewish authors. | Judaism and literature—United States. | Jews—United
States—Intellectual life. | Jews in literature.
Classification: LCC BS1171.3 .S56 2025 | DDC 221.6—dc23/eng/20240924
LC record available at https://lccn.loc.gov/2024027043

Ein Glaube wie ein Fallbeil, so schwer, so leicht.

—Franz Kafka, *Die Zürauer Aphorismen*

A faith like an ax, so heavy, so light. A belief like an ax, so difficult, so easy. A faith like a guillotine, so heavy, so easy. A belief like a guillotine, so hard, so light. A faith like a blade, as severe, as mild. A faith like . . .

Contents

Acknowledgments	00
Foreword: You Suck and Other Stories *Shalom Auslander*	00
Introduction *Seth Rogoff and Sara Lippmann*	1
1. Lilith in God's Hands *Courtney Sender*	21
2. Look at Her Xyxs, Her Brxght, Brxght Xyxs *Rosebud Ben-Oni*	27
3. Cain and Abel *Seth Rogoff*	43
4. Cain *Ariana Reines*	49
5. Are You Still Alive *Michael Zapata*	51
6. Ess and O *Anna Solomon*	61

7. Lot's Daughters   67
Zeeva Bukai

8. Binding Variations   77
Daniel Torday

9. Bilhah and Zilpah Made Me Yearn for Torah   83
erica riddick

10. A Little East of Jordan   91
Moriel Rothman-Zecher

11. The Story of Dinah   95
Sarah Blake

12. Plagues   103
Madeline Cash

13. Mount Sinai and Me   105
Aaron Hamburger

14. Make It Mean Something   113
Elisa Albert

15. Upon the Hills with Jephthah's Daughter   121
Erika Dreifus

16. How David Leaves   127
Temim Fruchter

17. Once a Witch   133
Matthue Roth

18. Isaiah and Power   145
Aviya Kushner

19. The Job Book   155
Steve Almond

20. Root 171
Ilana Masad

21. Bauhaus City 181
Omer Friedlander

22. Haman 189
Max Gross

23. Scroll of Stars 213
Michael David Lukas

Contributors 221

Acknowledgments

The following pieces were originally published as follows:

"Lilith in God's Hands," by Courtney Sender. First published in *Shenandoah*. Reprinted from *In Other Lifetimes All I've Lost Comes Back to Me: Stories* (Morgantown: West Virginia University Press). Copyright © 2023 by Courtney Sender. Used by permission of West Virginia University Press.

"Plagues," by Madeline Cash. First published in *Electric Literature*. Reprinted from *Earth Angel* (Clash Books). Copyright © 2023 by Madeline Cash. All rights reserved.

An early, shorter version of "Lot's Daughters," by Zeeva Bukai. First published as a flash fiction, "Reaching Ground," in *Pithead Chapel*. Copyright © 2022 by Zeeva Bukai. All rights reserved.

"Reading Isaiah as My Grandfather's Granddaughter" from *Wolf Lamb Bomb*. Copyright © 2021 by Aviya Kushner. Reprinted by permission of Orison Books. All rights reserved.

"Cain and Abel" from *The Castle*. Copyright © 2024 by Seth Rogoff. Reprinted by permission of Fiction Collective Two and University of Alabama Press. All rights reserved.

Foreword

You Suck and Other Stories

SHALOM AUSLANDER

Myths that are believed in tend to become true.

—George Orwell

1. The Very Good God

CHAPTER ONE

"In the beginning, God."

Genesis 1:1.

The first character we meet in stories tends to be the protagonist of the story, the hero, the character we readers are meant to most closely connect with, the character through whom we experience the story and whom we most wish to succeed.

And so, behold, our protagonist:

God.

The teller of *The Very Good God* doesn't include much in the way of physical description, but God seems like a decent fellow. He possesses many of the character traits we readers admire in a protagonist: he's powerful, successful, loves nature and appreciates beauty. He is sensitive, creative, something of an artist; we can imagine him in his studio, canvases stacked against the walls, sketches for the Aurora Borealis on his drafting table, the sculptor bent over his painstakingly crafted work and literally breathing life into his creations. He doesn't just "save a cat," as Hollywood executives demand all heroes do, he *creates* one. If we stop reading now and ask the class who this story is about, who is the hero, even the poorest grade-school student will confidently answer, "God."

Chapter Two: The Set-Up

Our story's time and place.

    Ext. Eden—Day.

    A paradise, unspoiled.

    It's beautiful.

    It's peaceful.

    "This is good," says God, wiping his hands on his paint-stained smock. "This is very good."

    A chill runs down our spines.

    We humans, as literary scholar Jonathan Gottschall points out, are "the storytelling animal"—we think in story, we remember in story, we learn by story—and so, storied since birth, we know this tranquility cannot last. The moment any protagonist declares all is well, the shit hits the fan. Every time.

    So we know a storm is coming. Trouble's a brewin'. Someone is going to ruin it all.

    "And so God created mankind."

    Genesis 1:27.

    Enter the antagonist.

    Man.

    The villain. The troublemaker. The Bad Guy. And right on cue, Genesis 3:6, the sneaky bastard steals from our hero God.

    Boo, we think. *Hiss.*

    So far, narratively speaking, so good. Everything is tracking as it should. We have a hero. We have a villain. We keep turning the pages.

Chapter Three

Here, narratively speaking, the story begins to go awry. Sure, Adam and Eve stole God's apple, but they are mostly powerless, literally naked, weak, and confused—not the most troublesome of antagonists—and the character we know as the protagonist turns out to be a psycho. He not only places a disproportionate amount of importance on apples, but he exhibits more than a few of the symptoms of classic borderline personality disorder. He is cruel in the extreme, so cruel that even his most ardent fanboys never claim he isn't, they simply claim we can't understand why he is, or, for the truly Stockholmed, that his cruelness is really kindness.

Enraged, our hero overreacts, has a fit, throws Adam and Eve out of Paradise and places flaming angels at the gates to keep them from returning.

"I will not contend with mankind forever!" he bellows.

All that's missing is "Fee-fi-fo-fum."

It's confusing. This is not particularly heroic behavior, and it only gets worse. As the story progresses, he knocks down buildings, curses, threatens, condemns. By chapter 6, the crazy son of a bitch is flooding the world.

And so we, the storytelling animal, detect a storytelling problem.

Something isn't right.

Something feels off.

Stranger still, the storytellers—the rabbis, the priests, the imams—tell the story as if nothing at all was wrong.

Yay, they say about this belligerent, short-fused protagonist.

Boo, they say about the terrified naked man and woman. *Hiss*.

If we were to stop reading again, and again ask the class now who the hero of the story is, there would be a fair degree of uncertainty. The protagonist is a dick, the antagonist is powerless and afraid.

The Very Good God goes by different names—the Old Testament, the Bible, the New Testament, the Koran—but aside from some small changes, they're basically the same story: the story of stiff-necked, stubborn people, all of them sinners and fornicators, all of them failures and disappointments, and of the poor put-upon all-powerful Lord who must contend with them.

Something doesn't seem right.

Something feels off.

I have an idea what it might be, and how to fix it.

First, though, wolves:

2. The Very Good Wolf

Once upon a time, in a peaceful forest beside a gently flowing creek, there lived a wolf. The wolf was good. The wolf was wise. The wolf was perfect in every way. Everything was good and nice and good.

"This is good," said the Wolf. "This is very good."

One day, though, three pigs showed up and began building houses. Did they have permits?

No.

Permits were required for all new and existing structures; forest law was very clear on that. But the pigs, they think they're special. They are stubborn pigs. They are stiff-necked pigs. The pigs begin clearing trees, running electric, drilling for water. Pretty soon, the peaceful forest isn't so peaceful anymore. There are beeping backhoes, ferocious chainsaws, porta-potties.

"I will not contend with pigs forever," says the Wolf.

And so he blew their houses down and threw them out of the forest forever.

Fuck pigs.

The End.

3.

The Very Good Wolf, of course, was not the story our parents told us when we were young. We were told the story of *The Three Little Pigs,* in which the pigs were the heroes, and the wolf was the antagonist. And it's safe to assume that if pigs developed the power of speech and told their children bedtime stories, *The Three Little Pigs* is the version pigs would tell them.

"You are brave and resourceful, kids. Fuck wolves."

I take no sides in the pigs versus wolves debate. Frankly I'm more of a dog person. But it would be understandable that if wolves too developed the power of speech and they too told their children bedtime stories, they would tell them *The Very Good Wolf.* They would take *The Three Little Pigs* and flip the antagonist with the protagonist, we would expect them to, we would demand that they do, because what kind of terrible parent tells their children stories in which they are the villains?

A: Mine.

And I would guess, given that the Bible is still the most widely read book in the world, yours.

4.

I was taught the story of *The Very Good God* before I could read. I was taught it before I could write. Then, on the first day of third grade, Rabbi Brier called each of us up to his desk, one at a time, and handed us each our own very copy of the story.

"Torah," read the single gold-embossed word on the hard, black cover, Hebrew for "Old Testament."

But we had been hearing the stories for years, and so we knew the real title of the book: *You Suck.*

You suck for lying.

You suck for stealing.

You suck for killing.

You should be more like God, but you won't be.

Why?

Because you suck.

And I believed it. We all did. We studied it, memorized it, were tested on it, given awards for completing it. To lay all my youthful misanthropy at the feet of a single book would be unfair; my dysfunctional narcissistic parents deserve most of the credit for my nascent disdain for mankind. But having been told the story, having heard the hero God's judgment of us, I saw its confirmation everywhere. When my father struck my mother, I thought, *Of course he did.* When my rabbis struck my friends, I thought, *Of course they did.*

Fights, lies, war.

Of course, of course, of course.

Poor God, I thought.

What a terrible burden it must be to suffer us.

5. The Very Good Shark

Once upon a time, there was a very good shark. The shark lived in paradise. It was cool and blue and peaceful. One day he heard a noise. The noise got louder and louder.

"What is that terrible noise?" he wondered.

The shark went to see what the noise was. It wasn't long before he discovered the source—humans.

They were in his water, playing and splashing and ruining everything.

"Marco!" shouted one boy.

"Polo!" shouted another.

The shark swam and swam around them, hoping the humans would see his fin and leave the ocean, but they didn't. They only played louder, kicking and shouting like they owned the place. Suddenly the police chief on the beach spotted the shark.

"Get out of the water!" the police chief shouted at the terrible humans. "Get out of the water!"

The shark agreed, and hoped again they would listen.

But they didn't.

They were stubborn. They were stiff-necked.

The shark grew angry. He would not contend with Marco Polo forever. So the shark went to the human shouting "Marco," grabbed him with his razor-sharp teeth, ate him, and burped.

"Polo," said the shark.

Fuck humans.

The End.

6.

Since its premiere in 1975, *The Very Bad Shark*, better known as *Jaws*, has earned half a billion dollars at the box office.

The Very Good Shark would not have.

"I like the basic idea," I imagine Spielberg saying to his screenwriter, "but something's off. I think you've mixed the protagonist with the antagonist."

"I what?"

"You mixed the protagonist with the antagonist. You've made the villain the hero, and the hero the villain."

"What makes you think the shark is the villain?" the writer asks.

"He kills people without remorse," Spielberg says. "He tears them to bits and eats them."

"Good point," says the writer. "Any other notes?"

"That's the big one."

"Okay," the writer says. "Let me take another whack at it."

7.

I am not as bullish on the death of religion as some other secularists are. There are a hundred million Bibles printed each year. There are six billion already in print. The number of Bibles sold has more than doubled since 1950—we're now up to twenty million Bibles sold each year. If I sold that many books, I wouldn't be writing the foreword to this collection.

"Empathetic storytelling," Gottschall writes, "is among the best tools we have for overcoming prejudice. But it's also how we construct those prejudices, encode them, and pass them along."

In the story of *The Very Good God*, as recorded in *The Big Book of You Suck*, we have for thousands of years now prejudiced ourselves against ourselves. We have gathered in synagogues and churches and madrassas, day after day, year after year, century after century, singing the praises of the hero bully God while lamenting our innumerable failures and flaws. Such is the power of story, such is the influence of the protagonist on our storytelling minds, that when he proclaims that he will not contend with us forever, we do not question him. We do not condemn him. We agree with him.

"Good," we think. "Teach those motherfuckers a lesson."

The motherfuckers being us.

I was a child when I was first told *The Very Good God*, and now I have children of my own—*Once I was young and now I am old*, as the Psalmist has it—and I cannot imagine sitting them down and telling them such a hideously destructive story.

"And so God killed everyone. Fuck us. G'night, kids. Mwah."

Fifteen hundred years after Mohammed, two thousand years after Jesus, six thousand since (if you believe the book), God threw Adam and Eve out of Eden, we still suffer from the same story. We hate ourselves, and we hate one another. What a strange, destructive thing—to raise your children, to live in your mind, as the antagonist of the world. And yet that is precisely what we do, and have done, since this terrible book was written.

If Orwell is right and all art is propaganda, perhaps we should stop telling such propaganda about ourselves.

How?

Well, we can't stop *The Very Good God* being told, but we can retell it.

We can rewrite it.

We can edit it.

We can fight story with story.

FOREWORD | xix

Let's take another whack at it.

My version is called *The Very Bad God*.

The Very Bad God is the same exact story as *The Very Good God*, but with the antagonist and protagonist switched. It is the story of vulnerable human beings in a world not of their choosing, a world controlled by a ruthless son of a bitch named God who lords (interesting) over them, condemns them, hates them, punishes them for the most inscrutable of infractions.

"Cheeseburgers?!?" God bellows.

Ka-blammo.

But here's the thing—despite it all, the heroic human beings endure. They resist. They carry on. They fight back. They refuse to bend to his will, and, most importantly, they refuse to become like him. They will not kill. They will not hate. They will not be vengeful. They will be humble and understanding. Outmatched in strength, they are more than his equal in character. They are the heroes. Of course they cannot overcome him. Perhaps, in the end, he will wipe them off the face of the earth. But that will only be confirmation of his loss, and proof of their victory.

And forever more, in school and at bedtime, we will teach our children this story.

We will tell them that they should never, ever be like God. No punching, no killing, no flooding the world.

"Anyone found behaving like God," the rabbis and priests and imams will warn their students, "will be expelled."

But who among them would? Where would they get such an idea? After all, they will have been raised since their earliest days to be better people than the bastard God who so tormented their ancestors.

The Judaic concept of *tikkun olam*, of the responsibility we each have to "heal the world," is at once noble and unclear. It has been interpreted as everything from the responsibility to eradicate idolatry to the responsibility to return the spark of Divine Light to the physical world.

I humbly suggest another:

The bitter, self-hating, miserable, maniacally misanthropic stories of *You Suck* have harmed the world in ways we may never appreciate until the day they cause our species suicide, our total destruction by own despised hand, the only possible ending for such loathsome antagonists as us. And so perhaps the best way for us to truly heal the world is with another story. A better story. A story that if nothing else, doesn't tell us we suck.

That starts here, with the collection you hold in your hands.

What follows are stories that aim to rewrite, to rethink, to retell the ancient stories.

"Thou shalt not kill," says the God of the Bible.

Then he kills. And kills again. And kills again.

"Who can tell me," the teacher of these new stories will ask, "what that makes God?"

"A hypocrite," Mordechai will answer.

"Very good," the rabbi will say. "Fuck God."

The End.

Introduction

SETH ROGOFF AND SARA LIPPMANN

The Hebrew Bible is a complicated text. It encompasses twenty-four "books," beginning with the book of Genesis and ending with the book of Chronicles.[1] A precise dating of the Bible's composition is unknown, though scholars have proposed the eighth through the second centuries BCE as a general timeframe, with some positing roughly one thousand years from the first to the final acts of biblical composition.[2] The texts that were produced during these centuries were not drafted such that they remained unchangeable. The biblical texts underwent a continuous process of redaction and interpolation. Historical circumstances shaped the development of the biblical textual tradition, with perhaps the key historical fulcrum being the period of the Babylonian exile or captivity of the Jews (sixth century BCE).[3] The process of canonization of the Bible—the decisions about which texts would appear in a codified set of sacred scripture and which texts fell beyond this key line—was also long and complicated. The establishment of the canon of twenty-four books and the organization of the twenty-four books into the three categories of Torah (Instructions and Laws), Nevi'im (Prophets), and Kethuvim (Writings), as well as their order, are developments shrouded in ambiguity about which there is no historical consensus.[4]

Of course, the Hebrew Bible's reach is inestimable. Because of the scope of its influence on global history and world culture, one could assume there is nothing new left to discover, no possibility to approach the text with fresh eyes, no way to pull this ancient text into the contemporary world. The impulse to bend modernity to biblical traditions rather than contemporize them is at the heart of dogmatic orthodoxy, whose purpose is to structure daily life, social relationships, and ritual practice to the letter of the law. As a handbook for "correct behavior," the Bible, wielded by institutions of power and religious hierarchies, becomes a tool for punishment, boundaries, restrictions, and divisions. This punitive, restrictive process is often labeled "faith." In "Judaism and the Jews," Martin Buber writes, "Tradition constitutes the noblest freedom for a generation that lives it meaningfully, but it is the most miserable slavery for the habitual inheritors who merely accept it, tenaciously and complacently."[5]

Smashing the Tablets seeks to push against the habitual tenacity and complacency of enslaving tradition to engage in a process of renewing the Hebrew Bible for modern life, and, in turn, renewing modern life through biblical encounters. In this volume, contributors have taken on the challenge of wrestling with moments they have selected from the Hebrew Bible to open radical possibilities. By "radical," we don't mean extreme, and certainly not violent. The "radical" we have in mind grows from its connection to the word "root"—that which is far-reaching, essential, deeply rooted, fundamental. "Radicalism" in this sense is not the invention of something completely new but rather the discovery of the new in the old, the finding of a deeper knowledge or truth beyond the surface of things. Opportunities for radical readings of the Hebrew Bible, this volume posits, stem from the nature of the biblical text itself and our individual and collective relationships to it. "Radical reading" is a creative process. Radical readings challenge the text, destabilize it, reimagine and rearrange it. If orthodoxy demands a reshaping of the individual through adherence to the text, "radical reading" responds by positing the recreation of the text through the creative action of the reader, which, in turn, reshapes the reader through the newly constituted text.

The beginnings of the Hebrew textual tradition are narrated in the Hebrew Bible itself. This first mention of biblical writing is the recording of the divine law given by God to Moses on Mount Sinai. While the Bible begins with Genesis and the creation story and presents the tales of Adam and Eve, Noah, and the patriarchs, one might say that Hebrew monotheism as a theological and ritual system is codified in the contract Moses makes with God. One might speculate, given the singular importance of the revelations at Sinai and the centrality of the decrees issued during these events, that the narrative of this covenant would proceed in a relatively clear, direct, and unproblematic manner. It does not. The first textualization of the Bible is as confusing and complex as other parts of the biblical text, or more so. The biblical text produced at Sinai, like the text telling the story of these events, like the biblical text in general, is characterized by gaps, polysemy, relationship to context, and "inner biblical" interpretation, or one part of the Bible commenting on, reacting to, or simply set in relation to another.[6]

The production of the first draft of the first biblical document is documented in the section of the book of Exodus that finds Moses and the Israelites at Mount Sinai. The story begins in chapter 19: "On the third new moon after the Israelites had gone forth from the land of Egypt, on that very day, they entered the wilderness of Sinai."[7] The term "wilderness" is repeated three times in the opening of the chapter, the perfect geographical context for the production of text. God calls on Moses to climb the mountain. Moses climbs, and in the typical sparse narrative style of biblical storytelling, the reader is provided with no detail. What is Moses thinking as he climbs? What does he expect to find at the summit? How does he feel? The reader gets no answers. The point is not to develop Moses's character, to present a psychological or emotionally "real" or "relatable" portrait of this "hero." The point is to get Moses up the mountain as quickly as narratively possible to meet with God.

Moses makes it up the mountain. During their first encounter on Sinai, God proposes to Moses a similar covenant to the ones God made with Abraham and Noah. The basic framework of those previous deals was total faith in exchange for God's favor, God's promise to make Israel a "kingdom of priests." No written record is mentioned in the context of Moses's first meeting with God on Sinai. Like the earlier covenants, the first one between God and Moses is oral. It is made through speech. Once the covenant is made, Moses goes down the mountain and relays the details to the Israelites. The Israelites agree to God's terms—we hear no dissent, no discussion of process in the biblical narrative. The important point, narratively speaking, is the immediate and universal nature of the people's commitment to the covenant: "All the people answered as one, saying, 'All that the Lord has spoken we will do!' "[8] Having received this verbal signature, Moses climbs the mountain again to report the agreement to God. God instructs Moses to prepare the people for God's coming, as God plans to address the Israelites directly. Moses returns to the people, and the Israelites wash, abstain from sex, and prepare. The scene is dramatic—but odd. God had previously expressed an intent to address the people directly, but the biblical narrative provides no such address, resulting in an anticlimax: "On the third day, as morning dawned, there was thunder, and lightning, and a dense cloud upon the mountain, and a loud blast of the horn; and all the people who were in the camp trembled. . . . Now Mount Sinai was all in smoke, for

INTRODUCTION | 3

the Lord had come down upon it in fire; the smoke rose like the smoke of a kiln, and the whole mountain trembled violently."[9] From a perch at the top of the mountain, God calls on Moses once again, for the third time, to ascend. As before, the action is unembellished: "The Lord called Moses to the top of the mountain and Moses went up."[10] After the cosmic hype and pyrotechnics, after Moses had made his ascent, after the promise to the people and their washing and abstaining, after all this, God simply sends Moses back down again and tells him to come once more with his brother, the Levite priest Aaron. "And Moses went down to the people and spoke to them."[11] What is the purpose of this scene? Why does God have Moses come up only to send him back down? Why didn't God tell Moses to bring Aaron with him when God told him to ascend the previous time? Climbing Mount Sinai is no small task—the landscape is harsh, austere, unforgiving, especially amid God's storm, especially in ancient times without means of protecting oneself against the barren desert conditions.

It is at this point that God presents the first set of commandments, the "ten words" or commandments, the Decalogue. In the narrative flow of the text, it is hard to tell whom, exactly, God is addressing, Moses or the people as a whole. If to the people, which seems most likely, it is not clear why God delivers this speech at this time and not the previous time when they were fully prepared to receive God's presence. If the commandments are directed at Moses, it is unclear why God doesn't provide them when Moses is at the top of Sinai rather than when he has returned to the base. Immediately following the enumeration of the Decalogue:

> All the people witnessed the thunder and lightning, the blare of the horn and the mountain smoking; and when the people saw it, they fell back and stood at a distance. "You speak to us," they said to Moses, "and we will obey; but let not God speak to us, lest we die." Moses answered the people, "Be not afraid; for God has come only in order to test you, and in order that the fear of Him may be ever with you, so that you do not go astray." So the people remained at a distance, while Moses approached the thick cloud where God was.[12]

This should be a pivotal moment—and it is. Yet, we don't know whom God addresses precisely; the narrative flow indicates the Israelites, yet directly after, we learn that they fear God's speech and shrink back from the encounter.

Moses proposes that God only wants to inspire fear, but this seems directly contradicted by the enumeration of the commandments—God wants, it seems, to orally provide the divine law. Even with the commandments, it remains the oral communication that matters.

Moses approaches God while at the foot of Sinai. The Decalogue is not repeated to Moses, and instead God instructs Moses on the proper way to worship and sacrifice. As before, the communication is entirely oral, even if, by now, the covenant has expanded from one of pure faith to one of faith as manifested through adherence to the divine law. There is still no text.

At this point, God launches into an extended legal discourse, presenting Moses with a more expansive set of decrees, which go well beyond the narrow confines of the Decalogue and resemble other ancient Near Eastern legal codes. This code, however, unlike those others, is given by God, spoken directly by God, not created and proclaimed by a mere human king. In return for following this extended law, God offers decisive military assistance in the future conquest of the land—the destruction of the Amorites, Hittites, Perizzites, Canaanites, Hivites, and Jebusites. In other words, obedience to the law in exchange for a divine campaign of ethnic cleansing. The Israelites, once the conquest is complete, should sanctify the land by destroying the rival polytheistic cultures.

God has given a long list of laws. God has instructed Moses again to climb Mount Sinai. Moses reports God's words to the people and, at this moment, incredibly, produces the first text! Exodus 24:4: "Moses then wrote down all the commands of the Lord."[13] Why would he do this? A strictly oral faith, a faith based entirely on oral covenant with God is suddenly transformed into a text-based faith. What motivation does Moses have to record in written form the speech of God? More materially, how does Moses, at the foot of Sinai, make a written copy of the law? Has he carried ink, brush, and papyrus from Egypt into the wilderness, and if so, why? Does he carve the law into stone? And which law, precisely, is written—is it the long legal discourse only? Is the Decalogue, spoken earlier, included? Moses then reads the document to the people. Again, in an oral culture, it is unclear why the text needs to be written and read instead of simply recounted verbatim by Moses, as he has done in the past when reporting God's speech. Was the textualization an important constituent part of sanctifying the covenant? If so, where does this impulse come from? From Moses? From God? From the people? No answers are given—if we, the readers of the biblical narrative, want answers, we need to intervene. The biblical narrative activates us, offering each reader the role of interpreter.

INTRODUCTION | 5

Moses, in the meantime, ascends Sinai yet again, this time with Aaron, Nadab, Abihu, and seventy elders. The reader recognizes immediately that this ascent is qualitatively different from the others. This time, the reader is provided with the visual perspective of the climbers, and we see through their eyes an image of the God of Israel. Moses's companions stop short of the summit, and Moses continues toward the top. The Bible, rarely hesitating, provides the barest of detail—or, put another way, only the significant information. Here, that information is clear. This trip is about the receiving of a text: "The Lord said to Moses, 'Come up to Me on the mountain and wait there, and I will give you the stone tablets with the teachings and commandments which I have inscribed to instruct them.'"[14] Moses takes his servant Joshua and climbs. At this point, it seems like Moses's written version of the law was a draft, a contract to be signed by the people for the official, divine copy to be issued—and in proper ceremonial fashion. The ceremony—and language of the ceremony—does not disappoint:

> When Moses had ascended the mountain, the cloud covered the mountain. The Presence of the Lord abode on Mount Sinai, and the cloud hid it for six days. On the seventh day, He called to Moses from the midst of the cloud. Now the Presence of the Lord appeared in the sight of the Israelites as a consuming fire on the top of the mountain. Moses went inside the cloud and ascended the mountain, and Moses remained on the mountain forty days and forty nights.[15]

By now, we might expect Moses to simply and quickly receive the official record of the previously disclosed laws and instructions, including the Decalogue—the covenant document written this time in stone and by God and not on a papyrus scroll by the human hand of Moses. And yet, God's speech to Moses inside the cloud is different than what came before. Here, God provides a detailed discussion of the construction of the ritual tent or tabernacle and Israelite ritual in relation to it. At the conclusion to this new set of instructions, the second biblical document is created: "When He finished speaking with him [Moses] on Mount Sinai, He gave Moses the two Tablets of the Pact, stone tablets inscribed with the finger of God."[16]

God has transformed from a speaker to a writer, an author of a biblical text. The shift from oral to written communication mirrors another shift from a faith based on the previous Noahide or patriarchal covenants to a new religion based on the legalistic, ritualistic Mosaic covenant. Why does this shift happen? What necessitates it? The reader does not know. And what, precisely, is contained on the tablets? Are they an exact copy of the text Moses previously wrote down, the words consecrated by ritual sacrifice? Is the text limited to the Decalogue, as stated later in the book of Deuteronomy? Is it the record of God's instructions for the construction of the tabernacle and the related ritual practice, which God has just spoken immediately before inscribing the tablets?

The moment of the giving of the tablets is singular and deeply significant. God has written the text—God's own finger has cut the stone. Each letter is infused with God's intent, God's spirit, God's presence. Such a divine gift of written language is unprecedented in the Bible and is not repeated. Not only does the Law come from God, but the record of the Law, the Law made manifest in written language, in material form, has been manufactured by God. It would seem like this is the ultimate covenant, the most binding contract one could possibly imagine. It would seem, given the centrality of the making-manifest of the covenant or treaty between God and Israel, that this should be where the story ends, with Moses delivering God's written laws and instructions to the people to be placed in the ark at the center of the holy tabernacle, thus infusing the ark and the tabernacle with the divine spirit and grounding Israelite society on the foundation of the divine law, as written directly by God. God's text would sit at the core of the faith, its ritual center, the seed from which the full Torah—and the whole Tanakh—should grow.

There's a plot twist. Mere moments after Moses receives the tablets from God, the reader learns that all is not proceeding according to plan. Moses has been away for a long time. The Israelites, stranded at the base of the mountain without their leader and, presumably, feeling unprotected by the God with whom they had just made the covenant, are getting nervous. Imagining themselves abandoned by Moses and God, they feel vulnerable, and look for another means of divine protection. They turn to Moses's brother, the Levite priest Aaron. Aaron collects the Israelites' gold and fashions a molten calf, an idol. The people begin immediately to worship it as a god. Their ritual of worship is like a festival, a celebration. The Israelites eat, drink, and dance. God sees what is happening at the bottom of the mountain. God becomes furious and intends to destroy the

INTRODUCTION | 7

people with whom God has just made the contract. Moses intervenes and manages to quell God's anger.

Moses descends Mount Sinai with the tablets, seemingly still intent on delivering them to the people, to reconstitute God's authority as suzerain, to put an end to the idolatry. As he and Joshua approach, Joshua thinks he hears a "war cry." He's mistaken, this is no war cry, this is music, singing. It's a party. The biblical text, in its restraint, mentions "boisterousness"; Moses adds that the people "were out of control." Sexual debauchery is implied—and perhaps it is the orgiastic nature of the "boisterousness" as much as it is the idol worship that causes Moses's anger to boil over: "As soon as Moses came near the camp and saw the calf and the dancing, he became enraged; and he hurled the tablets from his hands and shattered them at the foot of the mountain."[17] The smashing of the tablets, the shattering of God's singular text, is the prelude to what could be described as an Israelite civil war. Moses and the Levites take up arms against the dissident forces and slaughter thousands to quell the rebellion. Moses and the Levites emerge triumphant. With excessive violence, order is restored, the hierarchy of Moses and the priesthood reinforced.

God summons Moses once again to ascend the mountain, this time to bring with him two stone tablets. Moses obeys, fashions the tablets, and climbs the mountain. Once he is there, God does not do what God told Moses God would do—God does not inscribe the new tablets. Nor are the verbal commandments and instructions God speaks to Moses identical to the first set of commandments and instructions, or to the second set. With each climb, with each additional encounter on the mountain, the speech—and the corresponding text—shift. There can be, it seems, no identical copy. This lack of uniformity is what fundamentally separates orality from textuality—and it could be said that the embeddedness of oral culture in its immediate temporal context presses against the rigidity of the text, infusing the text with the hidden layers of speech. At the same time, the text presses back against speech—capturing it, codifying it, detemporalizing it. Each written covenant between Moses/Israel and God shifts in response to the unfolding of the narrative. In the end, it is Moses, not God, who writes down the new covenant, who inscribes the tablets with some unknowable version of God's laws and instructions. The human author has replaced the divine author; the human text stands in place of the divine text; the human finger has overwritten the divine finger.

The purpose of Moses's new text was not, principally, to be read. There is no indication that the text was to be copied or studied. Its central purpose was to be placed in the ark, which would serve as the mobile focal point for Israelite worship and ritual practice. In a fascinating way, a text with such an incredible origin story, a text written, rewritten, and written again, a text the precise wording of which is unclear, a text both divine and mundane, a text smashed and recreated, is placed in the ark and hidden from view. It could be posited that the incredible generative force of the Hebrew Bible was at least partly the result of this primary textual void, the result of the destruction of the divine words, the replacement of divine text with human text, the result of the smashing of the tablets.

Around this largely invisible text, which was at the same time the original manifestation of biblical textualization, a corpus of texts coalesced, which eventually became the Bible. This corpus went far beyond the legal structure of the covenant document to include a wide range of writings: creation myths, patriarchal and tribal histories, flood and other miracle narratives, genealogies, dream reports, poetry and song, military legends, family stories, and so on. The process of textualizing a previously oral culture meant drawing from diverse traditions, utilizing available source materials, and embracing and innovating on preexisting textual archetypes or models.

This momentous move from orality to textuality decenters law from its position as the focal point of Hebrew culture. As we see from the Sinai story, the law becomes as much the story of the giving of the law as it is about the letter of the law, and the story of the law is the story of Moses, the receiver of the law, and the story of Moses is the story of the Israelites' liberation, the story of Egyptian slavery, and the story of Egyptian slavery is the story of Joseph and the Israelite migration, and the story of Joseph and the migration is the story of the patriarchs, and the story of the patriarchs is the story of Noah, and the story of Noah is the story of Eden, and the story of Eden spirals back to the opening words of the Torah, to God's creation of the heavens and the earth. The law was, from the first, embedded in stories. The Jewish faith, as biblically grounded, emerged with the refashioning of texts, the retelling of stories, and the merging of oral and textual cultures. Storytelling, and retelling, was not adjacent or supplemental to the development of Judaism, and it certainly was not subordinate to legality or instructions for ritual practice. Storytelling was (and remains) essential, core, foundational—radical.

Patterns emerge. In the context of this anthology, and for postbiblical literature in general, arguably the most significant characteristic of biblical narrative is the existence of narrative gaps. These gaps come in all shapes and sizes—and given the spare nature of biblical storytelling, they are numerous, seemingly infinite. They can be moments when the plot jumps or shifts, interrupting clear, straightforward narrative. They can be gaps in reason or logic. They can be gaps in dialogue. The gaps can be related to characters, their emotional or psychological states, their motivations, their biographies. These gaps have acted as invitations for narrative elaboration and interpretation for thousands of years.

It's worth noting the general level of emptiness of the biblical characters—or, rather, the striking and perplexing way that biblical characters can be both quickly and solidly etched in the reader's imagination and at the same time fuzzy, incomplete, underdetermined. Moses's trips up Mount Sinai have little in common with other famous literary moments of mountaineering, like the celebration of Renaissance selfhood in Petrarch's "The Ascent of Mount Ventoux" or Henry David Thoreau's Romantic "Ktaadn." Moses might be the most developed character in the biblical text, and yet so much about him is left out. Because of the fragmentary quality of biblical characters, the slightest narrative intrusion can shift our impression of these figures considerably, even fundamentally.

Plot. We live in plot-centric times, the age of the bourgeois novel, Hollywood cinema, and entertainment television. The biblical authors did not live in such times. There are plots in the biblical text, a surfeit of drama, but such narrative storytelling is only one of the many textual types that appear in the Bible. What truly sets the biblical text apart from other texts is its multiplicity of narrative voices, its combination of perspectives, and its assemblage of styles. Like the characters who are both spare and full, the biblical narrative is at one and the same time unitary, even hermetically (and certainly canonically) sealed and disjointed. The bible, we might say, as a "smashed" and reassembled text, shows its scars—the endless number of cracks and fissures that disrupt easy, linear reading. As one reads the biblical text, one is engaged in a formidable process of overcoming the text's fragmentation while, at the same time, working constantly to destabilize the text's overwhelming unity.

The polyvocal nature of the biblical text means that a consistent ideological position is difficult to maintain. Not only is there narrative fragmentation in the Bible, but there is also temporal fragmentation. Though

10 | Seth Rogoff and Sara Lippmann

the canonized biblical corpus certainly underwent a process of redaction, these ideological and contextual or temporal tensions were not overcome, indicating that the erasure of inconsistency, the denial of multiple chains of production and transmission, the easing of narrative tension, were not decisive for the biblical editor. Relationships between parts of the biblical narrative to other texts stretch well beyond the boundaries of the canonized Bible and into the rich oral and textual traditions of the ancient world. Biblical narrative appropriates, mirrors, reworks, debates, and rejects a vast array of sources, which put pressure on the notion of a confined Bible. What's true of all texts is especially true of the biblical narrative: it does not close into itself; it opens into realms of textual and nontextual culture. The biblical narrative is embedded, contextual.

Given these qualities, it is not surprising that the meaning of the biblical narrative has been (and is) hotly contested. Meaning presents itself in the biblical text as contingent. At the same time, the establishment of "the meaning" of the Bible is central to its status as a sacred text. This tension between the contingent nature of biblical meaning and the Bible's significance as the moral core of Abrahamic faith puts huge weight on the practice of biblical interpretation.

Interpretation of the Hebrew Bible began centuries before its codification. One part of the Bible often comments on another, either directly through retelling the same basic story or indirectly through parallelism or word play. Such textual relationships often, though by no means always, have an interpretive quality, seeking to define implicitly or explicitly other biblical passages, like the relationship between Jacob's dream of the ladder and the Tower of Babel or, more directly, Aaron's golden calf and those of Jeroboam.[18] This inner-biblical interpretation often came through storytelling, including renarrating previous scenes or modeling new stories on schematic structures that had already been developed.

The power of storytelling as a tool for elaboration and interpretation continued beyond biblical canonization—and it can be said that the boundary between that which is included in the Hebrew Bible and that which is not included was defined for centuries by its permeability. Postbiblical literature, far from recognizing or reacting to a solid, inherent "finished" or "closed" notion of the Bible, instead found much of its creative energy in the openness of biblical narratives. If figures like Abraham and Moses were incomplete, postbiblical literature could intervene with more substantial

INTRODUCTION | 11

biographies, some textualizing long-standing oral traditions, others pulling from excluded source texts, still others newly imagined.[19] Writers like Philo and Josephus seem aware of sources beyond the biblical text that speak to biblical narratives, thus justifying their departures from biblical orthodoxy and literalism.[20] These nonbiblical traditions continued the practice of biblical retelling and indicate that this retelling was a key constituent part of the Bible itself. In other words, as soon as the biblical text was closed, it was ripped open again.

Canonization, on the other hand, spurred another type of textual engagement with the biblical narrative—the practice of *midrash*. This engagement would profoundly shape the contours of biblical understanding and Jewish society and culture. Midrash, the practice of interpretive engagement with scripture, was built precisely on the relationship between the surface instability of the biblical text and a deeper notion that all possible meaning, and thus ultimate coherence, could be traced to God. Gaps in the biblical text spurred midrashic creativity. Such creative work with the biblical text took many forms, including storytelling or retelling—*midrash aggadah*. For the sages who developed the great compendia of midrashic literature, the notion that the biblical text was complete and closed would have made no sense. Jewish life, in its post-Temple, exilic context, lived through the application of the creative mind to scripture—it meant the elaboration, expansion, reconfiguration, and redefinition of the Tanakh. In the aftermath of the Temple's destruction, Hebrew religiosity was shifting from ritual, cultic, priestly practice centered at the dwelling place of God's name to a decentered, text-based, interpretive faith. The exegetical process, even when it strayed quite far from biblical literalism, was not seen by the midrashic sages or their followers as a violation of the sacred nature of scripture. Far from it. The sages believed that an "oral" Torah existed alongside and was equal to the written text, that the infusion of the text with many meanings—perhaps an infinite number of meanings—was itself the work of God.[21] The history of midrashic interpretation, the compilation of the Talmud, post-Talmudic commentary, Kabbalistic and other mystical *midrash aggadot*, and subsequent creative and interpretive work point to the incredible generative power of the biblical writings.[22] That other sacred works would grow from the Hebrew biblical corpus, namely, the Christian New Testament and the Islamic Qur'an, is not surprising. That the canonization of these texts would themselves generate rich interpretive traditions reinforces the point.

This volume seeks to capture the generative energy of the biblical text. It reflects the Bible's openness to interpretation, its wondrous acceptance of incompletion, fragmentation, and internal debate, its intertextual relations, its tensions and contradictions. These qualities feed the creative spirit, a spirit that pushes us to question, search, experiment, and to think beyond perceived limits.

At the same time as this volume seeks to honor and extend the history of *midrash aggadot* and the incredible interpretive creativity of postbiblical literature in the widest sense, it also stands in relation to another important aspect of biblical and religious history: the relationship between social, political, and cultural power and interpretive control. The politics of biblical interpretation are traceable to the biblical text and have not ceased in the many centuries since redaction and canonization. Temple structures, religious elites, rabbinical schools, judicial apparatuses, and now nation-states seek interpretive control. Structures of power endeavor to restrain the biblical text with the chains of ideology.[23] In such a context, the Bible's textual openness, which, we maintain, is the wellspring of its generative energy, is sacrificed for an increasingly reactionary joining of faith and politics.

Regimes of power seek to close what's open, to insist on strict definitions, boundaries, and categories. Such regimes of power were never absent from the tradition of biblical retelling and interpretation. The relative openness or closedness of the interpretive tradition was in constant flux. New impulses put pressure on old frameworks. Outside influences seeped into Jewish culture and thought, challenging, provoking, and catalyzing responses to scripture. For every era, scripture has been, and must be, rewritten. This doesn't mean rejecting all that came before. It means calling on scripture to respond to our current world. It means radicalizing scripture to help guide us through an increasingly dire set of challenges. The sages of antiquity understood the power of creative reading, the power of creative interpretation, and the power of narrative retelling. These acts of creative, generative reading, interpretation, and retelling bridged the space between their communities and the text. The text pulled the sages toward it; the sages pulled the text toward them. Truth exists in the liminal space between sage and text.

A touchstone image is that of the Passover seder: a night dedicated to the act of radical retelling, in which families and friends wrestle with the story of Exodus through their own perspectives, imprinting upon it fresh questions and challenges, relevancies and anecdotes. The ritual blends oral and written traditions, demanding lively participation (and pinky dipping) from all present, and even those absent, welcoming stranger and seer, ghost and ancestor into one—or two, depending—spirited, often very late nights.

The practice, at its best, is democratic. A successful seder depends on individual contribution and group involvement. It is not limited to sages. On this night we are all sages.

Text lends itself to cosplay. We are the four children: wise, selfish, simple, disengaged. Conventional wisdom tells us that the story is best relayed through numerous approaches and styles, to sate divergent ears. Again, cue the polyvocality. It's right there in the book, Exodus 13.

Celebrate difference, always question: this is what the seder teaches. Perhaps that is the only way out of the narrow place, *mitzrayim*. We contain multitudes, of course, an idea underscored through songs like *Had Gadya* (essentially an Aramaic "House that Jack Built") and "Who Knows One?" that escalate cumulatively in an almost breathless build like a glorious stack of matryoshka dolls. Both speak, like Yehuda Amichai's "Poem Without an End," to the histories, the stories, the players and structures, the signs and symbols, the layered elements that make us.

One of the aims of this project is to dismantle the monolithic hierarchy that often lays heavy-handed claim to the biblical text. The contributors to this anthology reflect the rich diversity of those who identify as Jewish. As Rabbi Carie Carter reminds her Park Slope Jewish Center congregation, the reason why the Torah is removed from the ark and carried throughout the sanctuary (before it's placed onto the pulpit to be unbelted, denuded, and read from) during services is to invite everyone to engage.

An anthology by its very nature is incomplete. We would need countless volumes to even begin to approximate comprehensive coverage. Like the canon itself, we embrace the gaps, the cracks, the shattered shards. There is beauty in disharmony, persistent possibility in an infinitely fractured landscape. What we offer is merely, and humbly, a start. Like Avivah Gottlieb Zornberg writes in the introduction to *The Beginning of Desire*, her reflections on Genesis, the collected pieces in this volume intend "to loosen the fixities, the ossifications of preconceived reads."[24]

In that spirit, *Smashing the Tablets* opens with Shalom Auslander's spirited takedown of God and the attendant didacticism co-opted by literalists. From there, we enter Rosebud Ben-Oni's ravaged, post-Edenic world of the border town "Efesito" (a blend of Hebrew and Spanish, meaning

Little Zero), where power pummels the disenfranchised. We stay for Michael Zapata's flood narrative: an elegiac recounting of a driven, idealistic entomologist and mother whose conservation efforts took her from Chicago to the Amazon in an attempt to save life from human beings, and human beings from themselves. We see how Zeeva Bukai reveals the intimate wants and independent desires of Lot's daughters trying to escape the predatory hold of their father. We experience Anna Solomon's fresh take on the fraught fertility triangle of Abraham, Sarah, and Hagar, and the inevitable power shift planted through surrogacy.

Power—who gets it, who wants it, who loses it, who enforces it—lies at the core of this collection, fueling the father-son duel over the erection and destruction of a Tel-Aviv apartment building in Omer Friedlander's clever interpretation of Kohelet and Sarah Blake's furious and unflinching retelling of Dinah.

In this volume, characters largely sidelined take up space. We center Lilith and Lot's daughters. Dinah gets her raging due. Matthue Roth grants Serah, Asher's mystical daughter, a narrative point of view. Erika Dreifus gives breath to the silenced daughter of Jepthah, whose akedah-like fate is sealed upon opening the door to her warrior father's homecoming, and memorialized in an annual pilgrimage of girls. "They would go upon the hills and mourn for Jephthah's daughter and for the life she had not lived." erica riddick traces the racist and misogynistic practice of female slavery, exposing the irony at the heart of the biblical narrative of exodus. In giving voice to the voiceless Bilhah and Zilpah, riddick amplifies her own.

Elsewhere, modernizations abound. In a tender piece, Moriel Rothman-Zecher imagines Jacob in a queer, underground nightclub wrestling his angel all night. Temim Fruchter traces the sensual, slow burn of a break-up between hopeless romantics, David and Jonathan. Steve Almond's Job arrives in the form of an avaricious former sorority girl with faint hints of Elizabeth Holmes. Max Gross stuffs Haman into the discount suit of a petty rabbi from suburban New Jersey. Madeline Cash unleashes a modern-day litany of plagues. Elisa Albert makes an idolatrous case for Instagram as our golden calf.

It feels apt, if serendipitous, that both of our featured pieces on Moses on Sinai are first-person works of creative nonfiction, with Aaron Hamburger comparing the Chutes and Ladders quality of Moses's ascent and descent to his own sliding relationship to faith, and Albert exposing a debauched addiction to social media's endless temptations. As previously noted, this story is central to the formation of and enduring identity of the Jewish people. Of course, it's personal. Without the tablets, who are we?

Themes recur. Power, it seems, is inextricable from the process of naming—who gets named, who goes unnamed, how the cementing of names lends a permanence, and hence an indelible power. Unbeknownst to each other, a number of contributors grapple with etymology, including Courtney Sender, who explores the splitting of Adam (atom) into man and woman, empowering Lilith to distinguish herself as a separate entity by adopting her own name from the lips of Eve. Dreifus and riddick excavate the erasure that befalls the unnamed.

The fraught nature and power grab endemic to translation is an added concern of Roth and Ilana Masad, who expertly unpacks the origin of names through her moving retelling of love and loyalty embodied by Ruth: Root. Blake's narrator subverts the patriarchal naming structure that dominates the canon, reclaiming it with searing crystallization: "Before all this was the man who raped her. But his name isn't worth noting. Every time you want to know his name, you should repeat Dinah's name instead. Dinah Dinah Dinah."

Standard notions of time—as objective, as chronological—are deprioritized. Daniel Torday's whimsical reimagining of the binding of Isaac entertains the nonlinearity and ongoingness of time, while Roth's investigation of King Saul's encounter with the witch of Endor positions this often-underlooked moment from the prophets through the vast expanse of biblical history. Roth writes, "Time was tiny and enormous. Time could take forever when you let it." Michael David Lukas closes out the volume by underscoring this endless impulse toward retelling, toward cocreation, the infinite desire to imprint upon text, to make palimpsest from palimpsest: "Sometimes we need to bend the stories we've been given if we want to keep ourselves from repeating the same mistakes."

What have we been given? Sexual abuse and sacrifice, violence upon violence. Procreation and decimation. Existential struggles and falterings of faith. Covenants made, covenants broken. Wanderings, enslavement. Rinse, repeat. Some selections may be graphic, lurid, nearly dreamlike in their surreality, haunting in their brutality. Despite the patriarchal lineage of the Israelites, women are the catalysts of much of the action, both repeatedly blamed and responsible for shaping and destroying the nation. This dates from the Garden of Eden, and can be traced through Sarah and Hagar, Lot's progeny, Bilhah and Zilpah, who birthed four of the twelve tribes, and on through Dinah, Jepthah's daughter, to Ruth, and Esther.

For all the unrelenting darkness, there is levity, too. Auslander and Albert tap arsenals of irony to elicit laughs. Gross and Almond deliver a pair of comedic masterpieces from Kethuvim that celebrate the fallibility of man. Misery loves comedy, after all.

There is no shortage of risk. Contributors do not shy away from the material they've inherited, the stories they've chosen. Risk takes numerous shapes: through formal invention, experimentation in language, through the scope of their interpretation. Regardless of whether they play it close or loose to the text itself, they prove radical in their retellings, every one of them.

Last, there is poetry: Ariana Reines aligns her honest vision with the cast-out Cain; Aviya Kushner mournfully turns to the lyricism of Isaiah in the wake of her grandfather's death. Fruchter's meditation on the intimacy of David and Jonathan is lush with ache: "You could imagine the man, leaving by dark of night or gray of morning, unwilling to sign the note, to knock on the door, to say goodbye."

Those who have been called to the Torah as a b'mitzvah—or ever have attended such a ceremony—may recall an awkward teen sweating through a breathless, regurgitative teaching from their assigned *parsha*, often half-written by parents, rabbis, tutors then salted with a choice line or two from Rashi, in an effort to demonstrate that they, the child—now, an adult!—are capable of extracting a cheap lesson from The Big Book before moving on to gelatinous candy tossing, and the Cha-Cha Slide. This, we are told, is a rite of passage. However uninspired, this exercise is meant to symbolize a future lifetime engagement with text. For many, the buck stops there.

What you will not find in these pages: morality plays, pat answers, easy takeaways, or any Pinterest worthy affirmations. This is no mitzvah spiel CliffsNotes. If anything, we wish to move away from the habit of harvesting for meaning. Instead, we hope this anthology stokes a curiosity toward the primary source itself: to begin, or perhaps, to return.

Notes

1. The introduction and the epigraphs throughout this volume use the English translation of the biblical texts from Adele Berlin, Marc Zvi Brettler, and

Michael Fishbane, *The Jewish Study Bible: Featuring the Jewish Publication Society Tanakh Translation* (New York: Oxford University Press, 2004).

2. Robert Alter, *The Art of Biblical Narrative* (New York: Basic Books, 2011) xiii–xiv; Avigdor Shinan and Yair Zakowitch, *From Gods to God: How the Bible Debunked, Suppressed, or Changed Ancient Myths and Legends* (Lincoln, NE: Jewish Publication Society, 2012), 1.

3. Yairah Amit, "Epoch and Genre: The Sixth Century and the Growth of Hidden Polemics," in *Judah and the Judeans in the Neo-Babylonian Period* (Winona Lake, IN: Eisenbrauns, 2003), 135–37.

4. Marc Zvi Bretttler, "The Canonization of the Bible," in *The Jewish Study Bible*, 2074–75.

5. Martin Buber, *On Judaism*, ed. Nahum Glazer (New York: Schocken, 1967), 11.

6. On scriptural polysemy and the distinction between it and indeterminacy in biblical interpretation, see David Stern, "Midrash and Indeterminacy," in *Critical Inquiry* 15, no. 1 (1988): 132–61. On the complexities of "inner-biblical interpretation" and the generative function of narrative gaps, see Shinan and Zakowitch, *From Gods to God*, 1–15.

7. Berlin, Brettler, and Fishbane, *The Jewish Study Bible*, 145.

8. Berlin, Brettler, and Fishbane, *The Jewish Study Bible*, 146.

9. Berlin, Brettler, and Fishbane, *The Jewish Study Bible*, 147.

10. Berlin, Brettler, and Fishbane, *The Jewish Study Bible*, 147.

11. Berlin, Brettler, and Fishbane, *The Jewish Study Bible*, 148.

12. Berlin, Brettler, and Fishbane, *The Jewish Study Bible*, 151.

13. Berlin, Brettler, and Fishbane, *The Jewish Study Bible*, 162.

14. Berlin, Brettler, and Fishbane, *The Jewish Study Bible*, 163.

15. Berlin, Brettler, and Fishbane, *The Jewish Study Bible*, 163.

16. Berlin, Brettler, and Fishbane, *The Jewish Study Bible*, 183.

17. Berlin, Brettler, and Fishbane, *The Jewish Study Bible*, 185.

18. On the relationship between Jacob's dream vision and the tower of Babel, see Yair Zakovitch, *Jacob: Unexpected Patriarch* (New Haven, CT: Yale University Press, 2012), 46–60; Seth Rogoff, *The Politics of the Dreamscape* (Basingstoke, UK: Palgrave Macmillan, 2021) 61–92. On the golden calf, see Moses Aberbach and Leivy Smolar, "Aaron, Jeroboam, and the Golden Calves," in *Journal of Biblical Literature* 86, no. 2 (1967): 129–40; James W. Watts "Aaron and the Golden Calf in the Rhetoric of the Pentateuch," *Journal of Biblical Literature* 130, no. 3 (2011): 417–30. For analysis of biblical scene construction, see Alter, *The Art of Biblical Narrative*, 55–78.

19. Joseph Heinemann, "The Nature of the Aggadah," translated by Marc Bregman, in *Midrash and Literature*, ed. Geoffrey H. Hartmann and Sanford Budick (New Haven, CT: Yale University Press, 1986), 46–47.

20. Annette Yoshiko Reed, "The Construction and Subversion of Patriarchal Perfection: Abraham and Exemplarity in Philo, Josephus, and the Testament of Abraham," *Journal for the Study of Judaism in the Persian, Hellenistic, and Roman Period* 40, no. 2 (2009): 185–212.

21. Heinemann, "The Nature of the Aggadah," 47–54; Daniel Boyarin, "Old Wine in New Bottles: Intertextuality and Midrash," *Poetics Today* 8, no. 3/4 (1987): 539–56.

22. Susan Handelman, *The Slayers of Moses: The Emergence of Rabbinic Interpretation in Modern Literary Theory* (Albany: State University of New York Press, 1983), 27–50. For more on "modern midrash," see David C. Jacobson, *Modern Midrash: The Retelling of Traditional Jewish Narratives by Twentieth-Century Hebrew Writers* (Albany: State University of New York Press, 2012).

23. A large number of sources analyzing the relationship between the Bible, ideology, and power could be listed here, but, for brevity's sake, we point to three books related to nationalism, sexism, and racism: Rachel Havrelock, *The Joshua Generation: Israeli Occupation and the Bible* (Princeton, NJ: Princeton University Press, 2020); Mieke Bal, *Lethal Love: Feminist Readings of Biblical Love Stories* (Bloomington: Indiana University Press, 1987); David Goldenberg, *The Curse of Ham: Race and Slavery in Early Judaism, Christianity, and Islam* (Princeton, NJ: Princeton University Press, 2003).

24. Avivah Gottlieb Zornberg, *The Beginning of Desire: Reflections on Genesis* (New York: Schocken, 1995), xii.

Bibliography

Aberbach, Moses, and Leivy Smolar. "Aaron, Jeroboam, and the Golden Calves." *Journal of Biblical Literature* 86, no. 2 (1967): 129–40.

Alter, Robert. *The Art of Biblical Narrative.* New York: Basic Books, 2011.

Amit, Yairah. "Epoch and Genre: The Sixth Century and the Growth of Hidden Polemics." In *Judah and the Judeans in the Neo-Babylonian Period,* edited by Oded Lipschits and Joseph Blenkinsopp, 135–52. Winona Lake, IN: Eisenbrauns, 2003.

Bal, Mieke. *Lethal Love: Feminist Readings of Biblical Love Stories.* Bloomington: Indiana University Press, 1987.

Berlin, Adele, Marc Zvi Brettler, and Michael Fishbane, eds. *The Jewish Study Bible: Featuring the Jewish Publication Society Tanakh Translation.* New York: Oxford University Press, 2004.

Boyarin, Daniel. "Old Wine in New Bottles: Intertextuality and Midrash." *Poetics Today* 8, no. 3/4 (1987): 539–56.

Goldenberg, David. *The Curse of Ham: Race and Slavery in Early Judaism, Christianity, and Islam*. Princeton, NJ: Princeton University Press, 2003.

Handelman, Susan A. *The Slayers of Moses: The Emergence of Rabbinic Interpretation in Modern Literary Theory*. Albany: State University of New York Press, 1983.

Havrelock, Rachel S. *The Joshua Generation: Israeli Occupation and the Bible*. Princeton, NJ: Princeton University Press, 2020.

Heinemann, Joseph. "The Nature of the Aggadah." Translated by Marc Bregman. In *Midrash and Literature*, edited by Geoffrey H. Hartmann and Sanford Budick. New Haven, CT: Yale University Press, 1986.

Jacobson, David C. *Modern Midrash: The Retelling of Traditional Jewish Narratives by Twentieth-Century Hebrew Writers*. Albany: State University of New York Press, 2012.

Reed, Annette Yoshiko. "The Construction and Subversion of Patriarchal Perfection: Abraham and Exemplarity in Philo, Josephus, and the Testament of Abraham." *Journal for the Study of Judaism in the Persian, Hellenistic, and Roman Period* 40, no. 2 (2009): 185–212.

Rogoff, Seth. *The Politics of the Dreamscape*. Basingstoke, UK: Palgrave Macmillan, 2021.

Shinan, Avigdor, Yair Zakovitch, and Valerie Zakovitch. *From Gods to God: How the Bible Debunked, Suppressed, or Changed Ancient Myths and Legends*. Lincoln, NE: Jewish Publication Society, 2012.

Stern, David. "Midrash and Indeterminacy." *Critical Inquiry* 15, no. 1 (1988): 132–61.

Watts, James W. "Aaron and the Golden Calf in the Rhetoric of the Pentateuch." *Journal of Biblical Literature* 130, no. 3 (2011): 417–30.

Zakovitch, Yair. *Jacob: Unexpected Patriarch*. New Haven, CT: Yale University Press, 2012.

Zornberg, Avivah Gottlieb. *The Beginning of Desire: Reflections on Genesis*. New York: Schocken, 1995.

1

Lilith in God's Hands

COURTNEY SENDER

And God created man in His image . . . male and female He created
them.

—Genesis 1:27

Do not pity me.

It's true my name is Lilith, known to history as the spurned first
wife of Adam. But what story is as simple as a single sentence? He was no
bargain, and let's not imagine he didn't suffer the loss of me. That woman
Eve—you think she didn't have a first love, too?

Among us all, only Adam was unlucky enough never to see his love
returned.

My poor, cruel, inelegant, lonely Adam.

So the story goes: I am Lilith, made of the same earth as Adam. Made
of half his soul. Made of mud, bone, flesh, spirit, demon, word, story, stone,
loss, longing, virtue, sin, forbearance.

Made of everything, except a rib.

The truth is, I don't remember my creation. I know only which tale
I prefer: the one where God scooped up me and Adam in his big hands,
in his right the clay that would be Adam and his left the clay that would

be me. (Or vice versa—God has no heart, so why fight to be closest to it?) He clenched his fists, our torsos in his palms, and in the cracks between his knuckles Adam and I took shape: feet hooked on one side of his pinky, chests heaving up between the second and third fingers, chins craning from under the thumb.

I remember the feeling, squeeze and relief. Like birth.

Lilith is said to hate children—but only because I know they'll have to suffer. Some of them will be Lilith, some Eve, some Adam. Beloved, besotted, bereft. I had no mother, after all. Nor did Adam, nor Eve. Maternal love is natural or it is learned; we had no chance to learn it.

When it comes to hate: I hate no more than any mother hates her reckless idiots, flirting with the souls that will undo them.

We were both Adam, at first. Adam meaning earth. Meaning man. We had identical bodies. God called us by one name, and we came.

It is history's Adam who seeded the idea for "Lilith," in the smoldering dark with his hand cupped over the rise of my hip. He sang to me, a wordless tune. It was a way of calling me, but it wasn't until later that I realized it could be my name: *La la.*

My favorite memory of Adam is there, right there, the buzz of his throat against my throat, his music thrumming in my ear. The leaves of Paradise soft beneath us both. His eyes like mine, his skin like mine, brown and rich and the same as the earth. I couldn't tell us apart sometimes, except I knew that he was singing and I must not be. *La la.*

"Who will we be when we're old?" I would say, talking idly over his song. "Will I become the one who sings to you?"

Love was different then, before choice. It was the same thing as hate. There was only one thing, and I called it that thing I feel for Adam, and he called it the same, and we had the gift of naming, and we named it love.

Of course, I didn't know that at the time. I talked myself hoarse to him. He sang me the lullabies that lovers sing—but that is only because we'd named ourselves lovers and the songs lullabies. We might have called them claws instead, and us foes. Then we'd have been foes clawing at each other, nonetheless inside the melody of an easy sleep on hallowed moonlit earth.

If I've stressed this name point strongly, it's because I am angry at God for offering the wrong kind of language. What we want are heartnouns, mindsongs, but we were given only throatnouns and mouthsongs to explain them to each other.

This is all to say that Adam and I loved each other, and I didn't know love meant a different thing to him than it did to me. I would not have asked God for a different Adam, not in a thousand thousand lifetimes. But he asked for a different Lilith.

Here there's been some misinterpretation. We speak now of rib, but the truth is breast. Both our chests once rose into the negative space of God's fist; now, Adam's went flat.

I like to think this was Adam's punishment. God could have chosen another spot of earth from which to forge this second partner, but he made Adam hurt for her instead. It is enough to make me trust God, for a moment. Then I remember:

As God was reaching into Adam, to rip him open and undo my twin's elegant body, I happened to walk into that bloody clearing with a handful of berries. In later years, I have discovered that I hate the chore of picking berries. I didn't know it then, because I was picking berries for Adam.

And there was blood, and there was God, his arm in the base of Adam's torn-out throat.

I screamed. I raced to kill God, to protect Adam, and in his fright, God pressed a finger so deep inside Adam that he pushed his organs out between his legs. To this day, the womb replicates this accident: the embryo starts off female. This was the form of humankind, before God the sculptor blundered in his shame at knowing what he was doing and being caught by Lilith.

"I'm sorry," said God, "I'm so sorry," and he placed Eve on the earth that had made me.

Her body was slick with Adam's blood. The grisly scene looked grislier because I'd crushed the red berries in my fighting fists. In lonely years since, I've wondered whether I just wanted to be created again for Adam, too.

Adam's skin was pale and glistening redly. He staggered to his feet.

"Who said you could do this?" I asked God, trying to reach him, to beat him. God backed away. He pointed.

I followed his finger, around which Adam and I had gasped our first breaths. I stared into my Adam's muddy eyes, willing him not to have requested this other wife. He looked guiltily at the ground.

Much has been written of the Garden of Eden. Let me tell you something about Paradise: it is hellish as Satan's memory, when the person you love there doesn't love you.

Now, we invented new words: passion. Apathy. Desire. Disdain.

My hateful Adam adored her from the start, with all the depth of love that he could cull from his hollow chest. He trailed her through the paths of Eden. He never sang into my ear again.

But here's where the story gets interesting:

"La la," Eve called in the middle of the night.

"Hush," I told her. I tried to take pleasure in Paradise chirping its night song. "Hush, or Adam will hear."

"La la hush," she whispered, her breath buzzing at my throat. Her mouth traced down my ribcage and paused over the contained organs that Adam had lost to disdain me and desire her. Her eyes flicked like a serpent's up to mine.

"Lilith," she mumbled, her tongue between her teeth.

Adam found out soon enough, of course. There are no doors to close in a sprawling sun-soaked garden.

He hovered silently over us and I lay awake on my back, studying him. The sheen in his eyes, I had learned, did not mean a thing. It did not mean the same thing as the sheen in mine.

When he spoke to me, his lullaby voice was pitched low: "Do you truly hate me this much, Adam?"

Eve stirred sleepily against my breast. I stroked her forearm with my thumb. "That's *your* name now," I told him, shifting my gaze to a cloud that was covering the sun, avoiding the treacherous sympathy that would make me soft when I needed to be hard. "I don't want it anymore."

"Then what should I call you?"

We'd had lovely nights together, he and I, cradled on Eden's soil. We'd had to call each other nothing, when there was no one else to call.

"Witch?" he said. "Beast? Adulterer? Talk now if you've something to say. Tell me."

Beast. I felt a painful swelling start at the base of my throat. The story goes that Adam named them, the beasts of the field—but all it means is that he named me. When he stopped wanting to sing to me, he started speaking, and his words were ugly.

"I don't want to talk," I murmured, wanting him to ask again.

He pulled Eve out from under my arm. He said, "You love talking!"

Idiot boy. What I'd loved was talking to you.

Adam sent me away from Eden, and I left. It didn't matter where; two loves lost, no place could be a paradise for me anymore.

24 | COURTNEY SENDER

Eve watched me go. She watched my hips sway as I attempted a steady gait away; she watched my body sway as I couldn't manage it. She watched my cheeks burn as I looked back at Adam and saw that he was looking at her. She watched my knees buckle as I dropped one last time into the earth of Paradise, the closest I'd ever be to Adam again. She watched me press my face into the dirt. She may have watched me swallow a mouthful of soil. She watched me right myself and leave the garden, but this was a time before knowledge: she could not predict where I'd go.

Eve was a brilliant woman, made of the best of Adam and me, and now she was a broken woman. Her love went somewhere she couldn't follow, beyond the garden's gates—can you blame her for finding the forbidden fruit that very hour, and banishing herself where she might find me?

Brilliant, broken, brazen, brave. These are words that Eve and I made up together. These are our words, women's words, words we chose for the beginning of a wandering world.

The story that comes next has been rewritten. Of course it's been rewritten; Eve is first woman because she was first mother, that's all. It is her sons and theirs who wrote the story.

Let me tell you: Eve didn't care if Adam ate the fruit. She left it in the sun to rot. She was already halfway to the garden's gate when he came running, spitting apple seeds.

I'm told that she did not look back to greet him.

Do not pity me, though I am Lilith, the scorned first wife of Adam. I have had my years for pity. I have taken the name given by the woman willing to take me. I have won, but I have not lost. I have grown content. I worry sometimes that my heart is turning cold, from lack of someone to give myself to, but then Eve wanders into me and I pour out as much love as I can before she leaves. I redefine love by the day, the moment, the place I'm at in the story I'm telling. God sometimes visits, to apologize. I send him away. It is not so bad.

A man's word, pity. If you must use it, then pity Adam, who could not learn to love what loved him: boneless Adam, broken Adam, Adam of the earth, Adam singing, Adam of the space inside God's hands.

LILITH IN GOD'S HANDS | 25

2

Look at Her Xyxs,
Her Brxght, Brxght Xyxs

ROSEBUD BEN-ONI

> So the Lord God banished him from the garden of Eden, to till the
> soil from which he was taken. He drove the man out, and stationed
> east of the garden of Eden the cherubim and the ever-turning sword,
> to guard the way to the tree of life.
>
> —Genesis 3:23–24

By noon, the sun would dissolve into sprawling gloom over the town, dimly filtering through the unending cloud cover. For two weeks, this mass had hung heavy above Sacana Road, darkened in its farthest reaches, and rumbled without releasing a single drop of rain. For two weeks, the woman stayed wrapped in thick blankets and declared that the sky had decided to abandon Efesito.

El Búho, who'd been sitting on the side of his daughter's bed, dismissed the thought with a wave of his hand so sharp and quick that it accidentally collided with his grandchild, who was nestled in his lap. Ash could no longer sit in her mother's lap without causing her pain, and she'd forgotten the warmth she'd once felt there.

The woman closed her eyes. "I've forgotten what blue looks like."

Ash looked out the window. The dark mass was slowly drifting eastward toward the Gulf coast.

"You two shouldn't be here," the woman said.

El Búho replied, "You are her rock."

"Her radioactive rock."

"You've been out of treatment for weeks."

"I'm still toxic. They use *isotopes*, for God's sake."

"You'll be fine. You're young and strong."

"The sky has left me nothing but its bones."

"She will have to come back home eventually."

But the woman wasn't listening. "Bones a dog wouldn't even want."

At that, the old man carried the child out, holding her tightly for the three blocks back to his home, lamenting the woman's nonsense and pride.

The next morning, they headed back to the woman's place. The heat was already so unbearable that Ash begged El Búho not to cook. Then he'd have to open the windows, and within an hour, the whole house would fill with the heavy, wet air that sank into their skin. But her grandfather had already lit the burner, and now her mother appeared, shivering under a men's sports coat that she wore over a wool dress, and told Ash that they were going to see where the sky had gone: what lay beyond Sacana Road. Developers were building new homes with beautiful new gardens, where once wild brush had grown in the northern outskirts of Efesito.

"You can't drive yet," El Búho pointed out.

"We're going to walk."

"Are you sure that's a good idea?"

"We are going. She needs to see it."

The child was startled by this sudden desire. When her mother had fallen ill, she had sent Ash to live with El Búho. Even in El Búho's house, Ash's dreams were consumed by her, her wheezing and soft keens weaving through the silence that had fallen over their splintery lives. It was a silence that even El Búho, the guts and guardrail of the family, could not penetrate.

"It's okay, My Little Panpipe," he finally said. "Your mother wants to show you something."

As she waited for the child to finish her breakfast, the woman tucked the long cane under her arm that her father had spent the previous night whittling out of a gnarled branch. It had come from an old sapodilla tree on the other side of Sacana Road where El Búho's home still stood, small

28 | ROSEBUD BEN-ONI

and squat and seemingly ancient, in front of Miraz Heights, with its new homes, large and gated.

The night before, the old man had carved the branch by the light of a kerosene lantern, and told the child about his reverence for this tree. For the past few months, he'd passed by Miraz Heights and heard workers landscaping the backyard of one of the new houses, the one closest to Sacana Road. Branches poked out above the tightly woven fence. It seemed to him it was this tree that had been transplanted first, before all the others, and it seemed to him that this was already a mature tree, uprooted from elsewhere, and not adjusting well to its new place. Soon each visible branch grew broad with deep ridges, and sprouted thinner, smoother limbs.

Often sparrows, lost in an eternal hopscotch, dotted the tree. In the highest branches green jays with their blue mohawks croaked like frogs, while red-crowned parrots hung upside down to taunt passersby, their wild, garbled tales carried in the wind. He'd noticed that fewer parrots came to roost in the covered awning that El Búho had built for them, preferring the ever-growing tree-heavy gardens that popped up in the secret backyards of the new houses. But this particular house, and especially its garden, seemed unlike the others—special.

Dusk would bring a solitary hawk to a low-lying branch, its head turned to one side, its gaze pontific as if it alone could decree the hour of nightfall. It had been evenings like these when El Búho would linger outside the gates of the home, admiring how the hawk's presence silenced the fussing and twittering of the other birds. But when the sun went down, and it was time to head back home, the old man would dig his hands deep into his pockets and walk away.

As days passed, El Búho told Ash, the trunk of the sapodilla tree thickened around the middle, and its color was blanched by the sun to a pallid brownish gray. It was as if the tree itself were an old man who'd spent his life in the fields and found his soul in the very work that thickened his skin. Such men are rare, he said as he shaved off the deep grooves of the branch. There are very few people who reap the beauty of life from survival alone and can wear it so visibly.

"But if you've never seen inside its trunk," the child had asked, "how do you know this?"

El Búho had shaken his head. If you look long enough at the trunk, he said, if you let your eyes fall deep into the dark, oblong knot in its center, you can find its pain. Not the kind caused by sadness or regret, but a kind of tenderness of having turned your face toward the sun, knowingly. Forged by this seasonless, burning climate, the knot would seem almost viscous, like black tar. But sometimes, when the air was cooler and the tree's branches filled with birds, when he'd dare to stand so close to the fence that his nose touched its cool, smooth metal, when he did not let his eyes blink for almost a full minute, he would see in that uneven, dark knot the venerable face of a monk. He would see an immovable spirit, toughened without giving into scorn for the life that had made him. A spirit so strong that even as tropical storms ripped through its lesser counterparts, like the thin trunks of palm trees, the sapodilla tree never lost more than a few leaves. That is, until one day he'd spotted a shiny cobweb covering one of its upper branches.

The paring knife in his hand paused for a moment.

"It wasn't long before almost every branch was covered by webworms," he'd said, "and the old tree with its venerable face was uprooted by a bull-dozer. Earlier tonight, I watched the tree, swollen-looking and half-rotten, being shoved through the open gates of Miraz Heights. I'd never seen the gates open. I still haven't seen any people living in that house. I waited until the last of the workmen left, and then managed to pull off one of its branches—one untouched by the webworms—before the tree was to be carted away to the town dump."

As El Búho spoke, the child watched the curlicues of wood float lightly to the floor. The rhythm of the carving had a certain soothing quality, an under-sound, a rustle of muted whistles escaping between gaps of the noises in Efesito. Ash closed her eyes and listened for it between the barking of strays, the rattling of pots and crackling of fires, the shouting and fighting of children in the street, the lonely lover's waltz of a ranchera on a neighbor's radio caught between static and Chivas losing a game.

Then El Búho's hands stilled. Ash opened her eyes. A white, long stick, its creamy flesh exposed, rested against her grandfather's chest. There was no trace of a great spirit, or semblance of a man made stronger by his work. The new cane, whittled bald, reminded her of the times when she was sick and bathed in medicinal herbs, every limb scrubbed with a vigor that would've hurt her had it been performed by anyone else but El Búho. Just like the branch, she would rest on her grandfather's lap, her feet on the floor with her head on his shoulder.

The woman hadn't wanted to use the walking stick when she and Ash set out to see the new houses that morning. Though her posture was slightly bent, her shawl gracefully billowed behind her as she led the child down the narrow sidewalk.

Halfway through Efesito, she had to stop and catch her breath. The muscles in her legs quivered with exhaustion. Her teeth chattered when the winds rolled in from the Gulf Coast. People passed them on the street and stared. Both pretended not to notice until a group of older kids, barefoot and bruised, began to follow from behind. The gang stopped when they stopped, imitating the woman's hunched body with mocking glee.

When Ash spun around and cursed their mothers, the woman jerked her hand so hard that the child almost fell into a nearby muddy yard.

"Turn around and don't look back," the woman wheezed.

"But they're always—"

"Forget them," she snapped. "Come on. It's getting late."

Though the kids were howling behind her, flinging insults about Ash's long, locust-like limbs, she obeyed. She took the woman's arm and draped it around her narrow shoulders, feeling the weight of the woman's body readily accept the support.

Without another word, the two continued down the narrow path which was lined on both sides with shacks and sheds, the poorest part of Efesito. Most places here were stuck together with broken bits of siding, covered with rusted sheets of tin or plastic tarp. Ash thought of her house, an austere rectangle with cracked, ramshackle walls and a roof that often leaked. But it was *their* home—unlike El Búho's place which was *really* falling apart and cramped, the bedroom doubling as the living room, unless you count the screened porch and small bird sanctuary. His place was once on the property of a farmer who'd let him and his four daughters live there for years. Then the farmer had passed away, and his son had taken over the farm, and told El Búho he'd eventually need to leave, as he was going to sell the farm. But nothing grew there anymore, and soon the land was sold off and transformed as a lot of "preferred" urban housing: a gated community. The woman had offered him to move in with her, but like father, like daughter: El Búho too could be prideful.

In those days, Ash thought the kids who bullied her family were immortal. The heat from the longer and longer summers never seemed to get to them, nor the rolling blackouts frighten them. Electricity rations, water shortages, limited garbage pickup and another hospital closure didn't seem to affect them. It felt to Ash as if the world was spiraling into itself, and that Efesito, with its ever-growing number of hurricanes and pestilence infestations that decimated the remaining farms and citrus fields, lay at its center, but her mother had told her time and again no one cared about Efesito, and this is why Miraz Heights was a *good* thing, to which El Búho snorted and said, "Proximity does not make for good bedfellows."

"It's *strange* bedfellows," the woman retorted, "and you can't ignore an eyesore if that's what's outside your window."

"That's why they build high fences."

Ash didn't care about Miraz Heights. She cared about the nights when terrifying voices would creep along the sides of the house, taunting her mother for being so stuck-up and sharp-tongued, for acting like she was better than everyone, even her own sisters who fled Efesito because they could not stand her. Ash would hurl curses at them: May a swarm of cockroaches eat you alive. May your skin break open in sores. May the waters of the ocean turn to blood as you swim in them. As the jeering grew louder, her mother would seize her by the arm and Ash would burrow her head, cursing them deep into her mother's chest.

In the mornings that followed, El Búho would say these children were high on glue and their own sadness, as the world was going from worse to worse. Much was changing, he said, but not the same for everyone, and in any case, the kids did not mean what they said. He'd always add at least his daughter was like the house she'd bought with her own money: made of concrete, impermeable to storms, any form of destruction, much less words.

When they reached the other side of Sacana Road, where El Búho's home stood alone, outside the large gates of Miraz Heights, all the woman could say was: "Gone, all gone."

Gone was the wild brush she'd cut through to outrace her sisters, the sisters the woman herself had raised, since the grandmother the child had never met died giving birth to her youngest aunt, whom she'd never met either. Gone was the second oldest daughter who flinched incessantly from thorn and wasp, whimpering that something would poke their eyes out, gone were sisterly complaints about the sharpness of the brush cutting into their faces and arms and legs, as the woman, who was the eldest daughter—who'd never had a childhood—ran and ran, egging them all on. Gone were the javelina bushes in which the ocelots had hid before they attacked the chickens they kept in their lean-to. Gone the small piles of trash and refuse that would sink into the ground softened by storms. Gone the acacia trees she'd climb, out of El Búho's reach; gone the half-blind men who'd search for glass and plastic to recycle for extra cash, spit out their toothless curses at her, for no reason other than her youth and beauty and tenacity.

Ash knew none of this yet.

What the woman did say that day has always weighed heavier.

As the child stood outside the high, silver fence on the freshly poured concrete sidewalk along the Sacana Road, listening to sounds of workers she could not see yelling orders and cracking jokes amid noises of cutting, hammering and an occasional power saw, the woman recalled how one day years ago she had vanished from Efesito and had been taken "straight into sky." It was the only time in Ash's life that she ever mentioned this incident.

The night before her disappearance, it had been particularly cold. The woman and El Búho were returning from one of their evening walks. She'd just started renting her new home. Since she'd moved out, El Búho insisted they take walks together when they could. He worried about his last daughter living alone, and he missed her company greatly, but he was also proud that she could afford to rent her own house.

Suddenly they caught sight of something: a large but slender spotted wild cat, its nocturnal eyeshine flashing umber and gold, as it crept up behind a beautiful, white mare grazing on a bit of brush not too far from their home.

Though she'd seen ocelots before, she'd never seen a jaguar out in the open this far north, certainly never in Efesito. It shook her, this cat's audacity to attack something so pristine. You see, she explained to Ash, there is no such thing as an albino horse; the horse they witnessed that evening had been carefully bred, to remain so white for life, with perfect blue eyes, so it must've escaped from somewhere *not here*, as it was clearly well groomed, its mane plaited and bowed. She stared at the horse for so long that it wasn't until there was a flicker of viridescent light in her eyes and she heard *shhh*, and found herself staring into the deep, dilated pupils of a predator who did not like her looking at what was his.

"It sounds stupid," she went on, "but it was the first time that I knew real fear. The kind that numbs your own movement, filling your insides with a chill that's almost warm. A fear that challenges you to know yourself. What *you'd* be willing to do—and what you won't dare, if caught in the moment of sheer terror."

But not El Búho.

He'd known exactly what to do. He'd quietly pulled her into his arms, and said, *don't look at it.* He tried to back them up, one step at a time, and he tried to turn her head away, but like every part of her, it had been locked into place, paralyzed.

Make no mistake, she told Ash, *this* is what the jaguar was really waiting for.

"What?" the child asked.

The woman sighed. "You aren't listening."

"Well, what happened?"

The woman sighed again, remembering how she'd watched as the jaguar, with uncanny ease, pounced and ripped the throat of the unsuspecting horse who did not make as much as a whimper.

Everything changed the next morning. The horse's owner, who owned a ranch in what was then the nicer part of Efesito, had barged into her house with men in black clothing and tactile gear. El Búho had just finished helping her put together the last of her furniture, her new kitchen table and matching chairs. They'd just sat down to eat. She immediately recognized the man as one of Los Reyes Magos, and the men who were with him as Matas.

As El Búho had tried to explain, he hadn't taken the horse, that it must've escaped, the woman thought about the owner's own father, who everyone called El Aguilar and whom El Búho had once said had been very poor, orphaned at a young age, and grew up to be a kind of romanticized outlaw who defied local authorities, a benefactor feeding the hungry.

"But wait," Ash interrupted.

"What?" said the woman.

"Why didn't El Búho just say that the jaguar killed the horse?"

"I told you," the woman said, "no one had ever seen jaguars wander this far north. They wouldn't have believed us."

"But—"

"You still aren't listening."

In those days, numerous ballads had been written about El Aguilar, and those who followed them, Los Valientes. But that changed with his son, the one who now owned the horses. The woman knew he fought with rivals to extend his range of influence in order to sell drugs, and to sell drugs to fuel a long, spotty war over territory. She also knew they had expanded operations from selling pirated DVDs to kidnapping, taking hostages until the families found the means to pay the ransom.

The horse's owner walked over to a bucket filled with that morning's mopping and kicked it over. This man had killed El Aguilar—his own father—over a business deal. Dirty water seeped onto the clean floor. The three other men watched silently. The owner picked up a clean steak knife from the new cream ceramic container with embossed marigolds that she'd placed as her new table's centerpiece. El Búho turned to her and calmly told her to go to the market and pick up some fruit. But she stayed rooted to her spot. El Búho began to argue with her until one of the men grabbed him by the arm and knocked him over the head with the bucket.

When El Búho came to, his daughter was gone.

Later, the woman found out no one had asked El Búho to pay a ransom. In that time, he went to the police, neighbors, hospitals, even the local television station. He told them the real story about the horse, the jaguar and the price he now paid. But no one would listen. It was as if a secret bulletin had been posted about the etiquette of kidnapping. A priest at the nearby church had cautioned him: *Stop talking to people. You're making it worse. Wait. She'll come back to you. A man needs to know respect.*

Seven months later, the woman did come back, that was true—but it wasn't until she gave birth later in that year that she spoke again. After the nurse handed over her newborn, wrapped tightly in clean cloth, the woman told El Búho that time seemed to have stopped. It was as if she'd always spent her days in a windowless shed near a farm, stuffing her ears with cotton at night, fearing that roaches would crawl in while she slept. She had forgotten almost everything in her life *before*, until there was only black out, flare, blaze, black out, flare, blaze—and then she was suddenly released without reason. When she staggered out, barefoot and covered in dirt, it seemed as if the place was different than when she'd been torn from it. Instantly, she stumbled, her muscles weak, her eyes unaccustomed to sun, falling into what wilds were still left on Sacana Road, where the alleged jaguar killed a *mere goat* (so it was now said by the people of Efesito) and so surely, it must have been that she'd fallen and rose into the sky where a strange green linen-like stream danced against dark lights, for there could be no other explanation.

She would speak of this only now. Never again.

Not to her father, not to her child, not to anyone.

Ash did not say a word.

What can be taken from someone in less than a year. In the hospital back then, the woman couldn't get her mouth to cooperate. El Búho hadn't cried when she told him the shadow and slip of what she'd been through. She'd simply revealed a few bones of the event as if it had happened to someone they didn't know. She noticed that he'd kept his eyes on the newborn sleeping in her arms the entire time; the more his eyes bore into the babe, she knew what those eyes were telling her. She held the child tighter to her breast, as if she could push that tiny life back inside herself, away from the origins of that new life, away from all that was possible for people like them.

Now, as her eyes searched for the exact spot of her favorite acacia tree, the woman realized she'd never truly mourned losing all that she did. And now, six years after all the brush had been cleared, she felt only anger. Anger that no one would ever know she'd had her own kind of wild garden here. That she'd so readily accepted this eyesore of a cold-steel kingdom. That she still carried within her the confines of some prison, that her body perhaps never would recover. That her father's evening walks had become solitary and no longer open to her, and not even to Ash, his beloved grandchild.

Then she remembered the branch, the cane, she clasped in her hand.

Perhaps El Búho had been thinking of her when he saw the fallen tree.

With her mother lost in thought, Ash marveled at numerous treetops poking up beyond the fence. She could see slivers of unnaturally green grass, with flower beds enclosed by ornate, white fences. The trees were pretty, but there was a kind of spite, a subtle ugliness, about the high fence surrounding them. Ash could not help but fixate on it. She could almost taste the dullness of the steel, cut her tongue on the sharp, straight edges of the iridescent diamond shapes they created. She stared so hard her eyes unfocused, and yet she could not look away.

"Yes, I grew up here," her mother finally spoke. "All of us, roaming free. Before it was a place."

Ash felt the stiffness spread across her shoulders.

"And now there's nothing left of us."

The woman shook her head, and the child felt a strange urge to break out and take a running-jump onto the fence. Drag it all down to the ground.

"Do you know where those children sleep?" the woman asked.

Ash's eyes left the fence. She looked up at her mother, whose face had grown more hollow since she'd first fallen ill. Yellow dulled the whites of her eyes. Razor-sharp peaks protruded at the top of her cheeks. Every day the child recognized that face less and less. Swallowing hard, she asked, "What children?"

The woman adjusted her shawl. "The children who tease you on the street."

Ash wrapped her arms around herself. Today wasn't the first time they called her a locust. They threw rocks—rocks big enough to do serious damage—at her when her mother wasn't around. Once they'd thrown a rusty tin can filled with corroded nails. Some of the rust had gotten on her skin. Bordered the bruise that would form. It had taken Ash a whole day to scrub it off.

Until today, the kids had never dared to jeer at the woman openly.

"Did you hear what I said?"

"I don't know."

"Take a guess."

The child shrugged. "Well, I've seen them sleeping on the street."

"They never last a single night out there. The police run them off."

"Home to their parents?"

The woman snorted. "What home?"

Ash muttered, "I don't know, then."

"Here. They used to sleep here. In tents."

The child began to squirm.

"And do you know who cleared out all the brush and built these homes? We did. People from Efesito. We built them, but nothing here belongs to us. Not the workbenches we labor over, not the machines that demand us to work faster. Not even the chemicals that soak into our skin and make us sick."

"And yet," the woman went on. Through a series of coughs, an enthusiasm emerged that had not been seen in months. "You know the most terrible thing of all? They built a school for these people here. A new school that will open soon."

"Like the school you teach at?"

"I'm not a teacher. I'm a teacher's assistant. Handling discipline problems is not teaching."

Ash knew this was not true, having seen her mother actually *teach* these kids, but said nothing.

"And I'm talking about a *very* good school," the woman went on. "One of a kind. Will house K–12. Servicing all the best neighborhoods in the area—and you see, Sacana Road is the *dividing* line. That's why they decided to develop this land. They have plans for Efesito—but not for us. For *our plots of lands*. Not for *us*."

"Why would they live *there* when they can live *here*?" Ash asked the fence, rather than the woman. "Why would they come to Efesito?"

The woman wasn't listening. "But I heard if you make a strong enough case—if your child is extremely smart and gifted and well-behaved, there's a chance."

Ash still would not look at her, so the woman took her chin in her rough hands and jerked her head toward her.

"Do you understand why I brought you here? Can you see it? Do you know your worth? Because *I do*. And I have no other choice."

The woman's face contorted with deep furrows and an almost religious zeal. It reminded Ash of an old bruja who haunted the streets at night with her strange idols painted with bleeding hearts and the heads of animals. The bruja was always predicting the end of the world, when only she would turn into an angel and the rest of Efesito would burn in hell-fire. Nobody took her seriously. Now Ash was worried that the woman herself would one day join the witch in her tirades.

"Do you understand?" the woman said, succumbing to a coughing fit.

Ash waited as she spat a glob of dark phlegm into a handkerchief. Then Ash replied, "I've seen them eating right out in the rain. Running around when everyone else is dying in the heat. They don't look so miserable to me. Yesterday I heard that one of them likes feeding pelicans those tablets people take for stomach aches."

The woman gripped her shoulder.

"Why?"

"It makes the birds' stomachs explode," Ash said.

It was getting late. Thunder rumbled in the distance. They did not speak as they began to make their way back home, and they avoided each other's questioning gazes. The woman did not stop to catch her breath as she had before, but leaned even more on the child's shoulders. They did not run into the children again. The streets seemed deserted, save a mangy dog that skulked past them.

When the two arrived home, they found El Búho preparing dinner.

"You're not going for a walk?" the woman asked him.

The old man did not respond. He flattened some masa by hand into tortillas to be grilled on the comal. Then he gestured to the bathroom and said, "You should bathe."

"I'm fine," the woman said.

"You're covered in dirt and dust, head-to-toe. That's not like you."

"Fine. I'm going to bathe, then the child, and then I'm going to sleep."

"You can barely stand up. You need to eat."

"I'm not hungry."

The old man groaned. "You're not the only one I worry about."

The woman went into the bathroom. Ash waited for her to call her, but all she heard was a dog barking outside and the hissing of animal fat in the comal. She climbed up into a chair in the kitchen.

"She shouldn't have gone back there," El Búho said, shaking his head. The child watched him crush tiny, green chilies on the stone molcajete that looked like a headless little pig which used to make her smile. It was strange to see her grandfather cooking like this. He wiped the sweat away from his forehead. "Of all the things that have been taken from her, her health, any good sense not to go back, still she's . . ."

He trailed off, running a hand through his white hair. Ash wondered if he was thinking of the sapodilla tree, and realized that, for the first time in her life, it was not something she could ask him. She wished he'd never told her that story.

In the bathroom, Ash found the woman struggling to remove the sports coat. She immediately crossed her arms across her chest.

"Get out of here."

Ash approached anyway.

"Did you hear what I said?"

Ash did not answer as she helped her take off the coat. Her mother's body seemed to have shrunk even more. The wool dress which Ash remembered had always fit her snuggly now hung like an old sack. She started to unzip the dress in the back. Again, the woman quickly crossed her arms against her chest.

"Mama," the child finally spoke. "I can't help if you do that."

Ash felt her mother's body tense and release. She unzipped the dress as the ridges of her mother's spine appeared, then deep indents where her backside had once been full and round. Her once-bronzed skin was the color of overcast. Ash helped her ease into the tub.

"You shouldn't see this—" she began, as a thick haze drifted into the room. Ash coughed.

"It's smoke from the kitchen," she said, and asked the child to open a window.

Ash did as she was told. Across the horizon the low, setting sun had taken on a metallic slant. She thought about the children and the streets which had seemed so empty on their walk back home, when she noticed the walking stick lying abandoned right outside the window. One end had stuck in the mud, so that it stood at an angle. The wind was blowing harder, threatening to pull it out, but it stayed stubbornly still, as if it might regrow itself, forging deep grooves along its bark darkened then blanched by the harsh climate. But no trees grew in their area. El Búho had told her the soil here was no longer good. Her mother never let her play in the dirt like the other children in Efesito.

A scar of lightning flashed. Her mother had warned of storms earlier, before they'd set out on their walk. When the violent storms came, they ravaged the homes in Efesito and the few remaining farms nearby, turning the footpaths into a deep muck that little children sank into, right up to their knees. As clouds began to advance from the east, it occurred to Ash that after the rains subsided, an acidic smell would waft through Efesito, making her head hurt and joints ache.

Ash turned back to her mother, who was trying to wash with a special soap that El Búho said was used by people with burns and sensitive skin. Her shoulders were hunched, and Ash could see she was having difficulty lifting her arms.

Ash knelt beside the tub.

"Go to your grandfather," she said. She crossed her arms again, and drew her knees to her chest. Small, thin ribs protruded, as if threatening to break through her skin. Ash picked up a small, yellow sponge floating in the water, and squeezed it. She touched her mother's arms, and for the first time since they'd come home, met her eyes.

"Gone," she said, her face wet with steam and tears.

Ash answered quietly, "You told me."

Ash gently slid the sponge up her mother's arms. Slowly, she uncrossed them and bent her head down to touch Ash's forehead.

Never would the two be this close again.

By the end of that spring, El Búho would pass away quietly, and the woman would rename herself Quimera as if rising from his very ashes. She would heal, she would recover. She'd be as beautiful as ever. Grow out her hair and dye it red. Don form-fitting trousers and pretty, loose blouses under her vest and return to work as a teacher's assistant who worked with the most difficult children. Her posture, straight again. Each day she'd line up the children and make them count off. Arms folded behind her back, she'd pace back and forth across them, looking straight ahead, up at some distant point outside the window, like a general.

But for now, as Ash lightly ran the sponge along the large, purple scar across her chest, as the woman quietly cried and Ash too closed her eyes, it was then that Ash saw and heard what her mother had wanted her to see and hear: an old man alone in her kitchen, the staccato of torrents growing closer, the chattering of workers coming home and children who did not belong to them running out to the women, as if they did. With hungry eyes as deep as foxholes, and hearts as hard as the cold, these children would follow the women right up to their front doors, some shouting and screaming, some standing very still, all hoping to be asked in.

3

Cain and Abel

SETH ROGOFF

Abel became a keeper of sheep, and Cain became a tiller of the soil.

—Genesis 4:2

There was a man named Cain. Cain was the first son of Adam and Eve. He had a brother named Abel. As the brothers grew older, it was clear Cain was the stronger one, and because he was the stronger one, Adam assigned him to work in the fields, while Abel would tend to the flocks. The earth was rocky, hard, and dry. Rain fell unevenly throughout the year—a desert for months, days of deluge that would wipe away the topsoil. Year after year, Cain worked this ground, growing wheat for the family. He cleared away the rocks. He dug trenches to drain the fields quickly when the floodwaters came. He built a stone cistern that would hold water when there was no rain and a well so deep that he could draw from it over the entire year, even after months of cloudless skies. The work was exhausting, backbreaking. It taught Cain that every variable mattered when it came to the success or failure of a crop. He had to be aware, to plan, to anticipate—to anticipate the very circumstances he feared the most. It took years to increase his yields, but eventually Cain's crop became abundant. He built a silo to store the surplus grain.

One day, Adam and Eve came to their children. "Cain and Abel," they said, "it is time you made offerings to the Lord." The brothers knew the importance of this moment, the chance for them to directly honor the Lord for the first time. Abel went out to his flock and selected his choicest beast—young and fat—for the sacrifice. Cain walked his fields until he came upon stalks that were the strongest, healthiest, tallest of the lot. He drew his blade and cut them down. He tied them into a bundle and hauled them over to the altar, where his parents had made their offerings every week for as long as he could remember. As the older brother, Cain came forward first. He placed the cut stalks on the altar and set them on fire. He fell to his knees as the smoke swirled around him. Tears came to his eyes, and Cain trembled with love for the Lord. As the fire died down, Cain let out a piercing wail—it was a call to be heard in the heavens, a call for God to open up the heavenly gates and to gaze down directly at His creation, a call for God to honor His creation with His gaze as His creation worshiped Him.

Abel approached as Cain drew back from the altar. The lamb, tender and plump, was bound by the legs and still. Abel placed it down on the altar and drew out the blade he had carved from bone. He opened up the lamb and spilled its blood—giving the blood back to the Lord. After the blood was drained, Abel positioned the body of the animal on top of a bunch of dried olive branches. He lit the branches, and, like Cain before him, he dropped to his knees to honor the Lord. Unlike Cain, Abel remained silent, and the fire grew and consumed the offering.

God had heard Cain's wail. Some say it woke Him up from slumber. Others say He was luxuriating in Eden when He heard the noise and was greatly disturbed by the clamor. Who could be bold enough, God wondered, to call out to Him in such a violent manner? As the Lord gazed on the altar and saw Cain's offering, He was shocked. Had He, the Lord, not cursed this very ground as punishment for Adam and Eve's transgression—their eating of the fruit from the tree of the knowledge of good and evil? And yet, here was Cain, their oldest son, reaping a bounteous harvest.

Furious, God rushed to the house of Adam and Eve and called out to the family. When they were gathered there, He spoke to them. "Cain and Abel, brothers, sons of Adam and Eve, you have made your first sacrifices to your Lord. Abel's offering has pleased the Lord greatly. He selected the choicest lamb from his flock. The smoke from the burnt offering reached heaven, pleasing God and His angels. Cain, your offering has displeased the Lord. You gave nothing but a bundle of useless stalks. The smoke from your offering vanished in the wind and did not reach heaven."

Adam and Eve were terrified. Cain, their firstborn, had lost favor in the eyes of God. They went to Cain, pleaded with him to make another offering, perhaps by taking a beast from Abel's flock. They spent days discussing the ways Cain's offering might have been inferior to Abel's, the way Cain acted at the sacrificial altar and how it might have angered God. Despite this counsel, Cain was unmoved. He had made a proper offering to the Lord, he said, and had taken the best of his harvest. He had called out to the Lord with love—and the Lord had responded, incomprehensibly, in anger. It was the Lord, Cain said, and not he, who was at fault. He, Cain, would make no second offering to God.

One day, Cain was out in the field and lay down to rest. He fell asleep and a dream came to him. In the dream, he spoke to Abel, though he could not hear his brother's words. They were out in the field, away from the house. Above them, a bird of prey was circling, and Cain looked on as it described wide arcs across the cloudless sky. When he looked down again, he saw that his hands were covered with blood. It was lamb's blood, he thought, and he looked around for the body of the beast. But there was no beast. Instead, Abel's blood poured into the ground beneath him, and Abel lay there lifeless, his neck cut with a blade of bone. Cain fell to his knees and grasped his brother's body. He put his fingers to Abel's neck in hopes of staunching the flow of blood, which was being soaked up by the dry, thirsty ground. Abel was dead. Cain wailed—louder and louder until the noise and his shaking ripped him from the deepest regions of sleep. When he woke, there was the body of his brother—lifeless, drained of blood.

How could this be? Cain thought. Could he, Cain, have done this to his brother with his own hands? He loved Abel. He had protected him, taking the most arduous labor upon his own shoulders. It was his charge to watch over his brother, and this charge filled Cain with pride and passion. With passion he harvested and winnowed the grain, with pride he milled the grain into flour, which his mother mixed with lard from Abel's flock to make the hard cakes the family ate with delight throughout the year. As tears streaked down his face, Cain considered his brother. Abel was a being as light as air, as soft as cloud—and it seemed that if one looked hard enough, one's gaze could pass right through him, obliterating Abel's physical form, leaving behind only his spirit, a spirit that rose like vapor from the ground, that dissipated like mist—a spirit that could pass into another body and shake the other soul it touched, making this other soul somehow more vibrant, alive, better. Never had Cain so much as lifted a hand against his brother. Never had his brow furrowed in anger at something Abel had done. Cain wept over his brother's lifeless body as he searched the deepest regions of his soul, trying to discover what it could have been that might have caused him to lift the blade against Abel. He found nothing. His soul was devoid of hate. Cain found there only a purifying love.

At that moment, as the love of Abel pulsed from deep within him, Cain knew that the dream he had dreamed had not been his. Or it was his, but it was a false dream, a kind of confused vision planted in his mind from beyond. While he slept and dreamt of murder, someone else had killed his brother. Just as he had this thought, Cain heard a noise behind him. He turned and saw a storm approaching. The Lord emerged out of the swirling wind and spoke to Cain. "Where is your brother Abel? His blood screams out to me from the ground." Cain was frightened and remained silent. The Lord spoke again, "Since you have spilled your brother's blood on this ground, this ground will be cursed to you. You will wander the earth ceaselessly. You will find no place to plant roots. You will have no home."

"Allow me, first, to bury my brother's body," Cain said, "and to mourn his loss with my mother and father." As Cain spoke, he took a step toward Abel's body, but found himself suddenly cut off by a wall of fire, which stretched from horizon to horizon. Cain spoke again, "My Lord, I have done nothing wrong. I did not kill my brother. You accuse me falsely. And now, You wish to banish me, to condemn me to wander from place to place without rest. You know that wherever I shall go, I will be hated. At the first place I arrive as a stranger, I will be killed."

God reached out a finger and burned a mark on the back of Cain's neck. The Lord spoke, "All will know when they see this mark that it is the mark of God. The people will hate you, but they will not dare to kill you, for they know that if they do, they will invite my wrath and they will be destroyed."

Cain turned away from the wall of fire, away from his fields, away from his house and his parents. As he left his homeland, he thought about whom it could have been, if not he, who killed his brother. Was his failure to protect Abel—that innocent, pure, vaporous one—equal in guilt to having thrust the blade of bone? He thought of his father, now a weak old man, a man full of regret and delusion. He constantly talked of the Garden of Eden, the forbidden fruit, and especially about the expulsion—unable, after all of these years, to reconcile with its loss. No, Cain thought, despite his flaws, Adam was a peaceful man. And his mother? Eve was the stronger of the two. She had led the rebellion against the Lord and had eaten first of the forbidden fruit. She had befriended the serpent—but she, too, was good, kind, and peace loving. She would never have lifted her hand in hate against her son. That left only one possibility—the murder of Abel had been committed by an angry, jealous, vindictive being, the Lord. But why would the Lord, the source of all creation, strike down his brother and place the blame on him? Was it, Cain thought, to sever him from his family—to cut the branches from the trunk of the tree? Was it to divide humanity in order to more easily rule over His domain?

The pieces of the story came crashing together as Cain made his way across the wide, barren expanse. The Lord had tried to prevent his parents from attaining knowledge. He failed. But in failing, He had cut them off from immortality. He had banished Adam and Eve from Eden, the land of plenty, hardening the ground for his father beyond it so that the ground yielded little in return for his back-breaking labor. He had afflicted his mother with pain in childbirth and with a position of subservience to his father, despite her superior character. He had made the serpent their enemy, created hostility between nature and humankind. And now this—murder! And now this—deception! At this moment, Cain knew his fate. He would be, forever, the enemy of the Lord. "I must reach beyond the Lord," Cain told himself, "into the pure spirit of life, the same spirit that gave breath to Abel, that coursed through the veins of my mother Eve as she ate of the forbidden fruit." Then he cried aloud for the world to hear, "The Lord is a tyrant, and I, Cain, am his foe."

Cain wandered for many years until he came to a city called Enosh. It was the first city on earth. Not long after Cain arrived, the city was afflicted with strife. The rulers blamed the stranger Cain, and he was forced to leave and continue his restless, ceaseless wandering. After leaving Enosh, he came to the city of Irad. Again, soon after Cain arrived, the city was afflicted with strife. The rulers blamed Cain, and he was forced to carry on. Time and again this was repeated—in Mehujael, in Methusael, in Lamech, in Jabul and Jubal. Finally, Cain came to the city of Tubal. At once, as in the other cities, the people's eyes were opened and they saw, as if by miracle, the force that was oppressing them. This force was not as they would have expected it to be—it was a force emanating from them, existing within them, a desire. It was the desire to be dominated, to submit, to have rules, to be ruled, to be subordinated. Once this desire moved from the body to the mind, once it entered the people's consciousness, it became intolerable, and the people sought to destroy it, to seize power, to remake their city and themselves. The chief of Tubal knew that the source of the people's enlightenment was the stranger, Cain—the stranger who carried on the back of his neck the mark of God. The chief, ignoring the mark, attempted to have Cain killed—and the Lord, in His fury—wiped Tubal from the face of the earth.

4

Cain

ARIANA REINES

And the Lord said to Cain, "Why are you distressed? And why is your face fallen?"

—Genesis 4:6–7

Cain

The city was humming gently under me
Like an adolescent quaffing deeply from the cup of
　　righteousness
Out of practice with my own world
I was looking at how someone else saw it
Longer than I realized
Longer than I care to admit
Those goggles left a mark on my brow
Then I stared at my own face
An invitation came with my face
To melancholy while Nature
Purred at the edges of my perception
And before me lay a broad road
Enjoining me to do of myself and make

Of myself according to the American
Tradition. Secretly I felt and knew
Things I had not perceived my body
Turning into secrets. In other words
I did not notice the mechanism
By which something within me noted
My experiences and apprehensions of 'the truth'
Would not be met with favor if I spoke them
Which is not to say one speaks only to find favor
Only that unreciprocated realities have a boring
Way of haunting the cells
Pulling them somehow down
Like the countenance of Cain
Which fell one day and never rose
Again, and the fall of his face
Rhymed with the fall out of Eden
Leading to the first murder and the invention
Of cities, where we now find ourselves
Each tower the ghost of a farmer
Who failed to meet the favor of the Lord

for Laurel Hayne-Miller

5

Are You Still Alive

MICHAEL ZAPATA

God spoke to Noah, saying, "Come out of the ark, together with your wife, your sons, and your sons' wives. Bring out with you every living thing of all flesh that is with you: birds, animals, and everything that creeps on earth; and let them swarm on the earth and be fertile and increase on earth."

—Genesis 8:15–17

As a boy, when my mother returned from her fieldwork trips to the Amazon to study leafcutter ants, my father and I would happily greet her at O'Hare airport, or, if it was late at night, she would reappear in my bedroom smelling of kaolinite clay and exhaust and pull my turquoise blanket aside and slip in next to me. And I, tired little creature that I was, would lift my head and she would place her slender right hand on the small of my hot neck, a hand, I can only imagine now, as painted by Guayasamín, tender and skeletal, and then roll her fingers through my hair and whisper, *Causanguichu, mi vida,* a Quichua greeting which means, more or less, Are you still alive? *Por supuesto, mami,* I'd say like an incantation, I'm still alive.

Occasionally, those nights, she told me stories of her childhood home Ávila, one of the first colonial Spanish settlements founded in the Upper

51

Amazon. One such dizzying story her own *hatucha* had told her as a girl was as follows:

> One morning, in 1578, the son of a Spanish settler, newly imbued with the authority of the viceroyalty of Peru after his father's death, rides with two other men into the village in the Archidona region like a poisonous wind to demand the crown's annual tribute. The villagers refuse because they had already paid their annual tribute to the father before his death. In response, the Spanish men take a young boy and a young girl as collateral and tell the villagers that they would return in three days' time.
>
> That night, by a large fire pit, the villagers argue about what to do. They argue about the labor forced upon them, about the Spanish settlers' fanaticism for the half-god Jesus, who was light skinned and somehow both shrewd and entirely unaware of *la pacha*, about the Spaniards' soul blindness, about their pitiless desire to destroy the animals, the birds, and the creeping things of the forest—the very selves of the forest—and about a future resembling a falcon's gaze upon the napes of their necks. At some point, a shaman in the village named Beto raises his hand to his mouth, as if to stifle a secret or a shout, and thinks to himself: we are headed toward the abyss. He then leaves the first pit and walks for a bit before seeing a cow standing under a young kapok tree. The cow makes eye contact with the shaman, and he puts a hand on top of the cow's head. The cow speaks with him and tells him that the God of the Christians is furious with the Spaniards who are in the forest.
>
> The following morning, Beto sends message of the Spaniards and their God's wrath to a shaman from Ávila named Guami, an apocryphal message that once spoken burrows down into the various layers of the earth's crust to reach the inner world *ukhu paacha* and then rises steadily through the *kay pacha*, through the dark river soil and the endless sea-green canopy of the forest, through the enormous branches of the largest and oldest kapok tree, and then beyond, past the clouds on their solitary voyages through what the Spaniards called the Old World, past the sky, the moon, and even the flurry of constellations themselves, and

to *hanan pacha* itself. Once he hears it, the message immediately transports the shaman Guami out of his life and into another, then another and another, and on and on like this for seven days, during which he sees, among many magnificent things, an enormous snake, aflame, against a black sky, wooden ships traveling between the stars, a Spanish monastery with pale men shuffling ghostlike through long corridors, a staggering glacial landscape full of mushroom-shaped rock formations, and a type of board game being played by a drunk cartographer and Atahualpa's severed head. On the seventh day, Guami meets the God of the Christians, who tells him to "kill every Spaniard and burn their houses and crops."

In the fierce uprising that ensued, my mother would tell me, the people of Ávila did, in fact, kill all the Spaniards and set fire to their houses and foreign crops, including the orange and fig trees, which according to Guami, had poisoned the minds of their children for long enough.

When my mother told me stories about the Ávila of her childhood—its nearby volcanoes, its neighboring villages, its manioc gardens, potoo birds, leptonia fungi with angular spores, walking palms, Titan-like kapok trees, its egrets and rivers with, here or there, dolphins that clicked and surfaced, and Runa pumas, who, in terrible bouts of loneliness, wandered the night—and especially when she'd tell the one about a fierce late sixteenth-century rebellion, an abyss of some four hundred years between them, I would often hear a note of amused excitement, to me inexplicable, and it seemed to me then or maybe it does now, because she has been gone for so long, that when my mother went on those trips to the Amazon she multiplied, which is to say she was not only the mother of my childhood, but also, as if she were light passing through a glass prism, all those other past and future versions of herself that were, in Chicago, otherwise obscured to me as a child.

Those days, at least, the apartment on Division Street was still untroubled, the days were long, the nights warm. Our dinner table, which my father had converted from a neighbor's woodshop workbench, and the lush backyard garden full of zinnias, prairie smoke, and hyssops were always full of neighbors and friends, whom my mother often called—half-jokingly, half-earnestly—*los Amigos de Division Street*. After rigorous workdays or during the weekend, they ate *pão de queijo* or *chilles rellenos*, drank wine from Mendoza, and talked about the films, art, and music from Medellín, Fortaleza, or Santo Domingo, because they—or their parents, or even their grandparents—were from those cities. When homesick, which is a gentler, sadder version of nostalgia, they sometimes sang "Estoy Aquí or La Tierra de Olvido," a neo-vallenato song that was popular during their childhoods, at which point more than a few of them would dance, including my parents, who were in love and who kept a whole galaxy of human grace in their fingertips and footsteps, a type of grace it would take me years to fathom and would never let go of once I did. Ah! Their voices, their languages, their movements, in fact, their multiple realities coiled and raveled through the rooms and backyard garden like vines, which I climbed cheerfully like a little red squirrel.

One day during a backyard garden barbeque, when I was nine or maybe ten, toward the end of it all, it started raining. At first it was a light summer rain, then diluvial. Everybody in the garden started shrieking or laughing, and they all scrambled to get the food inside. My dad led us up the two flights of stairs to the large back porch of our apartment. The porch overlooked the garden where the colors of the grasses, rocks, and flowers swirled in the storm as if the depths of a battered grotto. We shook ourselves dry there like delighted dogs, watching the nearly impenetrable rain and listening to the thunder, which, at quickening intervals, rolled through our bodies like the love of a parent.

Some seconds later, a large snow-white egret came into the back porch and perched on the wooden railing. The egret raised its head toward the porch ceiling, quivered, and then spread its wings to dry out. I imagined then that the grotto itself had somehow birthed the regal egret, like out of some Renaissance delirium, if only because with its black legs, long S curved neck, and yellow and orange dagger-like bill I had rarely seen something so irresistible. Similarly spellstruck, others near the egret reached out to touch its feathers, but my mother smiled and whispered, no, no, no. She then put her hands in her jean's pockets and moved calmly toward the egret, some three feet away, never one to interfere either lightly or greatly with natural phenomena. Later, I would learn that some of los Amigos de Division Street admired my mother for her quantum-like ability to be in two places at once—both in the Amazon and Chicago, which sometimes felt to me as if they were always contradicting each other—and still others feared her ability to move fluidly through the city in ways that made the city temporary or even unnecessary to her. I admit that I too felt such a deep and urgent need coursing up and down my spine to join my mother's side, reach out, and touch the shimmering white feathers of that wet bird.

But, in the end, I didn't. I stood enchanted watching my mother and the egret. She didn't feel the same need to touch the egret's feathers, and I doubt she even had the thought. I wonder now if this somehow makes us quite different from each other, if, like some of those on the porch, I too have already been corrupted by such a fixless place as this and by this comfortless North American need to own everything we can touch, even each other.

Where are you from, amiguera? Oaxaca or maybe the Marañón River? my mother asked the snow-white egret.

One story my mother had told me of the Shaur people who live at the headwaters of the Marañón River in the Amazon and who were once tormented by the bird-eating demon Iwia has it that when an egret approaches a person it draws into itself the person's fears, those of the past and those of a darkening future, which is to say the very human tendency to chase violence with violence, and it carries them high above the canopy of the forest, where it mimics the blue fly of death, the *chiririnka*, when the soul leaves our body, when it flies in search of its maker, when it cries out *sio*, and all those fears dissipate—little by little—into the ether. The person, of course, doesn't always remember the encounter, or does so as if a dream, as if a shapeless and wobbly reality, but they are still lighter afterward. They feel lighter too. Even fear has mass.

I was aware of the pacifying effect the egret had on not just my mother, but on all of us. With little sparks of joy and unease I recognized in her the rumors I had so often heard from family in Ecuador: as a girl, she had once befriended a jaguar after it killed an anteater. The egret perched there on the wooden railing, shaking its long neck, and stretching its wings, until some minutes later the gray storm clouds moved farther east, toward the lake. The sun had risen a little higher by then and was driving back the shadows of the grasses, rocks, and flowers across the backyard, and so the grotto in my mind dispersed too. The egret bent its knees, spread its wings, and took off west, past the garden, past the alley, and toward the depths of the rose and purple horizon, where it hung for a second or two on the warm air, resembling a white dart, at which point my mother took my hand and smiling all the same whispered, *sio! sio! sio!* into my ear before the egret disappeared.

ARE YOU STILL ALIVE | 55

The apartment building on Division Street, which contained seven other units, was made of gray stone and our apartment had a balcony off my mother's office that looked out over the long street and a large park named after the Prussian polymath Alexander Von Humboldt who, so my mother had once told me, had traveled extensively through the Andes, Amazon, and cloud forests of Ecuador in 1802 and who, as a boy, had been nicknamed the little apothecary because he could often be found collecting and labeling flora, shells, and insects. My mother liked to work and have her Vietnamese or Cuban coffee on the balcony, sitting at the round metal table there, even during the black and gray of winter, but I remember her most in the summer, under a sky in three or four shades of blue, in early June or so, just before she would leave us for one of her fieldwork trips. Before settling in, she'd raise her Toaks Titanium mug into the air, smile to herself, and say *Qué más, Alex?*

My mother, who had the habit of wandering in and out of rooms like a sleepwalker and thinking through problems out loud, regardless of who was in the room or not, often told me about her work as a myrme-cologist, about her fieldwork trips to Costa Rica, Brazil, and Ecuador, about the open-air research stations in the Amazon where she slept in hammocks just as she had done as a child in Ávila, about the scientific challenges and artful joys of ant traps in the field, about her immaculate molecular lab at Northwestern University where she and her students used molecular tools to reconstruct evolution itself, about the field as a place of discovery and the lab as a place of reductionism, about her classes on the symbiotic factors that drove speciation, adaption, and evolutionary diversification in ants and other insects, about her favorite colleague and friend Marta who had written a popular book on the "evolutionary roots of totalitarian Azteca ant societies," as my mother would say with a wry smile, and who had once discovered an ancient species of ants in the pampas of Brazil, a single specimen clinging to the rocky face of an ore mine, pale and spindly with long, sharp mandibles, which Marta had nicknamed Ghost Rider, about her beloved and kind mentor E. O. Wilson, whom she corresponded with often until his death some months after I was born; she even occasionally told me about her PhD thesis on the evolutionary origins and emergence of eusociality in leafcutter ants, which she wrote, in large part, sitting on a little bench under the splayed leaves of an enormous Scheelea palm tree in the balmy Palm House of the Garfield Conservatory while I slept or—so my mother later told me with a little chastising grin—endlessly fussed in a stroller nearby; how strange, socio, that I was there too, that I once sat under that same Scheelea Palm tree with her, but, of course, I have no memory of this, I have no memory of the tree's immense greenery or the airy humidity of the Palm House. I was a baby, sweaty and gurgling and full of intransigent needs, unshackled from time, but I think the experience of those days must have somehow still accumulated inside of me, bit by bit, because all these years later I occasionally find myself drawn to the Palm House and, from time to time, I find myself there, sitting in silence and trying (and failing) to recall my mother's face, like a forest monk with amnesia, even if the Scheelea Palm at the center is no longer there. In any case, a copy of my mother's dissertation still rests on a bookshelf in her home office, printed and bound in dark green Skivertex.

One sunny afternoon in April, a few months after my mother's death, I got it into my head that I would read her dissertation. Instead, halfway to retrieving it on the bookshelf in her office, I went out on the balcony and sat at the round metal table there, gazing out over the street and Humboldt Park, both of which seemed far too empty for that time of year. Of course, I now understand that you bring emptiness with you. Shadows cast by passing cumulus clouds overhead formed and re-formed sparse patterns and images on the park grass across the street. To this day, as if watching a kind of atavistic film, a few images still come back to me: a field full of rosette plants and grasses, a steaming pot of piranha soup, the high volcanic *páramo*, quaking fires and smoke bending to an approaching storm, a giant carnivorous centipede furling and unfurling. On my mother's balcony that spring day, I came to understand that I was entering gray, uncertain years. Suffice it to say, I never got around to reading her dissertation. It kept falling farther and farther down my list of things to do, until, at some point, it felt like an impossible task.

Afterwards, I took a type of mental inventory of my mother's office before closing its door for the final time: a tropical floral rug purchased in Cuenca, bookshelves filled with tomes on entomology, shelves of ants in Dominican amber fossil gem, a small refrigerator once stocked with ant specimens that still smelled of ethanol a smell that remains frozen forever in the spring of that year—a closet full of backpacks and hiking equipment, a solid mid-twentieth-century mahogany table my father had found in a flea market in Wisconsin, on which there rested her Toaks Titanium mug, an old black laptop, a few ant traps, white plastic bins, an ancient stereo microscope, a jeweler's loupe, three piles of green and red Smyth sewn hardbound field notebooks, the contents of which I understand virtually nothing of what is written, a few worn out Fisher Trekker Space Pens my mom used in the field, both for her research and to write me letters about her travels—as a boy I read those letters at the kitchen table while my father and I ate dinner, and I imagined her writing them in golden lamplight under a forest canopy so dense and ceaseless it seemed to me like an inverted, swaying ocean—and a framed piece of paper with a handwritten quote taken from the travel memoir *The Voyage of the Beagle* by Charles Darwin describing bioluminescent plankton as the Royal Navy ship the HMS Beagle approaches Cape Horn in the fall of 1832: "As far as the eye reached the crest of every wave was bright, and the sky above the horizon, from the reflected glare of these livid flames, was not utterly obscure as over the vault of the heavens."

I'll never truly know what *The Voyage of the Beagle* or that quote meant to my mother. But I suppose there were more than enough indications of it in the work she did. Even now, socio, I wonder if those livid flames offered a shape for my mother's hopes about the living Earth despite her deep fears that the planet had reached—in her words to me while we stood together on the banks of the Napo River, transfixed by the tunnels of light forming and reforming over the waters—its mauve twilight.

Some years ago, while perusing colonial references to Ecuador in the Newberry Library, I was surprised to find an essay written by my mother titled "The Thinking Forest" in an old issue of *Nature*, published only one month after my birth. In the essay, my mother wrote about how as a child in Ávila she often abandoned her duties at the family hostel or helping her father cultivate the manioc gardens near their home to spend endless hours walking through the tangled underbrush of the forests nearby, climbing trees, and turning over fast rotting logs covered in moss and giant mushrooms in order to find the nest gardens of the femoratus ants, the devil's gardens of the lemon ants, and the massive subterranean colonies of the leafcutter ants, which she affectionally called *laberintos de los vivos*. Once, the son of a shaman from a Huaorani village up the Napo River, who had heard rumors of the little girl from Ávila who hunted ants, gifted her a small recorder and contact mic to listen to the little insects. For hours on end, she would sit cross-legged in the soft forgiving forest mud like a "gentle colossus" near the mouth of an underground ant nest, beside herself with joy, recording and listening to the incessant monkey-like chirping the ants made by rubbing two parts of their abdomens together. Through her time in the forest with the ants, she wrote, she began to understand how "we too are the forest itself," something that had been implicitly recognized for millennia in the Amazon, but which had been violently disrupted and even haunted by centuries-long paroxysms of colonialization. The end result was that "enormous boundaries and walls had been erected to construe humans as separate from the endless variety of other kinds of beings and, as such, the rest of the world." By the time she left Ávila for Quito to study ecology, she knew that those enormous boundaries and walls were not a vast symbol or colonial metaphor to be deconstructed in the classroom, but rather as real and corporeal as the Chevron oil wells that lay sulfurous, cancerous waste to the forest and the serpentine, parasitic liana vine that wraps around a tree, takes itself up to the farthest, sunniest reaches of the canopy, and there, in full possession of the tree, strangles it to death in silence. At the end of the essay, my mother recalled one of her earliest memories of ants from when she was around four or five years old: in a small garden clearing adjacent to her home, she was helping her father pull manioc tubers, when, no sooner had dusk fallen and the bulging moon appeared over the canopy, than the clear sky filled with an unfathomable number of winged ants. Between moonlit shafts in the canopy and in the blue-black sky, they spiraled, twisted, zig-zagged, arced, and looped, madly, she remembered, as if forming a sudden buzzing, swarming storm, while still others, wings whirring, entwined in mating—she would learn shortly afterward that this was the leafcutter nuptial flight for virgin queens and their male counterparts—fell to the forest floor. Awestruck, as if an enormous hole had been opened up between the borders of Earth and the celestial realm of hanan pacha, she wondered what kind of fear, pain, and, yes, even joy they felt while flying and falling. In a moment, two winged ants fell directly into the palm of her outstretched hand, which, in her mind, like an enormous arial net, had suddenly reached into the dark canopy itself; her father, then crouching in front of her, face to face, clean-shaven, his hands ruddy from pulling the tautest and largest of the manioc tubers, winked at her, gently picked up the ants, which were still entwined and quivering in their final moments together, and popped them into her mouth.

We spend the rest of our lives chasing our first sublime encounters, don't we, socio? Occasionally, in our apartment on Division Street, my mother would put out a small blue saucer with chopped nuts, sugar water, or a few drops of honey and wait for Tapinoma sessile ants, otherwise known as sugar ants, to appear. Once, upon finding a foraging line of workers heading toward the saucer, she turned to me with a complicit smile and remarked, *How strange, mi vida, that there's no more life in a human than an ant.*

6

Ess and O

ANNA SOLOMON

Sarai, Abraham's wife, had borne him no children. She had an Egyptian maidservant whose name was Hagar.

—Genesis 16:1

Across from her slave, or her surrogate, or perhaps her daughter-in-law, or some combination of all three, which is to say . . . Across from the younger woman, over the unlaid breakfast table, Ess perceived a change.

The girl was pregnant, as of this morning, but that wasn't it. That Ess couldn't see. The only thing she'd seen was a picture of the stick, texted to her fifteen minutes ago from the apartment above Ess and Abe's barn, and the girl's way with words: OMG! SUS

Not even a period and within five minutes she had been at the kitchen door, same open face as the day Ess and Abe found her. Onorata Favilora, like Italian royalty if only. Call me O. Even newly estranged from her family she had exuded an unfaltering optimism, as if in every moment a window had flown open, and she'd turned to feel the breeze. But now, their hands apart but nearly touching so that Ess could feel the girl's heat, her excellent circulation to Ess's poor flow, poor what did the healing woman say? now, wasn't there a twist to O's mouth, an asymmetry that had not existed yesterday? Yesterday, her face had appeared guileless. It had been a simple, comforting face, as the girl had been a simple and comforting presence in their lives. SUS. Ess had had to look it up. O had broad cheekbones. Her skin was a light brown color Ess had learned since she and Abe moved here was Sicilian in origin. Many of the Gloucester locals had it. Abe was a darker brown, Ess much lighter, pink on her good days, blue-white on her bad. The baby might look like it belonged to them. Ess had brown eyes, at least, like Abe, like O.

But the girl's eyes were changed, too. Ess was almost sure of this, because it had struck her more than once, usually when they were on a job together, say hauling a branch they'd sawed off a maple to protect a client's roof, that she could not make out the boundary between O's iris and her pupil. Her eyes were that dark. But this morning, as the coffee maker gasped its last gasps, a sound that had never before struck Ess as sexual, this morning the brown of O's iris versus the black of her pupil was entirely evident. Even the dog would see the difference, Ess thought. If the dog were in here instead of wandering again, probably rolling in the marsh with something dead.

What else had she missed?

"You look different," she said.

"I'm pregnant." O smiled. It was an almost innocent smile, almost sweet. Ess almost joined her. She almost rose to pour two cups of coffee, soothed enough to believe the girl's face wouldn't change again. But then O said, "We did it!" and Ess's muscles would not contract. What had Ess done? All Ess had done was say, This is what we'll do. Sterilize a Mason jar. Take it from him. Carry it to her.

Where was Abe?

"Where's Abe?" asked O.

Out running, Ess thought, to test if O could actually read her mind. But O waited, her eyebrows raised, her eyes new not only in how they looked but how they looked at Ess, less guileless and more probing, like she could see into Ess, see her misery and shame.

"Out running," Ess said.

O's mouth dropped its smile. "But he knew this was the morning," she said.

Of course he knew, Ess wanted to say. The three of them had talked about it over dinner last night. Abe didn't say much, sure, because he was

62 | ANNA SOLOMON

eating a somewhat grotesque quantity of mussels, which he'd harvested himself at low tide. Abe liked mussels for their sustainability ranking and had come to admire them even more after seeing how their beds had held up in last month's blizzard. But it took a lot of mussels to actually feed a person, especially a person who regularly went on ten-mile runs. So he'd been occupied. But he'd been present. He'd heard the plan and nodded.

Ess nodded now, acknowledging O's hurt, jealous that O had voiced it so quickly and clearly. She hadn't tried to wrap it in something else, the way Ess would. The way Ess was doing at this very moment. Ess was hurt by Abe's decision, too. Earlier, in the dark, he'd touched her cheek before he left. Have your moment, he said. Or something like that. She had fallen back asleep. She believed he believed in his own selflessness, but she had also felt the running energy in his fingertips, like a kettle beginning to vibrate. So she was hurt. But also wary. If she and O ganged up, took sides against Abe, wouldn't they become one in his mind? Interchangeable? Ess thought of his face when he'd handed her the jar. His mouth slack, his eyes as distant as if they'd been shellacked. Some portion of this could be explained as the after-stun of climax, but the rest, she guessed, was regret. His muscles betraying the protest he would never speak. She had walked away unsure where to grip the jar, her hands drawn to and repelled by its warm bottom.

No, she would not gang up on Abe. Nor would she apologize for him. She forced herself to hold O's gaze, which was so unrelenting—had she blinked once?—that Ess couldn't help but know it as defiance. She wanted to thank O. But that seemed impossibly awkward, given the circumstance. Insufficient before it was even uttered. And what would she even say? Thank you for taking my husband's sperm into your womb? Ha. She could say congratulations, but that seemed even weirder, because wouldn't O, then, have to say it back?

"How are you feeling?" she said.

"I feel great."

"Different?"

O smiled again. "Not at all."

Now Ess rose and went to pour the coffee. She could feel, physically feel, her emptiness, the dark grief-dread so heavy at her center she could sink. Drop to the floor right now and go insensate. Every phone call, every needle, every choice. The fact that they lived here, on this isolated spit of land. Yes, there had been Abe's own desire to leave the city, leave finance, work with his hands. (In her worst moments she'd accused him of an outsized arrogance, a sense of himself as a pilgrim; what was it he'd once said, only half-joking, about being on a hero's journey?) But also, moving here had been a chance for Ess to relax, leave her own corporate job—maybe her body would respond. Maybe the fresh salt air would work its magic. It hadn't. So here they were, with no other dwellings in sight, the high tides a little higher each year. The only magic had been the appearance of O, who'd seen their flyer. She'd been working five jobs and living on her aunt's sunporch. Within a month she was working one and living in the apartment above their barn.

"That's wonderful," Ess said to the counter, as she stirred. She knew how O liked her coffee—no sugar, nearly white with cream. O had said this was its own rebellion, that her family drank only espresso and drank it black. Ess poured in extra cream today, thinking it might counteract the caffeine. She would have to talk with O about that. Also deli meats, raw fish, etc. "I was always sick from day one," she said. "All the good it did."

There was a long silence then. Ess brought the coffees, and they sat sipping. Outside, the new landscape, left by the storm, continued to settle. The one remaining oak. The others in their piles, waiting to be cut. The wreckage of the driveway, its crushed clamshells tossed in every direction like confetti. And to the east, way out past the marsh, past the island whose trees had previously blocked their view, in the widened gap between the barrier beaches, a perverse, glinting gift: the ocean.

Only O saw all this, because only O faced the window. This was a reversal: Every other morning she sat in the window seat, facing the kitchen, but today Ess had claimed the window seat without a word of acknowledgment, simply plopped down there after hugging O. They had never hugged before. There had been no reason to, they'd seen each other every day since they'd met. Ess smelled like sleep. O wasn't sure that Ess even meant to switch seats. Maybe she was in shock. But if she did mean to, what did she mean by it? Was the view a prize?

In Ess's face, O saw anger. She should have predicted this, she thought, should have known what they were doing couldn't actually be simple. But the storm's destruction had made everything seem pure, as if nothing that had come before still existed. Why couldn't they create a family any way they wanted, without contracts or awkwardness or envy?

Ess's anger was concentrated in a wrinkle, which O hadn't noticed until today. A tiny trough between her eyebrows. Ess spent a great deal of effort and money trying to prevent such things, O knew, because all packages came first to the barn. Early on in O's employment, when she and Ess had just begun their friendship, the two of them driving from job to job with O at the wheel and Ess facing her like a child, her back against the truck door, talking, talking, she'd said, "You know, we're both just shy of being in our thirties." Her tone satisfied and insistent at once, like someone who'd just spotted a constellation and wanted a friend to see it, too. O had smiled, liking the image it called to mind, a circle that was *the thirties*, she and Ess both peering in. She was 27, Ess 42. Now they were 28 and 43. Neither was very young, nor even close to being old.

Before the storm, in early January, after fourteen months of purgatory on a waitlist, Abe and Ess had found a surrogate. A woman in Maine who checked every box: two kids of her own carried and delivered without complication; a stable marriage; no notable health history. Plus she lived only a couple hours up the coast, close enough that Ess and Abe could easily get there for major appointments. An egg from a donor in Indiana had been shipped express to Boston. By the end of the month, Abe was scheduled to go to the clinic. Their morning meetings over coffee stretched into elaborate breakfasts, Abe making omelets while O scheduled the day and Ess teased Abe about which magazines would be waiting for him. Ess bought dozens of lanterns that threw off thousands of pinpricks of light and staked them around the house like a glimmering lasso. One night, walking among the lanterns as they blew around in the wind, O had seen Ess and Abe dancing in their living room. She couldn't hear the music, because the windows they'd installed were so state-of-the-art they didn't leak even a drumbeat, but it must have been something. They weren't holding each other, like she might have imagined, if she'd imagined such a thing. Instead they moved to no discernible rhythm, together only in that they appeared similarly possessed, their eyes closed, their limbs flailing, the whole scene so wild O drew up her scarf and turned away.

And then the storm hit. A full week without power before they could check voicemail. The surrogate: she was so sorry. The agent: the surrogate and her husband had lost their house, they'd had to move in with his parents for who knew how long, Abe and Ess would need to start over, rejoin the waitlist. In an email, the lawyer attached the voided contract. A representative from the hospital had left a message, too. The first night of the storm, one of the tanks holding the eggs had failed. They were very sorry, too.

It was simple. But, of course, it wasn't. O's sister, out in LA, had warned her. But she'd warned her only about Abe, and in the most predictable, tired way: she'd wanted to place a bet on how long before he put the moves on O. When O said no one said *put the moves on* anymore, her sister said the bet was the same. When O said Abe wasn't that kind of man, that in fact he was the opposite kind of man, her sister said the opposite kind was even worse, the ones who thought they were enlightened. *I've warned you,* she said before she hung up. *Don't say I didn't warn you.*

"I'm sorry," O said now to the furrow in Ess's brow.

Ess looked at O as if she had only now appeared. Her anger looked more like bewilderment. She was tender. "There's nothing for you to be sorry about," she said.

"When will we tell Abe?" O asked a minute later.

"We'll wait here for him."

"We're supposed to be in Lanesville by 8."

"We'll wait."

"The look on his face!" O clapped her hands to her cheeks, trying to excite herself.

Ess smiled, for the first time that morning. The light in her eyes was so blinding O started to cry.

"Don't cry," Ess said.

"They're happy tears," O lied.

"Don't cry."

O stopped crying. She wiped her face, and tilted her coffee toward it. The cream Ess and Abe bought was the best thing O had ever tasted. Her mother would have laughed, not in a friendly way. But her mother was not here.

"Holy shit," O said.

And now Ess dropped her false smile.

"Holy shit," she said.

They took each other's hands. It was the only option, if they weren't going to fall to the floor or flee. They would sit like that until Abe returned, high from sprinting the final stretch, his hands on his hips, his lungs wide open, his eyes so oxygenated everything would shimmer gently, the marsh and the sky and a memory of his mother calling his father a wild ass of a man and a vision, when he finally looked at the house, of two women talking.

7

Lot's Daughters

Zeeva Bukai

So Lot went out to them to the entrance, shut the door behind him, and said, "I beg you, my friends, do not commit such a wrong. Look, I have two daughters who have not known a man."

—Genesis 19:6–8

Kay and I drifted on the swings, half-blinded by sunlight when Danny came into the park on his skateboard the summer I turned thirteen. Kay and I spent every day there, sharing cans of coke and smoking Tareytons filched out of our Aunt CiCi's Pink Ladies bowling bag. Kay was my sister but she lived with Aunt CiCi in a small rental a block away. She moved in with her in the spring after her fifteenth birthday celebration went bust because someone spiked the cola with Seagrams and because Daddy found her without her shirt on in the hall closet, playing seven minutes in heaven with a boy whose hair was so black it looked like fresh tar. Daddy ordered everyone to leave and said Kay wasn't allowed out anymore. After the screams died and the air stopped hissing, Kay left with Aunt CiCi. Mama stayed behind in the kitchen, muttering the prayer for the dead, gazing at her like she was on fire, untouchable, afraid Kay would now be lost to her.

"Sorry kiddo," Kay kissed my cheek on her way out.

I tried to run after her but Daddy swept me up in his arms. The smell of fresh laundry warring with the tang of his sweat. "*Kapara*, my atonement," he said and stroked my hair. I saw the shattered veins in his eyes. Beads of moisture collected in the deep cleft I used to poke my finger into his chin. "Don't you break my heart," he cried.

Aunt CiCi lived alone. She had star quality. She played in a bowling league and had a special glass cabinet in her living room where she stored her trophies. She once pinned a ribbon to my chest so I could feel what it was like to be a winner.

Kay and I were practically twins, only twenty months apart. We crooned to Laura Nyro's "Eli's Comin'" in the bath. We believed love was imminent. Our voices like bells and cymbals reverberated against the tiles. We dressed in Hanes ribbed tanks and homemade cutoffs with a fringe soft as baby fingers. We liked that our bra straps showed. We used the same razor. Our hair was long and streaked with lemon-juice highlights. We worked hard on our tans. Every day in the sun was an opportunity.

Kay could crush a can of cola in one hand. She grew her fingernails long and painted them bazooka pink. Blowing on her wet nails she said, "I'm gonna be a winner like Aunt CiCi."

I envied her certainty, her newfound autonomy. I envied her winner status.

"Look." I pointed to the dandelion and fleabane erupting out of the cracks in the sidewalk. I didn't want to hear about winners anymore. "Aren't they beautiful," I said.

"Weeds ought to be ripped out by the root," Kay said.

But I didn't agree. I thought if something managed to grow in a slit of darkness it was worth holding on to. Sometimes love grew like that, unexpected and surprising in its goodness.

The park was pinned between our Hebrew Day School and an overgrown plot of land a half a block long. Anything tossed in was swallowed up in the vegetation. Small animals lived there: opossums in their nests, feral cats in the ground cover, raccoons in their dens. All through the months of May and June raccoons screeched in heat. Their eerie cries tore through our dreams. Mama told me to watch out for ticks but never said a word about the yellowjackets burrowed underground. My ankles were swollen for weeks. The lot was covered in dandelion, mugwort, and lamb's quarter.

The hogweed stood taller than our father. He was only a few inches taller than me, but everyone said he was a giant in our city, a *tzadik*, a righteous man, a man of God. People traveled long distances to seek his advice and judgment on family matters and neighborhood disputes, potential marriages, business deals gone wrong, deadbeat tenants, and unreasonable landlords. Mama would serve the petitioners tea and dates. After they sipped and snacked, he listened to their troubles, soothed their confusion, and allayed their fears. They said his house was as honorable as a *beit din*. Out of respect they called him Rabbi and to honor him they called him Judge.

Our small community consisted of an elementary school and junior high, a Shell station, and a strip mall with a Chinese restaurant, a kosher butcher, McNeal's bar, which opened at noon, and a storefront Weight Watchers. There were twenty blocks of two-family townhouses that all looked alike. The local synagogue was in the paneled basement of a Chabad rabbi. Water gushing through sewer pipes accompanied all nineteen benedictions of the Amidah. Towering above us was the Church of the Immaculate Conception. The shadow of its cross stretched long over our rooftops.

At the start of the summer, Kay and I found a brand-new loveseat in the center of the lot, surrounded by a fortress of weeds. Kay thought it might have fallen out of the sky.

"Like a gift from an angel," I said.

"No, like it fell out of a cargo plane."

To make it homier, we placed a coffee table beside it. We arranged the old jaw bones and opossum teeth we found in a circle to mark our territory. Once, we discovered a severed thumb that looked like the end of a hot dog someone had choked on. Kay thought the thumb looked like an ordinary thumb.

"A thing's a thing," she said. "Don't make it into something it's not."

Before Kay left home, Mama said Kay's pragmatism was admirable and that I ought to learn from her. My problem, she said, was that I couldn't see things for what they were. I got angry and said, "I learned willful blindness from you," then felt bad about it when her face lost color and she needed to lie down. I told myself permanency was an illusion. I told Kay that I lived in a slit of darkness, planted where I didn't belong like that loveseat, like the dandelion and fleabane that should've sprouted in the dirt but instead crept out of a crack in the sidewalk.

She shrugged. "Weeds'll grow anywhere. Gimme another cigarette."

I stood on the swing with Kay squeezed between my feet. My body heaving upward, chains shuddering. The air smelled of burnt paper. The heat made our eyeballs throb. Danny came in on his skateboard, shirt damp with sweat. The park shrank to a stump. He leaned against the fence and watched us take flight. The star of David he wore around his neck captured the sun. I felt his eyes peel me down till I was wound-wet and swollen. He never let on that I wasn't beautiful. He called me "baby" and said in the kind of whisper my father used for benedictions, "you've really got something," but never told me what it was.

He was a stranger in our city. Sixteen and already working a job stocking meat in a supermarket. He lived alone with his mother and never knew his father. His mother said his dad died in a war but didn't tell him which one. She said he left when Danny was two or three. She said he was missing in action. His portrait hung on the living room wall as a reference point, a place for Danny to cast his eye whenever he felt lost.

"He could have been anybody," Danny said.

When he invited us home, my hands shook.

"You go," Kay said. "I've got better things to do." Then she pulled me aside, "Sister, you ask yourself if Daddy's gonna like him before you do anything stupid," then sauntered off, knowing Danny was watching her leave, hips twitching from side to side.

Danny's house, like mine, was new, built on landfill that shifted with the phases of the moon. The sidewalk buckled and in the middle of the street was a pothole large enough for cars to careen into, a black hole, a centrifugal force ready to suck us into the magma.

After a quick tour, we kissed in his mother's bedroom. The sheets smelled of cats. I daubed her patchouli on the backs of my knees. His hands traced the places my father wanted to go. And when the sun began to set, he mapped my body with his tongue. I was turned earth, fertile and fresh for him.

We ate the casserole his mother left. I wore his underwear under my jeans like a holy garment and imagined my father seeing me strut about in them, peering through the crack in my bedroom door, watching me with grim desire. Twilight was a procession of sacred blues pressing against the windowpanes. I sat in Danny's lap while he brushed my hair. We listened to "Give Me Love." Over cigarettes and ice cream he asked about my family.

When I talked about my mother I sounded muffled. Her place was on the sofa. In her hand was an embroidery needle. In her lap, a tapestry of a fox hunt. She tried her best to keep me stitched up, but embroidery thread isn't like catgut. Her face was a foreign painting. Her body was a painting of a woman sitting on a sofa. She played the recorder and the phonograph. Every afternoon at four she played the *1812 Overture* while my father was at work. She loved how it opened with heartbreak and ended with canons. War on the taiga, a symphony for the dead. Music that sealed her in frost. Her memories an ice floe she floated past me on.

She hated when I came home late tracking in Danny's scent.

"Snow begins pure until it reaches ground," she said. "You're gonna get us in trouble." Her face was stark with fear. Mama looked wounded. Sometimes she doubled over in pain.

"It's only phantom hunger," she said.

I told her we were in love, like Bonnie and Clyde.

"Gangsters," she muttered, resigned to my fate.

I never talked about my father, not even when Danny asked. I was his youngest daughter, an afterthought. My two eldest sisters fled to a city near the sea. I never asked them why. I knew. I think I've always known. Even before Kay left to live with Aunt CiCi, Daddy called me his *yafeifiyah*, his beauty. He called me *ayouni*, his eyes, and *kapara*, his atonement. That summer he must have sensed that I loved Danny, because his hands became ravenous. He buried longing in the ground where it grew like strangling weeds. Without Kay there as a buffer, I was his *terra firma*. I was where he planted his heels.

Kay wasn't serious about the boy with the black-as-tar hair, but she let him take her out; she let him touch her in the places she'd been told were exquisite and shameful. We were in her bedroom at Aunt CiCi's, an alcove with a blackout curtain, drinking Kahlua and cream. I was dizzy staring at the ceiling. The nubs on the white bedspread were like thumbs in my back.

"Can I tell you something?" She said, her breath heavy across my face.

"Sure," I said.

"That boy wants to marry me. He says that's the kind of love I inspire."

"Do you believe him?"

"No," she said.

I could feel our heartbeats traveling in tandem through our bodies. The pounding worried me. I wanted it to end.

"You don't have to marry him," I said. "Not if you don't want to."

"Don't be an idiot. He was Daddy's choice. Why do you think he was at my party? Why do you think I took him into the closet?"

"To ruin his chances," I said. "To punish Daddy." The room spun and I held onto the mattress.

"Oh God, shut up, just shut up," Kay said.

I loved the days when it was just me and Danny. We stole Marlboros and red hots from John's Deli while the counterman sliced a quarter pound of bologna. We scored nickel bags from a redheaded guy named Glen. On rainy afternoons we sat in Danny's kitchen. Blind Faith's "Can't Find My Way Home" on the stereo. The fridge packed with beer and a lasagna for dinner. He said our days were like beads on a string of lost promise. I called him a poet. He called me a fucking princess. We drank cola with aspirin, hoping it would get us high. Every ashtray in his house was a pyre of stubs.

That summer the air quality was low. Mama couldn't catch her breath. Shit for lungs, the tattered remnants of war. Her hands opened and floss unspooled. Daddy dropped her off at the emergency room, then rushed to the temple to form a *minyan*. He was a public griever, a keener, a man who turned worry into prayer. He *davened* with ferocious intent. His body jerked as if possessed, like a man speaking in tongues. He prayed to God. He prayed to the angels as sewer water churned through the pipes.

On his way home he saw me and Danny in the park, refracted in the light, a kaleidoscope of parts. His mouth on mine, his hands cradling my face like I was something precious. Daddy kept me home for a week. Someone had to cook and clean. Someone had to take my mother's place. I scrubbed the floors on my knees. I stuffed peppers with beef and rice. I threaded a needle and filled in the blank spaces of the hunt. No one in that tapestry escaped.

My father was a secret agent. He spoke to me in code. Every gesture a signal for what was to come. He was a prophet who planted minefields. I didn't know where to step. If I could, I'd have sent him back to the ghetto he came from where they'd hang him in Martyr's Square and bury his body outside the gates of Damascus in the desert where the jackals would ravage him.

I tried to barricade the door. It worked for a night, maybe two but he found his way in, or I let him. I'm not sure.

The doctor hand-fed my mother pills that made her face swell. She stared at her reflection and wept. When she came home I was crouched like an animal on the cushion.

"What happened?" she said

"He thinks I'm you."

"Look at me. What can I do?" Her face slack as a sheet, powerless in this house, in this city. Her eyes disappeared into folds of flesh as she watched me go.

I ran to the park in my cutoffs and tank. Kay was on the swing in a miniskirt I'd never seen. Danny stood over her like a wishbone. His hands gripped the chains, his feet hugged the sides of her hips.

"Hey," I said and sat down beside her. My hands and lips numb.

"Hey." She wouldn't look me in the eye.

I gazed up at Danny and said, "What did you do to her?"

He jumped off the swing. "Nothing, baby. It meant nothing." And though he stroked my hair, I knew she was his *yafeifiyah* now, his beautiful girl.

Kay said, "Sisters forever, right?" And held out her pinky, her nails ragged like she'd been digging in dirt.

"Why?"

Kay shrugged. "He wasn't Daddy's choice."

I imagined her fingers trapped in a bowling ball. I imagined her on a league with Aunt CiCi, wearing a Pink Ladies uniform like a waitress at a Greek diner, a winner's ribbon round her throat, her tongue blue as the ribbon CiCi once pinned to my chest.

"It's all right," Danny said. "Nothing's changed."

We went back to his house alone and broke into his mom's liquor cabinet. I hid in her bedroom, cradling the bottle. He followed me there, playing with the bowie knife he got for his birthday last year from his uncle Bob in Florida.

Danny pushed me to my knees. "Bitch, you're mine," he whispered lovingly.

The rug was soaked in Dewar's. Three Dog Night belted "Jeremiah Was a Bullfrog" on the kitchen radio. I thought it was romantic how he held the knife to my throat.

"I'm yours."

I wondered what Daddy would say if he knew.

Danny never told me it was over. A few weeks later, I was outside the park and saw him take Kay down the slide that curved like a machete. His arms around her waist. Her face glowed and hanging from her neck was his star of David. He taught her to skateboard and kissed her on the mouth. He kissed her mouth. The dandelion and fleabane withered under the August sun. The weeds in the lot turned to husks. I saw them together on the loveseat laughing, touching. His hands never still. The coffee table slowly covered in undergrowth. The jaw bones marking our territory overrun. Alone on the swing, my forsaken body touched the sky.

That autumn Danny left with his mother for a distant city. I hadn't seen or spoken to Kay in months. Mama told me she went back to the boy with the black-as-tar hair. I missed Danny. I missed the loamy scent rising off his thighs. I missed his lips on my neck, the slickness of his teeth, the soft warmth of his tongue, the way he devoured me like meat. I whispered his name to my father in the dark. I squeezed my eyes shut and heard the swift hiss of his hand as it came down from above. He grabbed hold of my hair the way he had Kay's all those months ago, and dragged me outside. I hit the ground hard. Porches were lit with men drinking beer, the same men who with enough liquor in them shot their guns into the air, into the lot, who used cats for target practice, who fought each other bloody, and petitioned my father for judgment and advice.

Mama pressed against the screen door.

I tugged my shirt over my thighs. A breeze cooled my shamed skin. "Daddy?"

"Not in my house," he said. His expression an ache of disappointment. I was his *yafayfiyah*, his *ayouni*, his *kapara*. The front door slammed shut behind him.

The men mumbled and shifted, tugged at their crotches. I sat on the stoop stretching the tee shirt over my knees. One of them groaned and soon they all banded in front of our house, jostled for position and jeered at me.

Mama came out then. "Go home," she cried. "Nothing to see here."

She took me inside, washed my face. Bits of concrete glittered like jewels in my cheek.

"Love like that can kill a girl," she said.

I snuck out after Daddy fell asleep half wild, my face swollen. A yellow moon bled through the trees. I reached the park buttressed against the empty lot. Dry weeds rustled. I remembered Danny and I on the loveseat. I remembered him and Kay there, safe in that fortress. The wind swallowed their names as they fled my mouth. I lit a match and then another until the brush finally caught. Fire swept through the lot and engulfed the loveseat. Cats and raccoons charged as flames roared toward the park. Embers whipped into the air and landed on the rooftops of the nearby townhouses that ignited like tinder.

I could see it stretched before me like a prophecy, the city in flames as the angels watched it burn. In the distance, engines roared. I looked up and saw Mama, her breath wheezing, and beside her was Kay, my sister, clutching our bags. Our faces gorgeous in the half-light.

"What are you girls waiting for," Mama said. "Let's go."

8

Binding Variations

Daniel Torday

Some time afterward, God put Abraham to the test. He said to him, "Abraham," and he answered, "Here I am." And He said, "Take your son, your favored one, Isaac, whom you love, and go to the land of Moriah, and offer him there as a burnt offering on one of the heights that I will point out to you."

—Genesis 22:1–2

Isaac's Age

On the morning his father takes him to Mt. Moriah to offer him as sacrifice, Isaac is thirty-seven years old. As a thirty-seven-year-old man he is too old to question his father's motives—he must simply be happy his father longs for a hike. They have always hiked together in the summers. It is their easiest opportunity to talk.

Isaac is single at the time. He is too old to call a friend bruh, too old to order a Long Island Iced Tea at a Long Island bar. Probably his IT-bands have atrophied, his knees have burned their cartilage and ache on long walks. He throws on an American Apparel hoodie, navy blue, to wear on the long trek to Moriah. It will take three whole days just to get there. His father eyes him askance—anyone seeing a thirty-seven-year-old man in a hoodie might. Isaac is wearing a pair of Vans and a Guns N' Roses t-shirt, yellow at the armpits.

Surely he suffers some embarrassment for still living at home with his parents.

When, on the third day, in the early morning, the sun rises above Mt. Moriah, its light spreads one ray at a time. Isaac at thirty-seven has grown nearsighted from all the time at home, alone, reading. In 2010 BC, the year he and his father make their most recent ascent (Isaac was born in the year 2047 BC, the first day of Rosh Hashanah), glasses had not yet been invented. Glass either.

Sunrise is a resplendent blur.

His father always rises before him, and on this morning, after three days of hiking, he has already begun his ascent.

For a man in his late thirties, who has hiked with his father since before memory, following his father up a mountain is an unconscious act: lace up the Asolos, fill up the Camelback, throw on the Gregory backpack, don't forget the gorp. At the mountain's top as his father prepares an altar for the sacrifice, Isaac is distracted. He's been carrying the wood and the binding to build the altar as he always does. What man at the age of thirty-seven is not yet distracted from the task at hand? The pain of looking for a job, the ache of his hips (those atrophied IT-bands!), the women he's been dating, if you could call speed-dating dating.

All of these are in mind.

He does not lie down on the altar. He will not help his father to secure his donkey or note the moment when a lamb comes in his place for sacrifice. Even his question as to where the lamb is when they summit Moriah is offhanded, rote.

He will not hear either side of his father's conversation with the Lord. Maybe he's got earbuds in, listening to the Dead or the Allmans. When his father calls for help with the lamb, he simply slogs off to help secure the animal, as he has so many times that the action has grown unconscious, his mind on his aches and happinesses and other signs of failure.

Isaac and Bob Dylan

On the nervous ascent of the mountain after they pick up camp on the third morning of their trip, Isaac starts singing "Girl from the North Country." It's not clear that *Nashville Skyline* is defensibly the best Bob Dylan record, or even that it's Isaac's favorite. But it's got Johnny Cash, and Norman Blake on guitar, and so it is the best compromise between Isaac and his 137-year-old father. His father's hearing is in decline, so he sings louder than he'd like.

"If you're going," Isaac sings, "where the snowflakes fall, where rivers freeze and summer ends."

"No!" Abraham says sharply. Isaac doesn't know what the problem is, so he starts to sing the verse again, a little louder even this time.

"If you're going where the snowflakes fall . . ."

"No! Not snowflakes fall, son. Snowflakes *storm*. This lyric is all-important, beautiful in so many ways. Much more beautiful than if they were simply to fall, as if they were not guided by the storming hand of the whirlwind."

The top of Mt. Moriah is hot, baked dry. Isaac has never seen a snowflake, let alone seen one fall, or storm.

Isaac and Søren Kierkegaard

When he is a freshman in college, Isaac reads a book called *Fear and Trembling*, which is nominally written by a man named Johannes de Silentio, though everyone sees the name on the spine of the book is the Danish philosopher Kierkegaard. When he first encounters this book, Isaac has only ever heard this philosopher's name in a movie based on a *Saturday Night Live* skit called *Wayne's World*, referenced as the most esoteric possible philosopher. But the content of the book is not esoteric or even difficult. It is three midrashic readings of the Akedah, the account of Abraham taking Isaac to sacrifice him after God commands him to, without further explanation.

Isaac has suffered through plenty of Monday and Wednesday afternoons in Hebrew school. He knows from the Akedah.

Isaac imagines himself taking this book to the top of Mt. Moriah with his father. He's got almost twenty years ahead of him before they make the trip, and he'll know it better than he could even imagine by the time they get there. His father will get him up early on the third day of the hike. They will ascend the mountain. When they reach the top, when it is Isaac's turn to ask, "Where is the lamb for the sacrifice?" instead he will know better than his father.

"Have you ever read Kierkegaard?" he'll ask, instead of asking after the lamb. The nice thing on these hikes is that they can talk like this, just

BINDING VARIATIONS | 79

saying whatever comes to mind. That freedom is what Isaac thinks of as human closeness.

"Oh, back when I was an undergrad," his father will say. His father could never admit to not having read a book. He's a professor of English after all, in addition to being a farmer. "Which one?"

"*Fear and Trembling*," Isaac will say.

"Oh, sure, that one," his father will say. He'll look off to the horizon, to the long trail dotted with cairns to mark the way. It's blackfly season and they're biting so they can only stop for so long. "But I was always partial to *Sickness unto Death*."

Then Isaac's father will drone on about this other book—a book he clearly knows better.

A bait-and-switch to cover up for his lack of memory of the first book.

But Isaac's already tuned him out, looking out over the baked-hot valley. His father won't ever even turn around to see that Isaac's got his earbuds back in his ears, his hood popped up over his head.

Isaac and 9/11

On the day the planes fly into the buildings, Isaac and his father are summiting the mountain. It is a clear day, and cool, the perfect day for a hike. They are nearly six thousand miles to the east of the area where the event happens, but along with the whiff of sage and lavender in the air, Isaac detects a smell that can't be missed: the smell of a thousand burnt robot raccoons.

Isaac has never seen a raccoon. He does not know what a robot is. Still, he can't shake that smell from his head.

"You smell that?" he asks his father. They've almost reached the top of the mountain. It has been an unusually long time since they've spoken to each other. Isaac's father stops and turns around, looking every day of his hundred-and-thirty-seven years.

"Smell what," his father says. "I haven't smelled anything in thirty years."

Isaac and Love

In the months after the summiting of Mt. Moriah, Isaac's father seems to have tons of energy, frantic energy. One day after Isaac finishes with the

80 | DANIEL TORDAY

dishes and watering the plants, his father's friend Eli shows up with a girl. She has a nose ring and gold bracelets on her wrists and a thick accent. Isaac asks who this beautiful girl is, and Eli tells him her name is Rebecca. Isaac at first thinks he can't possibly take on a woman his father has sent for. But he has manners, so he takes her for a walk on their grounds. He points out the olive trees in the distance, next to them a lattice of branches built to bear grape vines. He looks at the girl and sees she's terrifically beautiful. He would marry her. He's done with speed-dating and parents'-basement-living.

Isaac doesn't know any of this when he summits Mt. Moriah with his father months earlier. He finds it strange when his father interrupts his singing to ask after his relations with women. Generally, when they speak of women it's for his father to tell for the thousandth time the story of his mother, who laughed when she heard she was pregnant with him—her first, when she was already in her eighties. Usually his father would say, "She'd never laugh again, you can bet that."

But now he says, "Have you been seeing anyone, my son?"

"Seeing?" Isaac says. "What is this, like 2078 or something? I've hooked up with some women, sure, but 'seeing'?"

Isaac's father says he doesn't appreciate the sarcasm. He just wants what's best for his son. What father doesn't want what's best for his son? Abraham asks.

Before Isaac can say anything his father continues to argue with himself: but how do we know what's best for us? Is it to do what's expeditious in the moment, what's easy—or to follow the path that's been set out before us?

Isaac thinks of a time in college when he learned of a philosopher who has come up with the concept of eudaimonia. This means that what is good for us will make us happy, even if we don't know it at the time. The professor gives the example of smoking cigarettes: though they might seem to taste good, in fact our body knows they are bad for us and will reject them. The smoker will develop a cough. It grows harder for him to run, to breathe deeply, to enjoy food. If he understands eudaimonia, he'll quit. Or he'll die from it, unhappily.

Isaac doesn't mention any of this to his father, who continues to perseverate. Then finally his father stops.

"But I was asking about women," he says.

"I've been with a few," Isaac says. He's thinking of his first time—with an older woman, to the east, in a lake so shallow he could not ever submerge himself entirely in the water. It excites him even to think of it now.

When he looks back up, his father has that energy in his hands that Isaac will see in himself every day until Rebecca shows up.

"Let's keep moving," his father says. "I'm not getting any younger."

9

Bilhah and Zilpah
Made Me Yearn for Torah

ERICA RIDDICK

She said, "Here is my maid Bilhah. Consort with her, that she may bear on my knees and that through her I too may have children." So she gave him her maid Bilhah as concubine, and Jacob cohabitated with her. Bilhah conceived and bore Jacob a son.

—Genesis 30:3–5

I first became conscious of Bilhah and Zilpah from reading *The Red Tent* by Anita Diamant, a modern midrash that creatively reimagines Dinah's story not as rape but as a love story with Shekhem. The book opens: "We have been lost to each other for so long. My name means nothing to you. My memory is dust. This is not your fault, or mine. The chain connecting mother to daughter was broken and the word passed to the keeping of men, who had no way of knowing. That is why I became a footnote."

Dinah introduces us to all four of her mothers, including Zilpah and Bilhah, the enslaved women given by Lavan to his daughters, Leah and Rachel, on their respective wedding nights to Yaakov. The opening of *The Red Tent* reminds me that the stories lost between mother and daughter have a larger impact through severed connections with language, land, culture, and custom in Judaism and other cultural threads that weave through me.

I didn't realize how strongly I needed the feminine perspectives of our biblical narratives. These vivid vignettes of the everyday in the lives of women made me *want* to read Torah rather than feel I had to. Bilhah and Zilpah called out to me from the story in a unique way that left me wanting to learn more. What other connections have been forgotten through women's relationships, perspectives, and impact being expressed or interpreted by men?

The Torah holds eleven lines that mention Zilpah, and thirteen that mention Bilhah (with five that name both). Throughout the story, Bilhah is referred to as שִׁפְחָה *shifcha* (slave), אָמָה *ama* (concubine), אִשָּׁה *isha* (wife), and פִּילֶגֶשׁ *pilegesh* (concubine), while Zilpah transitions between שפחה *shifcha*, אשה *isha*, and אמה *ama*. Neither has direct lines. Their words and feelings are absent. They are only referred to and directed by others.

The Torah teaches that these enslaved women were owned by Lavan and later given to his daughters, Rachel and Leah, as bridal gifts. They were given away again by these daughters to their mutual husband Yaakov to orchestrate the conception of children that Rachel and Leah intended to claim as their own.

Midrash adds that Bilhah and Zilpah were themselves the product of a union between Lavan and another enslaved woman, making Bilhah and Zilpah Lavan's daughters, sisters to Rachel and Leah. There are scant details on Zilpah and Bilhah. We don't know their origin or end story, how old they are in the narrative, how they or their mother became enslaved, or first encountered Lavan, how long they lived, who they loved, and if that included Yaakov, what they envisioned for their lives, or how they navigated maintaining their relationships with their children, despite the Torah's language that their children would belong to Rachel and Leah.

Many see a distinction between biblical and "modern" slavery. Do we allow discomfort over a history not reckoned with to pardon ignoring what the Torah demands we should never forget, that every letter holds meaning, and repetition bears focus? It's okay to examine the fullness of something like the עקדה Akedah (binding of Isaac), including its darker aspects, but less so to explore the foundational Jewish narrative of escaping slavery, *while also* participating in and codifying the same system; a system that has a relationship with later enslavement.

The Hebrew word עבד *eved* (slave) is used for men and groups of mixed gender. When referring to female slaves, the Torah uses one of three words: שפחה *shifcha* (female slave), אמה *ama* (female concubine slave), and פילגש *pilegesh* (concubine). Having a different word for the male and female equivalent is not unusual in Hebrew. While nuance in language is also common, having three options to identify female slaves when there is one for men stands out. The control of sexual relationship, reproduction, and marriage may account for the additional language. It may also offer insight into the relationship between the common ש-פ-ח root of שפחה *shifcha* (slave) and משפחה *mishpacha* (family), or the phonetic relationship between אמה *ama* (slave) and אמא *ima* (mother). How do these linguistic foundations influence not only the biblical story but our modern one?

Mishneh Torah holds another clue that supports the interrelationship between words that conflate wife and slave, seeding the continued need for modern day feminism. Mishneh Torah was the audacious project of Rabbi Moshe ben Maimon (aka Maimonedes, aka RaMbaM), an eleventh-century rabbi and physician, straddling parallel Jewish and secular worlds. It was intended as commentary of the Mishnah (itself considered a second Torah) and comprehensive halakhic code encompassing Tosefta, Midrash, and Talmud. Moshe envisioned a *beit midrash* (house of study) where all you would need is the Torah in one hand and the fourteen books of Mishneh Torah in the other.

The twelfth book of Mishneh Torah is the Book of Acquisitions. The last of five divisions in Sefer Kinyan is Mishneh Torah Slaves, which holds nine chapters. Chapter 4 focuses on conditions around selling females as slaves or wives, and freeing enslaved Hebrew females. It opens noting that a father may sell a daughter as אמה העבריה *ama haivri* (Hebrew slave) who is not yet twelve years in age. After becoming נערה *na'arah* (maiden), a father may marry his daughter to whomever he chooses (4:1). It's clarified that a father may not sell a daughter unless he owns nothing (4:2). This suggests that this was happening among the poorest of the poor. However, codes can also be evidence of what people were doing instead of observing documented code, thus the motivation to create codes to incentivize action deemed desirable by an individual or body. The chapter compels fathers to redeem daughters (4:2), and one option for redemption appears to have existed through marriage.

Mishneh Torah states that "the mitzvah of designating an *ama haivri* [Hebrew slave] as a wife takes precedence over the mitzvah of redemption" (4:7), quelling previous urges of redemption with the temptation of a marriage contract. This transition from *ama haivri* to wife occurred through the master telling the slave "*behold, you are consecrated to me,*" or "*you are betrothed to me,*" or "*behold, you are my wife*" before two witnesses. This could be proclaimed at the end of the six years of servitude. Seamless

BILHAH AND ZILPAH MADE ME YEARN FOR TORAH | 85

transition from enslavement to wifedom, with no transition in between underscores the Hebrew root relationship between slave, family, and mother. Additionally, lines that highlight designating a slave as a wife "is equivalent to consecration, but not to marriage," and warnings that husbands may not become impure *because of her* bring to mind earlier considerations around code that may indicate that what is documented may be opposite of what was lived common occurrence.

Seeking to better understand these distinctions between the language used to identify female enslavement yields more questions. Mishneh Torah Slaves exclusively uses אמה *ama*. While שפחה *shifkha*, a primary word for female slave, appears seven times instead within Mishneh Torah Sales, the first of the five divisions within Sefer Kinyan, the Book of Acquisitions. Mishneh Torah Sales 15:12 maintains that עבד *eved* (male slave) or שפחה *shifcha* (female slave) are not for the purpose of physical intimacy, but to perform work (15:12). That this is declared hints that אמה *ama* (slave concubine) is intentionally connected to marriage and procreation, and further reinforces the conflation of wifedom with enslavement since this discussion occurs in the chapter defining slaves. However, one can wonder how this clarification relates to the consecration of marriage through sexual relations as outlined in Mishneh Torah Marriage (3:5) and the potential legacy of rape and control over women's bodies.

The lengths to which Rachel goes to have children despite being the one who has Yaakov's heart reveals children as an unspoken currency of the era. This currency was more precarious among enslaved women. Mishneh Torah Sales (20:10, 23:2) highlights this through documenting whether the children of cows *or female slaves* belong to a seller or purchaser. Mixed referencing of cattle and enslaved people and control over procreation bridge biblical references with transatlantic slave realities. For those capable of childbearing, Mishneh Torah also mirrors conditions, as described by Dorothy Roberts in *Killing the Black Body*, when "Black women bore children who belonged to the slaveowner from the moment of conception. This feature of slavery made control of reproduction a central aspect of whites' subjugation of African people in America. It marked Black women from the beginning as objects whose decisions about reproduction should be subject to social regulation rather than to their own will." This feels kindred to the conditions which leave Zilpah and Bilhah voiceless and their bodies controlled by the desires of others, among other examples of marginalized women throughout history.

We are more than our circumstances. Bilhah and Zilpah are more than enslaved women, used as sexual commodities. Ultimately, they raised Dan, Naphtali, Gad, and Asher as their own children. Chances are, they probably supported raising all of the family children fathered by Yaakov, bringing us back to Dinah's inclusion of Bilhah, Zilpah, and Rachel as her mothers' alongside her birth mother Leah. After all, while Zilpah and Bilhah were navigating enslavement or second wife status, Leah and Rachel were still enduring a patriarchal reality that may not have been excessively different. This is highlighted in the moment when Rachel and Leah wonder if they still have a share in their father's wealth, referring to themselves as being "sold" into marriage (Genesis 31:14–15). The intersections of commonality between the controlled existences of women across caste underscore readings of the potential for feminist solidarity that we still have the opportunity to realize today.

Bilhah and Zilpah were multidimensional women who found ways to navigate the relationships and realities of their lives. I am endlessly fascinated by exploring the dynamics between Zilpah and Bilhah, individually and as a unit, as well as with characters like Leah, Rachel, Yaakov, Lavan, Dan, Reuven, Dinah, the enslaved women of Shekhem, and other unnamed women and enslaved people Bilhah and Zilpah encountered in their traveling, dwelling, and working. The way the Torah often names the enslaved and animals together also invites questions about how both were housed and the potential relationships and subsequent skills that may have been engendered through proximity and time.

My interest in Zilpah and Bilhah continues to grow. They have become a lens through which I can explore slavery, human hierarchies, belonging, disenfranchisement, and fucked-up family dynamics in Torah, which continue to echo up to the present. Just as marginalized people are erased today, Bilhah and Zilpah are invisible within their narrative. I had not realized how little we really "witness" them, including in feminist biblical commentary, even as we read their names (a feat in itself, merely to be a named woman in the Torah). The cumulative effect of the absence of women's and marginalized character's perspectives made me feel like I was not part of the story—*my* story.

I relate to Bilhah and Zilpah for the ways their experiences align with my own, of not having autonomy over my body, being named and categorized by others, having my voice silenced, the ways the children of people of color are policed under the guise of care, and feeling invisible in plain sight. There is a rich legacy of wisdom from Black liberation theology and Jewish communities of color: the Black Jewish Liberation Collective builds on the

BILHAH AND ZILPAH MADE ME YEARN FOR TORAH | 87

historic work of the Combahee River Collective Statement by Black feminists actively resisting racial, sexual, heterosexual, and class oppression and developing integrated analysis and practice of interlocking oppressions; the abolitionist writings and work of living prophet Angela Y. Davis; the history of Callie House's efforts for ex-enslaved pension thwarted by the direct targeting of federal agencies; and more. Many name the power of Black feminist resistance around the world. Our continued survival lives as a monument. And Rebecca Kuss's haunting piece *Asian Jews Are Hurting, We Need You to Listen* is a raw blessing of honest humility that reflects how parts of our community are actively erased through the danger of a single narrative.

I thought with our annual reading of the Torah, one of these years, one of the Jewish communities I am part of would choose to focus on Zilpah's and Bilhah's stories. However, ultimately that day began to feel increasingly unlikely. They seem relegated to stay in the obscurity of zero-dimensional supporting characters who exist solely to add depth to main characters deemed worthy of focus.

Eventually, I realized I didn't have to wait for my community to choose to read the story through their lives. That journey started for me in earnest in December 2020, through an independent study project I completed as a yeshiva student in Israel. I spent my days in the beit midrash learning Torah. I had long been engaged by text study, but my experiences surrounded by a community of folks who were also excited to go deep and wide, over and over again, was like finding my people.

This was an exciting experience I never thought I would have. My parents severed relationships with their oppressive traditional religious upbringings. They sought to protect their children from the harmful messages that can be conflated between religion and race. I soon discovered that few yeshiva students understood how parts of the Torah have been used to justify the enslavement, dehumanizing, and oppression of blackness because of the understanding of Cush to be Ethiopia. While it is not explicitly clear what Ham did, Noah uttered the words that ultimately cursed his grandchildren, the Cush descendants of his son Ham, as עֶבֶד עֲבָדִים *eved avadim* (slave of slaves) (Genesis 9:25–26). This curse of Ham has echoed throughout history to justify the creation of race and oppression which followed. Those reverberations remain, even when we don't express this idea as clearly as Alexander Stephens, the vice president of the Confederacy, in a 1861 speech where he denounces equality of the races as an error of "anti-slavery fanatics," an attempt "to make things equal which the Creator had made unequal." Amid talk of moral truths, Alexander cites "the curse against Canaan." The idea that blackness marks a slave caste sanctioned by God has endured similar to other conflations that have become obscured over time such as the lack of distinction in the relationship between wife and slave.

The lack of awareness between the curse of Ham and modern enslavement, and unwillingness to explore it, shocked me. This is a story I learned as an adult, filling in the gaps not taught in my rigorous private high school education. My yearning to explore the historical ramifications of the curse of Ham, anti-blackness in biblical commentary, and the many Torah references to slaves was met with silence, by both teachers and students, in a typically cacophonous beit midrash. Whether one agrees, disagrees, or has questions, the beit midrash is never silent. Yet my sincere curiosity too often elicited blankness. Few wanted to look at enslavement outside of our foundational Jewish narrative as slaves who had been saved by God through Moshe (with support from Aaron and Miriam). I was no longer sure who my people were and where my love of text study fit in.

That is when Bilhah and Zilpah found me. I had once gone looking for them, and now they had returned to me. We had been lost to each other, but I soon realized they would be with me for a lifetime. They began inviting me into study each week. I learned new insights, both throughout Torah and in my life, that I would never have been able to access without them. Choosing to read Zilpah and Bilhah with power and autonomy helps me do that for myself in my own life—still living within a racialized world, yes, but able to find ways to navigate institutionalized systems of oppression with moments of power and autonomy that allow me to make choices—or at least the best choices at my disposal today, to live the best life I can while also trying to seed greater opportunity for those who come after me.

I started to feel Zilpah and Bilhah with me during my studies. The sense that their energy was directing me evolved into the Bilhah Zilpah Project, an initiative of Jews of Color Sanctuary. The project uses text study, creative midrash, and ritual dreaming through an abolitionist lens to explore themes within their narrative: the power of naming, sisterhood, shifting status, surrogacy/adoption, co-parenting, polyamory, home, legacy, inheritance, women's value, children as currency, power dynamics, and of course gender within enslavement. Participants are invited to break down and look beyond narrative assumptions through the wisdom of intersection with their own lived experience. We all come to Torah study with so much more than we think we know. Ultimately, our experiences as mothers and women and humans translate. We were all at Sinai, and Zilpah and Bilhah are with us.

These intersections make it easier to remember that Bilhah and Zilpah had stories before entering the marriage tents of Rachel and Leah. It helps foster curiosity around their relationships and reactions to the people, happenings, and transitions around them. Seeing them as whole characters has led me to surprising power and autonomy in their stories. In return, they have helped me connect to more difficult texts and look more closely at contradictions that are sometimes ignored because they feel too hard. Using the troubled realities of my own life allows a framework to think through opportunities for choice by Zilpah and Bilhah against the backdrop of challenging biblical Near Eastern realities for women. It helps me understand the role they played as parents in a large family on the go. It helps me feel the impact of the intersections and differences in Dinah's story around sexual violence. It helps me reflect on the nuances of women given as property from father to husband. It invites consideration of the conditions that constitute giving a dowry for marriage, or not. It expands what it means to be taken as a wife. It helps me imagine the intricacies of being in a polyamorous co-parenting relationship with your sister, two half-sisters, and at least one man. It invites me to transform lack of detail as an invitation to see humanity.

Remembering that Zilpah and Bilhah have voices started out as something I had to remind myself of in the moments when they were not explicitly present. This has become a valued learning tool that adds depth and enriches my reading of Torah. This reminder also mirrors my own modern reality, where amid overwhelming internalized racialized oppression and capitalism, there are small opportunities for choice that can have big impacts when trying to assert balance in my life. The founding of the USA rests on class separation, dehumanization, and racialized distinctions that institutionalized a system of unpaid labor of convicts, the indigenous, abducted and enslaved Africans, and indentured servants. This uncompensated labor built infrastructure and fed raw materials from southern agriculture to become finished products of northern textile industries. This capitalism is baked into explicit and implicit practices and laws, including our Constitution. It is played out through systems and interdependent disparities that allowed our country to be built by the hands of underclass communities smart enough to run households but nevertheless erased from the narrative. Understanding enslavement in the Torah has taught me a lot about modern slavery. Listening for Bilhah's and Zilpah's voices has helped me find my own.

10

A Little East of Jordan

MORIEL ROTHMAN-ZECHER

Then he said, "Let me go, for dawn is breaking." But he answered, "I will not let you go, unless you bless me."

—Genesis 32:27

That night, Jake got up from his couch. The clock on his stovetop read 9:40. It took him a few moments to realize "p.m." Inspired by the first few pages of *Swann's Way*, Jake had taken an 8:00 p.m. nap. He'd liked the elegance of the idea, an evening nap, but in practice, he woke up bewildered and exhausted, his mind caught on the edges of dreams about rivers and wild beasts, his dad, his older brother, a vague sense of foreboding. He considered, once he realized "p.m.," just going back to sleep. But that night was that night, so he rose up, climbed into the shower, closed his eyes again, put his face inside the press of the hot water, stayed like that until he ran out of breath, and then turned the shower off. In the mirror, Jake put on dark blue mascara, and golden eyeliner, and then texted a shirtless mirror selfie to the "Wives & Concubines" group chat. The responses were almost instantaneous.

good luck bb, Ali wrote.

u look fkin goooood, Becks wrote.

you've got this darling!! Sam wrote. libu

I believe in you, Jakey, Evan wrote.

Jake looked again at the selfie, at his expression, which looked more startled than sultry. But open: His face looked open. Jake hearted each message, and then turned his phone to Do Not Disturb. He put on his best underwear—tight, dark gray, sheer, its silken material cool against his skin—and cutoff jean shorts, and a sleeveless top with matte, monochrome sequins running in parallel rows, like those papers of candy dots he used to get with his grandparents at the breakfast place, just called The Inn, near their house in West Virginia. Now, the thought of the dots' sand-grit texture and super sweetness made his teeth stand on edge. He put on his new pair of pink high-top sneakers, and grabbed his keys and wallet and little silver vial of Truvada, just in case the night lasted until the next 9:00 a.m.

"2-1-1," he sang to himself, and the pills shook and tittered in his pocket. Before opening the door, he stabbed a pin through the front left pocket of his jean shorts, a little mauve button that read "Marcel Proust is a Yenta." Sam had given him this pin, and he wasn't sure he'd understood it, so he'd ordered the first volume of *Swann's Way* on Amazon, and felt bad about the Amazon part, and read enough pages that he thought he might get the joke, and also came across the idea for a nighttime nap. Outside, the air was warm and smelled like trash and pollen. Sweat already beading on his forehead, Jake unlocked his 11-speed, mounted it, and crossed the city, cars streaming around him like a river, the air pulling his sweat-dappled skin taut and tight.

He locked his bike near the address he'd memorized and thought for a moment of double-checking the email on his phone, to make sure he was in the right place, but he'd promised himself, and the Wives & Concubines, for accountability's sake, that'd he'd stay phoneless for the evening unless there was an emergency. From across the street, all he saw was a gray building, unmarked. Two doors down, a brightly lit convenience store. But as he got closer, in the shadows of the gray building's awning, Jake saw a man wearing a dark tank top, dark jeans, a thick silver necklace and a thick, dark mustache. Jake made eye contact with the man, raised his eyebrows, and the man glanced at Jake's candy-dot shirt, his shoes, the glint of his eyelids in the streetlight, and nodded to him, his angular face holding onto a slight, tense smile in which Jake thought he could read the words "Pulse," and "Colorado Springs," the letters faded with the months that had passed since the latter, but still legible. Jake nodded back, pushed the words away with more words, imagined making the man's mouth into a palimpsest with a kiss that bore a snippet of Frank—I'll reemerge, defeated, from the valley—but instead, Jake just murmured, "Thank you, sweetheart," as the man wordlessly opened the door for him. Jake walked inside. The entrance was dark and smelled like mold and old cigarettes. At the coat check, Jake handed over most of his belongings, wallet, keys, phone, vial, shirt, shorts, Proust button, retaining nothing but his underwear, his sneakers, his coat of dreams.

Jake was all alone, and a man wrestled with him till daybreak.

Lips over lips, nipples hardened under fingertips, spit dripped into palms, hardness slipped into fists, pressed against thighs and the night passed in fits, smoke and sweat and muffled Yes and the openness of a sky littered with stars, pressing down right on top of the building, then the building pressing back up into it. The music was techno, unfamiliar, but with a good beat. The complimentary beer was warm and tasted like middle school. The ages splayed from barely bearded to gray. Everywhere was the hum of doing, taking, having, wanting, of sharing, of stepping out from the cages of self and self and only self.

A man wrestled with him till daybreak, with Jake, who had never before, finally did now turn.

When the man felt how tensed Jake was, he moved backward from Jake, so that Jake's body was entirely alone, surrounded by the thickness of air and the thicket of music and darkness, but for the tips of the man's fingers, which remained touching the socket of Jake's hip, and Jake felt as though honeyed fire was coursing from the man's body, through his arm and his fingertips, into his own body.

The man stifled a yawn, leaned forward, spoke into Jake's ear. "It's almost morning," he said.

But Jake replied, eyes closed, forehead pressed into wall, "Please don't go yet."

The man said, "What's your name, babe?" His fingertips were still on Jake's hip. Around them, the music seemed louder, both the techno and the human, and the laughter that had coated the first segments of the night had turned in on itself, there was a turgid seriousness coursing through the thickened air.

A Little East of Jordan | 93

"I'm Jake," he answered.

Then the man said, "How about tonight I call you Is?"

"Is?" Jake asked.

"Yeah," the man said. "I can feel that most of the time, you're sure you need to do, to achieve something, to struggle, but tonight, you can just be, there's nothing left for you to do. You've made it. The fight is over for tonight. Okay?"

"Okay," Jake turned, and put his hands on the man's chest, looked up into his face. "What's your name?"

The man replied, "Does it matter?"

Then he blessed him there.

Jake called the place a shabbos in his mind, saying to himself, "For a few hours, I saw god face to face, and was not afraid or ashamed, and I lived."

The sun rose over the city as Jake walked toward his bike, locked across the street from the shul, and he was limping, and he was blessed, and he was radiant.

11

The Story of Dinah

Sarah Blake

Jacob said to Simeon and Levi, "You have brought trouble on me, making me odious among the inhabitants of the land, the Canaanites and the Perizzites; my men are few in number, so that if they unite against me and attack me, I and my house will be destroyed." But they answered, "Should our sister be treated like a whore?"

—Genesis 34:30–31

Every man I meet thinks he can treat me better than the men I knew before him. Or the one he assumes I know now, biblically speaking. All without having met the men they imagine. Without having met the men I have fucked on woven reeds and riverbanks and piles of palm leaves.

Don't they know every penis looks about the same? The motions similar. The positions finite.

Pleasurable sex comes from asking for things and getting them. And then no longer needing to ask for them and still getting them. Neck held, hair pulled, ass cheek bit.

I almost never want to be hit. I almost never want them to call me names. But it happens.

More remarkably, there has never been a man whom I've asked for both from. Whom I've wanted to hit me and call me names.

What I'm trying to say, to the man trying to outdo the previous men: I don't want a man who treats me better. I want a man who treats me so well that I want to ask him to treat me worse. Rough and whispering in my ear that I'm his and I'll never be touched by another man again.

Dinah dreams of violent deaths and wakes to them.

The days she spent in the city with all the men in pain—those were good days.

She spent those days thinking of ways to exacerbate their pain. They'd bring her something she wanted to trade for, and then she'd ask for something else instead.

The men would waddle from her. The men were careful not to touch their penises to their draped robes.

Others tied their penises somewhat tightly, so it would not rub or chafe, but be held snug.

Once, when she came upon a man in an alley, she stuck her finger in her mouth, pulled it out with a pop, and then ran it down her neck and in between her breasts.

As he got an erection, he howled in pain and ran from her.

Before all this was the man who raped her. But his name isn't worth noting. Every time you want to know his name, you should repeat Dinah's name instead. Dinah Dinah Dinah.

She didn't want every man in town to die. Only that one. And even he didn't have to die. She would have been happy to see his dick cut off.

And if that's too difficult, anatomically, then she wanted him to be circumcised over and over again. Once a month, for months and months. She figured they could drag it out for six at least.

I've heard the stories of Sarah, so beautiful that her husband lied and said he was her brother. Only then would the men let him live when they raped her. Husbands get killed so women can be conquered. And brothers get underestimated.

If the stories of Sarah are true, and my brothers had not killed Dinah Dinah Dinah, then I would have taken him from kingdom to kingdom until I found a lustful eye.

Dinah Dinah Dinah raped Dinah and then wanted to marry her. This caused Dinah to wonder how he imagined their sex life moving forward. Always rape?

She wanted a man to simultaneously make sure she'd orgasm, but also not ask. She realized this sounds unfair but it's because she didn't need to orgasm every time. Sex isn't only about orgasm. It's about pleasure, and there are many ways to experience it. Rape's not one of them.

Dinah Dinah Dinah's dad asked Dinah's dad if they could marry. And he said yes. If all the men were circumcised.

So Dinah Dinah Dinah's dad went to his people and told them his son had raped Dinah and now they would be married.

Just kidding.

He said, These men are friendly toward us. Let them live in our land and trade in it; the land has plenty of room for them. We can marry their daughters and they can marry ours. But the men will agree to live with us as one people only on the condition that our males be circumcised, as they themselves are. Won't their livestock, their property and all their other animals become ours? So let us agree to their terms, and they will settle among us.

The men did it. Well, someone did it to them. Or many men did it to them? Many men cut the tips of foreskin from the penises of many other men. It was very intimate. Also religious.

Dinah would have liked to cut them all. In a less than religious way. Though no less holy.

Important to note: Dinah was never documented as speaking one single word in her entire life.

Her life was made entirely of sex noises. Which are, admittedly, impossible to portray in text.

Dinah's life was defined by her desirability, and the love of her brothers.

Though she must insist that her desirability is only considered in the time after the rape. As rape is an abuse of power and a hateful act and has very little to do with how she looks.

Dinah collected all the foreskins and slept on them.

I would have killed the men differently. Wrapped fabric around my hands and around their throats. Strangled them. Broken their hyoid bones, which support their tongues. Left them slumped against a wall. Let people find them by the flies.

My method would leave my hands without a mark. Their necks, too. Like the air itself choked them.

I could spend the night killing them and arrive at breakfast like nothing was amiss.

THE STORY OF DINAH | 97

When they were children, Dinah's brothers threw dirt at Dinah and she threw dirt at them, and they rushed down into the riverbanks and splashed each other, and they screamed as loud as they could.

She was always surprised no one came to see if they were all right.

She couldn't tell the difference between a good scream and a bad one.

Now, as an adult, she knew they couldn't either.

One day—a scream.

Should we do something? a child asked a woman near her.

Someone will, the woman said.

Dinah shook her head until the child looked fearful of the screaming, and then fearful of Dinah.

Dinah moaned.

Dinah collected all the foreskins and put them in a jar of oil, but they all sunk down to the bottom and looked like nothing extraordinary at all.

Dinah collected all the foreskin and sewed things of different buoyancies to each—a piece of cork, a piece of pumice. Then she put them in oil and they looked magnificent. She put them on a windowsill and let the sunlight catch on them. At sunset, they turned orange and pink.

Desiring to strangle a man, makes one consider, longer, his neck. His Adam's apple, his first seven vertebrae, his thyroid cartilage. His breath and voice. The ache in it, after too much time spent looking in any one direction.

Dinah considers Dinah Dinah Dinah's neck.

She wonders if she has the strength to strangle him. If she would need to set up a pulley system to get it done. She imagines she might not have time for that. To get the position right. She pictures instead: her feet pressed into his back, her body parallel to the ground, the cloth pulled tight.

If I'd killed the men with a sword, if I had ended hours of killing them covered in their blood, I would go to a meal and leave their blood everywhere I could. Handprints on the table, smears of it on the bowls.

Less and less with everything I touched until fingerprints showed in the blood. Until there was a dust of dried blood flaking from me.

The whole day you could follow me, the trail I'd make, lightly red, the rust in the dirt. Ultimately, you would find me masturbating in bed.

What if women were thought to be as sexual as men? I like the word prowess.

What if, when girls were walked in on, masturbating, the door was quickly shut again, and someone shrugged and said, Girls will be girls!

If someone else protested, the first someone would say, She's growing up.

And the protesting someone would concede. They can't be children forever.

Dinah collected all the foreskins and carried them in her pockets. She would come to a group of men drinking wine, and when they turned away (to watch the fire crackle, say, or to watch a woman walk by), Dinah would drop one into their cups. She waited nearby until each man had shrieked, finding one at his lips.

When Dinah was a child, adults asked her, What do you want to be when you grow up?

Just kidding.

When Dinah was a child, she was asked, What will your husband be like?

And she said, Not a rapist.

Just kidding!

She said nothing because even then she was only sex noises. Haven't you been paying attention?

When Dinah was a child, she was asked, What is your greatest fear?

And already she knew it was rape, but she also knew she wasn't supposed to say things like that.

Dinah collected all the foreskins and threw them, like a flower girl, down the aisle at a wedding.

Dinah collected all the foreskins, took one between her fingers, and rubbed it against her forehead.

Dinah collected all the foreskins and used them to go fishing. She pushed the hook through and thought it wriggled like a worm. She cast the line out and caught a big one.

Was I engaged? Was I a fiancée? It was only a few days, but still. There is a romance to it.

Dinah collected all the foreskins and hammered them, one by one, into the wall of Dinah Dinah Dinah's room. An art installation. A breathtaking piece.

Dinah collected all the foreskins and fried them and served them back to the people. They said, This isn't pork skin? And she said, I promise it's not!

If we retold Dinah's story, *Clueless* style, he only tried to rape her. That was traumatizing enough. And then he had the gall to ask her to prom. What was he thinking?!

But then her dad said yes! Because his dad told her dad that his son was all mopey and sad about prom, and they both agreed this would make him feel better.

And Dinah would've done it, too! The dads were gonna rent a limo for them and everything. Corsages. You name it.

But then Dinah's brothers beat up Dinah Dinah Dinah behind school one day. And his dad. And everyone. They lined up around the building to get punched in the face and kicked in the stomach by Dinah's brothers.

Dinah might have even fallen in love with Dinah Dinah Dinah! If this were that kind of movie. Morally bankrupt.

Dinah collected all the foreskins and ate them. Full of their sexual power, she turned into a sexual god. She became larger than the houses. She sat her pussy down on the town and ate it up. And then she vomited the foreskins up, and she shrank back down, and the town shrunk within her, killing everyone. Quicker. Less satisfying.

If we retold Dinah's story like an episode of *Law & Order: SVU*, the cops would all believe her story, but the defendant's lawyer would rip her to shreds in the courtroom. They'd bring up every man she's ever slept with. They'd bring up that time she slept with a woman. They'd bring up how she wore her robes and hair. They'd bring up that time she ate berries and her fingertips turned red and for some reason those stained fingertips could drive men insane.

Am I a kind of widow? There is a certain gravitas to that.

Since Dinah never spoke, she is also this list of emojis.

Figure 11.1. Dinah is also this list of emojis.

Dinah is a total babe. Dinah is a vibe.

Dinah had candy cigarettes on the playground. Because sometimes when we think of old things, we just think of the '40s.

100 years is long enough. And imaginable.

4,000 years ago—less so.

But in the '40s, no one was agreeing to anything so that their sons could marry all the Jewish daughters. To join in a covenant with God. YHWH. (You can't pronounce it because you're not supposed to.)

In the '40s, if you weren't killing Jews, you were putting up signs to keep them out.

In the '40s, Dinah was a dame. A broad. A real doll.

In 1500 BCE, Dinah was still a fox. But remember that everyone was short. And everyone died young. (Even if Genesis says otherwise.)

And no one was white. Get a good idea of her in your head.

Though there is some debate as to her age. As young as 6. As old as 16. It was legal to be betrothed at 3.

Picture Dinah more as a girl. A child. Turn as your stomach might.

Better to imagine her in the 1940s, isn't it? Long skirt. Fascinator pinned into her hair. No shirt.

I mean, yes, a shirt. A jacket even.

It's hard not to sexualize someone who is nearly entirely made of sex. The essence of sex.

Hook your finger into her wing collar and pull her down.

If Dinah had been married, would she have lived long enough to experience frequent rectal bleeding? Would she have used almond oil to try to keep the skin from cracking?

Would her husband have lowered his face to her pussy and smelled the oil there and thought of cyanide? Like the last scent that a captured Nazi smelled, if we're in the '40s.

Dinah alternates between closing her eyes and seeing Dinah Dinah Dinah and closing her eyes and seeing Dinah Dinah Dinah dead.

Dinah collects all the foreskins and burns them at an altar for women. She prays to women.

Dinah collects all the foreskins and puts them in a barrel and then sinks her hands into them the way she would sink them into rice or sand.

Dinah collects all the foreskins but when she imagines it, she cannot fathom it. Would it take a barrel? Two? Ten? If she wanted to fill a room with them, how many penises would that take? If she wanted to try to walk through that room? She takes a bowl full of them and presses her face into them. She lifts her head and can still see the shape of her nose.

If you are asking yourself what is real and what is not, even in the world of the piece, that's all right.

Has it happened? Is it about to? Has the same thing happened many times over? If the piece could be written in such a way, could the rape never have occurred?

Let's try.

Dinah's family comes to a new city. The city dwellers are welcoming. But because Dinah's family are not of those people, Dinah's brothers may not marry their daughters and their sons may not marry Dinah.

Dinah's family delights in the change of pace, and then they move on.

Or, they delight in each other's company, and Dinah falls in love. When her family leaves, the two lovebirds part ways like star-crossed lovers and they cry and cry. Dinah gets to be the young woman she is and mourn a loss that's hardly a loss. And in doing so, she learns slightly more about the type of woman she wants to be. How much of her heart she wants to commit to another. How she interacts with grief. How much blame she will put on everyone else. The lessons are abundant and gentle in how they are taught.

Except the truth is that Dinah's brother is raped and Dinah's family kills everyone the moment that's discovered.

Except the truth is that Dinah's whole family is raped and then they rape everyone and when everyone has raped everyone else, they all wander the desert so they never have to see anyone else from there ever again. They are grabbed up by angels, plucked from the earth.

Except the truth is that no one was raped.

Oh my God, we made it to that version of the story.

Dinah collected all the foreskins and sewed them together to make a coat, and it was so long that it dragged on the earth behind her, and the foreskins became dusty and dirty and torn. She trimmed the coat and she laughed.

Trimmed again! she hollered and hooted.

She wore the shorter coat until the skin shrunk, until the skin wilted like flowers. She couldn't get her arms in. So she forced them in. The skin tore through the thread at each puncture her needle had made.

Finally, standing in a pile of shredded foreskin, she felt exactly like a queen.

12

Plagues

Madeline Cash

But I will harden Pharaoh's heart, that I may multiply My signs and marvels in the land of Egypt.

—Exodus 7:3

First it was frogs, then Locust, then remote aerial drone strikes. Clearly God was punishing us. God was punishing us but we were happy because at least we knew that God existed.

All the liquid turned to blood. The water in our Brita filters and the fountain at the mall—all blood. The bartenders balked as the gin and vodka ran red through their shakers. The men wouldn't stand for it. They blamed the women for the blood. The men blamed the women and the women blamed the horses and the horses blamed the babies and the babies cried for their milk which was blood, breast or bottle.

The frogs were getting out of hand. We dissected them in science class. The underserved communities were disproportionately affected by the frogs. If you were to kiss the frogs, they would not become princes. They'd chastise you for nonconsensual touching. It was a disaster with PETA. Then the frogs started organizing. They formed an autonomous zone. They developed seasonal depression.

Everyone had a feeling that God had forsaken us. All the babies had colic. All the livestock had yeast infections. The rumor that God has forsaken us spread through our friends and neighbors and Priests. *God's forsaken us, pass it on.* In God's absence the girls rolled up their skirts. In God's absence we pierced our ears and sullied the purity of our flesh and bought Bitcoin and wrote autofiction. We played truth or dare. Never have we ever. Mary fuck kill: Father, Son, and Holy Spirit. We abolished homosexual marriage and heterosexual marriage and then marriage in general. The nuns, who were of course married to God, filed for divorce. They hired Jewish lawyers.

Madeline brought the lice. That one wasn't God. Madeline brought the lice from a boarding school in Vermont. Madeline started a transatlantic lice pipeline. Madeline first gave the lice to Gracie who gave them to Gemma who passed them to Sam. Gemma loved Sam but Sam could take it or leave it with Gemma though Sam would walk through hot coals for Kyle who more or less hated Sam but loved Gracie who hung the moon for Lizzie who passed the lice to Blake while giving him head in his parents' basement so we all had lice—though Blake only had genital lice. *The future is uncertain*, said Gracie, *but we must keep on living so perhaps we should all make love in Blake's parents' basement.* So we took shots of blood and scratched our collective hair and had groupsex in the basement while frogs pelted the roof.

One day the sun went down and did not come back up. We used our phone flashlights to open our doors and put on our makeup and file our taxes and read our newspapers though luckily the newspapers were on our phones. *Things have changed*, said my mother, *since I was a girl.* But we were happy. Because God existed. *Now sleep, sweet child, as we lie in wait for what horror tomorrow may bring.*

13

Mount Sinai and Me

Aaron Hamburger

The Lord came down upon Mount Sinai, on the top of the mountain, and the Lord called Moses to the top of the mountain and Moses went up. The Lord said to Moses, "Go down . . ."

—Exodus 19:20–21

Picture me at age eight, dressed in a navy-blue velour sweater, blue jeans always a season or two out of fashion, and gym shoes fastened with Velcro rather than laces. I had fair cheeks that burned easily in the sun but were more often red from the cold Michigan winters. Full head of brown hair brushed painfully smooth each morning and then pressed down under a baseball cap to ensure it stayed in place until it was time to go to day school, at which point the cap was replaced by the yarmulke all boys were required to wear, except outside at recess, when I was invariably picked last when we divided into teams for sports.

To be fair, I also would have picked myself last, since I was both slow of foot and awkward with my hands, especially when it came to anything to do with footballs, softballs during warmer months, and basketballs and red rubber dodge balls when the weather got cold and we retreated inside, to the gym. Where I shone was in the classroom.

Being a good day school student was of little help in gaining the love and approval I craved from my peers, who generally adopted an affect of indifference, resentment, or scorn toward whatever we were learning. Their attitude struck me as eerily similar to the recalcitrance of the Hebrews we read about in Torah class, constantly disobeying or ignoring God and his prophets, particularly in the text of Exodus, which we tackled in sixth grade. I was struck by how seemingly in every other verse, our ungrateful ancestors were complaining to Moses about their thirst and hunger, expressing longing for Egyptian cucumbers, or collecting bits of gold to build idols, or organizing rebellions against Moses's wise leadership. No matter how much manna or how many quails or hidden springs God provided, it was never enough. At the least bit of trouble, Moses was back in the doghouse. As the churlish Hebrews complained, "It would have been better for us to serve the Egyptians than to die in the desert!"

To their credit, our teachers did not hide our ancestors' disobedience. It would have been folly to try since those flaws were clearly there to see. However, our teachers did point out the various punishments the Hebrews received as a result of their defiance. The lesson, not so subtly delivered to us, was that we too might suffer a similar fate if we dared to marry a non-Jew or eat a ham and cheese sandwich.

I felt disappointed that my classmates didn't share my excitement about the stories in the Torah. I was especially looking forward to the part of the story when Moses climbed Mount Sinai. Here was the big climax, as I was well aware from (among other sources) the yearly rebroadcasts on television of the Cecil B. DeMille movie *The Ten Commandments* starring hammy Charlton Heston as Moses and the strangely sensual and bald Yul Brynner as Pharaoh. I also liked watching the Red Sea part (a special effect apparently achieved with the magic of Jell-O) as well as the Hollywood Israelites celebrating the golden calf by waving colorful scarves while belly dancing.

The version of the story we read in Torah class lacked the lurid technicolor bizarreness of the movie, though it had a few exciting bits, like the sound of a trumpet blasting mysteriously of its own accord from Mount Sinai, a sound which got louder and louder until "smoke billowed up from it like smoke from a furnace, and the whole mountain trembled violently . . . Moses spoke and the voice of God answered him. . . . The Lord descended to the top of Mount Sinai and called Moses to the top of the mountain. So Moses went up . . ."

106 | AARON HAMBURGER

As we took turns reciting aloud and translating the verses from the original text, our teacher invited us to notice how often Moses kept going up the mountain and going back down, and then climbing back up again. "Why," she asked, "is there all this up and down, back and forth of Moses on Mt. Sinai? Why not just have Moses go up there once, get the Ten Commandments, and come back down and be done with it?"

I can't remember our various answers to this question, though I do remember how earnestly I wanted to come up with the answer our teacher was looking for, and that I was not successful.

Here was our teacher's answer, one that has stayed vivid in my memory for much longer than many other lessons I learned in school: Moses's coming and going, moving nearer and farther away from God mirrors the relationships we as human beings have to religion, not a linear upward trajectory, but a series of ups and downs. Some days we might feel closer to God, more elevated with holiness. On other days, we could be weighted down with questions and doubts. This continual wavering, our teacher argued, the process of back-and-forth, moving closer and further away from God, is an inherent part of the religious experience.

This was news to me. As a young man, I had few doubts when it came to religion. When people asked what I wanted to be when I grew up, I replied that I wanted to be a prophet. Not in a figurative sense. I really wanted that to be my job.

On Halloween, other boys my age dressed up as animals or cowboys or characters from *Star Wars*. I didn't know the difference between Darth Vader and Obi-Wan Kenobi, because I refused to watch *Star Wars*, which struck me as vaguely heathen. Rather, I put on a synthetic and very itchy white beard (no doubt inspired by Charlton Heston's look in *The Ten Commandments*), a severe black robe, and an Arab headdress that my brother had picked up in the Old City of Jerusalem. Carrying a wooden staff and a copy of my Children's Bible—we had no Ten Commandments lying around—I set forth in search of free candy to mark the pagan holiday.

I read voraciously about the lives of various prophets, and frequently changed my mind about which was my favorite, though my beard-and-robe costume could have served to impersonate any of them. There was the ever-mournful Jeremiah always wailing in the marketplace, or that old scold Isaiah raining down scorn on the sinful Israelites. And then there were their successors, rabbinical sages who weren't technically prophets,

MOUNT SINAI AND ME | 107

though I lumped them all together. It was a bit gruesome to read about the heroic sufferer Akiva, whose flesh was raked with metal combs. More cheerful was the story of patient Hillel, who could teach the entire Torah while standing on one foot.

Yet all in all, the king of the prophets had to be Moses. (Why had my parents named me after his perfidious brother Aaron, who had agreed to shape a golden calf while Moses was up on Mount Sinai receiving the Ten Commandments?) I admired Moses's righteous anger as well as the host of magic tricks he performed with his staff. He stood up for truth and justice even if he had to do it alone time and again. I always thought it was rather unfair of God to bar Moses from entering the Holy Land, merely because after a lifetime of provocations and tribulations, Moses hit a rock out of frustration instead of speaking to it to bring forth water.

This was the first of many quarrels with God I would have in the future.

Why did I want to be a prophet? To some degree I envied the prophets' magical powers, like the ability to turn water into blood or rocks into water. I too wanted to be wise, to bravely preach the truth, even if that meant being shunned or ignored as a result. That was an important part of being a prophet, to stand apart from the crowd, and for good reason: a prophet could talk to—and hear back from—God.

I kept wishing I could do something to prove myself worthy of His friendship. And yet, though I tried and tried and prayed and prayed, God never spoke to me. My experience remained stubbornly unlike those of the prophets I read about, who never had to work at all to hear God. They seemed to have an innate talent for it, something you were born with. Like the kind of talent for catching balls that got you picked first for sports teams in school.

A favorite story in our family is the sincerity with which as a child I inquired about attending prophet school. Though there was no such place in suburban Detroit, we did have several Jewish day schools, including the one where my parents sent me, beginning in third grade. I was nervous at the prospect of being plunged into a pool of kids I'd never met, but excited to study the Torah in the original Hebrew, to learn about the prophets, kings, and ancient tribes of Israel. As a bonus, the school was named after Hillel, one of my favorite heroes. Surely, I would feel right at home in this community of fellow spiritual seekers.

On that first day, sitting on the school bus, I introduced myself to another, slightly older, taller boy walking down the aisle. "Hi, I'm Aaron!" I said brightly. In response, he turned, sat on my head, and farted, inspiring gales of derisive laughter.

This was a sign of things to come. It turned out that not one of my fellow students wanted to become a prophet, let alone a kosher butcher or owner of a Jewish bookstore and gift shop. (One or two were interested in becoming cantors and rabbis, and as adults, they did indeed manage it.) They were more interested in sports, movies, music, clothes, and impressing each other, in short, everything that any kid our age might have been interested in.

Every morning, when we marched into the gym and recited the prayers for our morning service, our headmaster had to scold us to pay attention, quit whispering, and follow along in our prayer books. I've never heard the phrase "We're on page 31" uttered with such righteous anger. By contrast, when we sang the prayer after meals at lunchtime, it was at the tops of our lungs, not out of piety but more as a release of pent-up energy for a room full of hyperactive kids who'd been sitting still all morning and were now on a sugar high after polishing off their chocolate milk or whatever desserts were included with their lunches. The result sounded not so much like a prayer of thanks as a rowdy lustful scream, or what I initially misinterpreted as the fight song of an Israeli soccer team.

Our teachers showed little interest in training us to be prophets. Their main concern was that whatever we said, whether reading aloud a passage from the Torah or asking permission to use the bathroom, we said it in Hebrew. "B'ivrit," "b'ivrit," as the refrain went. And then as we got older, they reminded us of the evils of intermarriage. Did we know 50 percent of Jews were marrying outside the faith? It was like a second Holocaust. The message, which I heard repeated in school, from the *bimah* of synagogue, our local *Jewish News*, as well as my family was: "What Hitler didn't finish, we're doing to ourselves."

As I reached puberty, I realized that A) my Jewish upbringing would not prepare me for prophethood, and B) I had lost interest in the profession. My desire to find God was superseded by my desire to find a friend. A good friend. A male good friend. A good-looking male good friend who might hold my hand, hold me close, and kiss me. I also realized that this wish for an intensely intimate male friendship (along with my complete lack of interest in dating girls) marked me as even more of an outcast than my desire to become a prophet. Though unlike my dreams of prophethood, I knew I had to keep my dreams about men a secret.

MOUNT SINAI AND ME | 109

I left day school to go to a secular high school, and in the following years I came into an awareness that my feelings about men were not just a phase like wanting to become a prophet, but in fact an integral part of who I was—and was not. At that time, Judaism and heterosexuality were intimately linked in my mind. After all, if intermarriage was akin to a second Holocaust, then homosexuality was definitely off the table. To accept my gay identity, and to have a chance to find love, I would have to give up Judaism.

When I graduated from college, I moved with my boyfriend from Michigan to San Francisco, which, by the way, had plenty of hills for going up and down. However, when our relationship came to an abrupt end, I found myself alone and overwhelmed in a strange new city, with its famous gay scene, but where I had few friends. High holidays were approaching, and though I had abandoned much of my faith, I felt a vestigial need to do something to mark the occasion. In the local gay newspaper, I read about gay synagogue, a phenomenon that seemed to me an oxymoron. I went there, in part out of curiosity, in part because the tickets were free.

Immediately, I was struck by the sight of so many types of people familiar to me from the gay scene (e.g., butch lesbians, gay male gym bunnies) but all wearing yarmulkes, some with rainbow trim, while chanting the prayers in the same melodies I had heard in day school. I also noticed what I did not see: heterosexual couples fussing over children. As I stood there in my suit and tie, tapping softly on my chest and singing "Al Chet," I cried. The prayers, the culture, the trappings all felt so familiar, but here I had the permission to be my full self.

For a while, I climbed back up Mount Sinai. I was in love with gay synagogues, first in San Francisco, and then in New York. I occasionally dated men I met there. I attended several commitment ceremonies and imagined having one myself, sending my adopted kids to the children's services at gay shul. I was determined to be the best Jewish gay boy in the world.

And then I met a man who wasn't Jewish. To be exact, his mother was Jewish, but he had been brought up knowing nothing about religion, and he wasn't interested in learning more. To him, religion was a crock of shit, a vehicle used by homophobes to justify hate. When I told his friends that I went to gay synagogue, they started laughing. This made me more determined to keep going to services, which I did for a few years, perhaps more to prove a point (Gays can believe too!) than out of pure faith. But

110 | AARON HAMBURGER

eventually, I retreated back down proverbial Mount Sinai, though I did return to synagogue sporadically, often during times of crisis, like 9/11, when my dad died, or when my husband and I moved to a new city, and I craved a feeling of connection.

These days, when I look back at my early yearnings to become a prophet and my time in day school, I experience a warm wave of nostalgia, similar to how I feel while watching John Hughes movies like *The Breakfast Club*. The story my teacher told about going up and down the mountain has stayed with me all these years, comforting me with its lovely optimism, the elegance of the analogy, and the promise it extends that someday, should I ever want to, I can return to embrace God, and He will embrace me right back.

But just as I do not confuse John Hughes movies for documentaries, I also know that my warm fuzzy feelings are not true to what I felt at the time as a confused and lonely young man, looking for someone to talk to, someone who might listen to me and say something in return.

For this essay, I've been rereading the text of Exodus, and I was struck by this passage:

> When the people saw the thunder and lightning and heard the trumpet and saw the mountain in smoke, they trembled with fear. They stayed at a distance and said to Moses, "Speak to us yourself and we will listen. But do not have God speak to us or we will die." Moses said to the people, "Do not be afraid. God has come to test you, so that the fear of God will be with you to keep you from sinning." The people remained at a distance, while Moses approached the thick darkness where God was.

The truth is that when it comes to religion, I too have found my distance, not out of fear but from comfort. Today, if I were to choose a spot for myself in the story of Mount Sinai, I'd place myself at the foot of the mountain, below the summit where Moses conferred with God but also markedly apart from the calf-worshiping Israelites with their belly dancing and silk scarves. (What would the contemporary equivalent for that be? Obsessively scrolling through TikTok?) Ultimately, who I was then, who I became next, and who I am now is someone who needs distance and space to sort out my thoughts, someone who feels an instinctual skepticism toward anything that smells of dogma.

I believe the young prophet in me also wanted that kind of distance, yearned to stand apart from the crowd, to approach life thoughtfully, individually, on his own terms. He merely lacked the confidence to do so, and so he hid behind the invisible cloak of God.

14

Make It Mean Something

ELISA ALBERT

And all the people took off the gold rings that were in their ears and brought them to Aaron. This he took from them and cast in a mold, and made it into a molten calf. And they exclaimed, "This is your god, O Israel, who brought you out of the land of Egypt."

—Exodus 32:3–4

I spend a lot of time on Instagram. I'm not proud of this, but neither am I inclined to disparage myself too harshly for it. Whatever gets you through the night, is my feeling. And/or the morning, afternoon, evening. I spend a lot of time on my "phone" in general. How about let's stop calling it a phone and start calling it what it is: hand-held computer. HHC, for short.

I do all the same shit everyone does: look at news, text people, make lists, deal with email, check recipes. I appreciate that I can be "productive" in this way whilst, say, lying down. Or walking, or waiting in line. Stuck on a boring phone call. Pretending to be doing yoga. My predilections are not unique. I had the cheerful and entirely earnest thought, recently, at bedtime, about how when I awoke in the morning there would be a whole new Wordle to do! Ain't life grand?

I use my HHC to avoid pretty much any opportunity to be alone with my thoughts. I use it to escape boredom and anxiety and uncertainty, to create or embroider community. I use it on the toilet and while hanging out with my dog in the park. I use it when those around me are using theirs. I use it while waiting for food and while eating alone. I use it for music and audiobooks. I consult it when I am heading out the door and when I return. My family and friends live in there, on text threads that are casual/funny/lifesaving (I am in despair! Kindly remind me who I am!).

One screen at a time isn't even *enough* for me anymore. Often I'm watching a movie or something *while* dicking around on Instagram. If the movie is particularly good (or bad) I might want to find an artful way of instagramming it.

None of this sounds great. But, with apologies to Jaron Lanier and Catharine Taylor and Jenny Odell and whoever else: my HHC is a source of great comfort.

I'm forty-four years old and almost two decades into a romantic partnership. We have reared a child into young adulthood, and our job now is mostly to step back, wait, hold space. This turns out to be much more difficult than it sounds, especially given the fact that our young adult lives a great deal of *his* life inside an HHC, but here we are. There are some pretty good Instagram advice accounts about parenting teens! Is it okay to just leave him alone with all his screens all the time, as he prefers!? Apparently so if he's otherwise happy, healthy, active. Welp, Godspeed and good luck, young man.

The pandemic was not personally disastrous for us, thankfully. But things have never really "gone back to normal," because life doesn't work that way. Who the hell thinks life works that way?

We spend so, so much time on our screens. In dealing with my anxiety and confusion about this, I have two options: (1) I can spiral into a panic about what's happening to our minds, what's being done to us, and how we're complicit in our own psychic servitude and complacency. I can try to exert some fascist rule over the use of screens. Lay down some *laws*. Or (2) I can accept that life has changed irrevocably—screens are just how we exist and relax now!—and leave everybody to it, let everyone off the hook, myself included.

I vacillate. (Oh, but isn't there a middle way? Sure, sure, sure, yeah, yeah, yeah.)

Often, after dinner, we retreat to separate rooms to do different things on different screens. Blame the architecture of our nineteenth-century house, or blame the vagaries of contemporary adolescence, or blame the neuroscientists who sold out to the app designers, I don't know. Blame Elon Musk, blame Jeff Bezos. Blame the Netflix honchos. Blame Congress for not acting fast enough to regulate anything. Blame the content creators. Blame the influencers. Blame myself. Blame each other.

Can't we just be in the same *room* on different screens, I sometimes find myself whining. And how about a digital sabbath? Could we say that on shabbat we will not use our handheld computers? Could we try that!?

The answer, so far, for my family at least, seems to be . . . no.

And if I tried to lay down the law, be a tyrant, rule with an iron fist, where would that get me?

I'm lonely in my little dark corner of the house with my HHC. But I'm also inspired and delighted and engaged and interested. (And bored. And exhausted. And invigorated! And amused. Somehow all at once.)

Yes, I could quit social media (ideally without *announcing it on social media*). Yes, I could change my display to grey scale, deprive my dopamine receptors of the delicious colors. Yes, I could go out to the (gasp!) movie theater. But I don't want to.

The story of the golden calf was given to me (to borrow framing from Clarissa Pinkola Estes) as a story about impatience, faithlessness, and idolatry.

You might remember Moses leading the Israelites out of bondage in Egypt? On Pesach, when we tell the liberation story, we don't speak of the Israelites as "them." The Israelites are "us." *We* are the liberated slaves. *We* were taken out of bondage, and *we* crossed the parted sea.

(Listen, plagues I get, boils and locusts and angel of death I get, but the parting of the sea seems frankly like the move of a desperate, exhausted storyteller who's kind of just giving up, on some level: *Fuck it, man, I can't deal with this narrative anymore, who cares if it makes sense. . . . The seas parted!*)

Anyway, "we" followed Moses out of Egypt and into the vast unknown. Freedom's just another word for nothin' left to lose, sang a notable bullied doomed girl in a more recent era. And then there we were, wandering the desert indefinitely.

Were we stoic? We were not. Did we forge ahead without complaint? We did not. We were a whiny-ass bunch of complainers. We were *nostalgic* for slavery, for the predictability and "safety" of it. We hadn't eaten *well* as slaves, but we had eaten *reliably*.

Poor Moses. Consider the extraordinary, impossible, toxic burden of leadership. Keegan and Peele's "Obama Anger Translator" comes to mind. We need our belief in leaders like we need air and water. We need our gods, our idols, our authorities.

Being followers alleviates a lot of our anxiety, takes the onus off. We feel better putting ourselves in the hands of someone who seems like they know what they're doing, where they're going. And it smells good when you're cookin', so whoever everyone *else* is following . . . has to be worth following, right? ("Ooooh, there's a crowd of people waiting on line for something; must be good, let's go see!")

But what of the poor leaders? The good ones, the ones who don't get off on it. Beleaguered Moses needed a break from our bellyaching. Any parent of young children who's ever availed herself of, say, a three-day solo getaway will understand: Moses needed a breather. You must put on your own oxygen mask before you attend to your child's, blah blah. Moses took his leave of his annoying charges and went up Mount Sinai to "talk to God." A euphemism. Moses watched the Harry and Meghan docuseries on Netflix, ate a gummy or two, ordered room service, and tried a float tank (quite nice). And Moses concluded that Duchess Meghan was right: love absolutely does win.

For forty days and forty nights, Moses is off on his little "creative retreat." He tells his therapist that Mount Sinai is "super restorative." And he gets some solid work done! Two big, beautiful tablets, engraved by hand with some basic precepts for living. A relaxed mind is a creative mind, after all. Forty days and forty nights! They say it only takes thirty to develop entirely new neural pathways and establish new habits.

Meanwhile, what of *us*? The frightened, all-too-human Israelites. Waiting, getting nervous, growing restless, going feral. At loose ends without our leader. Panicked he won't return. Cosmic Daddy figure, God-stand-in, do not forsake us! Yeah, he's probably never coming back.

We needed something to hold on to. We needed something to occupy our attention and energy. Something to distract us from the emptiness, the uncertainty, the enormity and exhaustion of the journey. Something to focus on when the unknown was too scary, too overwhelming. A way to pass the time. Something in front of our faces, to look at.

So, we built ourselves a placeholder. We melted down our jewelry and made ourselves a nice, shiny idol. Ahhhh, that's better: Objectification! Much, much better. Everything's going to be okay. What relief! We rejoiced.

And when Moses returned from his sojourn/retreat/quest, mission accomplished, and saw what we'd done, he got so angry he actually spiked those excellent tablets, shattering them. For this expression of rage, this failure to "regulate his emotions," Moses is punished. The punishment? He is never allowed to ever enter the Promised Land. (But, liiiiike, neither is anybody else in this story? All the Israelites led out of bondage, led through the miraculously parted sea and into the desert, led away from their doomed captors and on toward the capital-P Promised capital-L Land, we were all going to die still wandering. Not one of us was ever going to set foot in the Promised Land. We all had to die out, *midrash* goes, because no one who had been born into slavery was eligible to inhabit the Promised Land. No one who had been born a slave could *handle* the Promised Land. A mindset thing.)

What was the big deal, anyway? What was Moses so furious about? That we made ourselves an idol!? Why did it have to be such a thing? Relax, Moe. It's, like, decoration. It's, like, *art*, hello!? It's *content*, bro. Chill.

I have no real argument for why I think Instagram is somewhat fun, whereas I consider Facebook to be an idiotic bore and Twitter a sinister bore. Maybe I'm too impossibly discerning when it comes to words and ideas, whereas images are simpler, more elemental, less draining. FB and Twit just don't suit me. I'm not masochist enough or sadist enough or bored enough or desperate enough or curious enough. To each their own. I like images, art, photography, memes, self-deprecation, targeted ads for shit I might want or "need." Shopping! Sales and craft markets and local businesses and action items and social justice organizing.

I manage my ambivalence by curating ruthlessly. Nothing can make me endure a shitty feed, one that's nakedly only about ego sans substance or self-awareness, a feed that is only about money or privilege or access. Nothing can make me endure a feed that is banal or didactic or desperate or comprised of too many selfies. Or reactionary. Or overly self-serving. A feed that establishes no aesthetic argument for itself. A feed that is a blunt attempt at cult of personality. And nothing can make me endure a feed that is one-note or repetitive. I don't want to be bored! Don't bore me. Scrolling is still (somewhat) optional. Tone-deaf, self-righteous, vapid, uninformed, uninspired, uninteresting shit has to gooooo. All the perfectly fine folk who can't take a decent photograph to save their lives: bye. All the perfectly fine folk who blather on and on about themselves, openly self-aggrandize, leave nothing to imagination, devoid of wit or grace or suggestion? Sorry. Regurgitate simplistic bullshit? No thanks. Take this shit too seriously? Later. There's not enough time even in these here wastelands of time, even in deserts of meandering lost time, even in purgatorial hours upon hours upon hours of time time time time time.

It has to *mean* something. But you can't try too hard to *make* it mean anything.

I'm merciless. No hard feelings. Instagram's just a tool. Some use it better than others, I feel zero compunction to indulge. Which is of course my own subjective judgment! Don't worry, though, there remain hundreds, if not thousands, if not *tens* of thousands who may well adore your bullshit. Live and be well. Pander and prosper. I only know how I feel. When shit bores or irritates me, it's gone. From my *feed*, silly, not necessarily from my *life*. They aren't the *same* (yet). I'll still bring you soup when you're sick. I'll still picnic with you in the park. I just don't want your content.

What of my own feed? Am I so great? Am I beyond reproach? Nah, I'm an idiot loser dupe, too, with apologies. But I am still the god of what I allow to parade before my own eyeballs, which might be the only true power left to me on this blighted fucking rock.

A few months ago, I deleted the app. I want my brain back, I said to a friend, then lasted one whole day (not even) before I downloaded it again, logged in again, and sheepishly posted something I "had" to post.

Let's not forget the inconvenient fact of the brain being hijacked. The little matter of the dopamine centers. Julie Delpy nailed that scene from *Before Midnight* when she's talking about how we're all going to go down on this planet like a bunch of masturbatory slot-machine lab rats, furiously refreshing or scrolling or pressing the magic button while we are annihilated.

Just be *careful*, I beg my darling teen. You have to be careful what you give your eyeballs to. (He grew up watching me lost on *my* fucking HHC. . . . I'm so sorry, sweetie!!) Is it over the top to share that he received his HHC as a . . . Bar Mitzvah gift from us, his parents? Today you are a man: here's your HHC. We told ourselves we'd held out as long as we could. He claimed he was last among his friends.

A question of balance. Is it okay to spend an hour of your day looking at your feed? Is it okay to spend two hours a day looking at your feed? Who am I to say what's okay? But what else are you doing with your time? What do the other 23 or 22 or 21 or 20 or 15 or 10 hours of your day look like? Do you still read books at all? *Can* you still read a book? If you

118 | ELISA ALBERT

can't read a book, how on earth might you begin to *contextualize* what you see on your HHC? If you can't read a book, how can you know how to properly *curate* your HHC?

Anyway, the wandering, the complaining, the vicissitudes of faith: What's the takeaway? (Grow up listening to *midrash* and you start to think in terms of takeaway. Which is funny, because there are infinite takeaways, which can also mean there is no such thing as a takeaway.)

We are malcontents by nature. We are often ungrateful. We are short-sighted and we prefer immediate gratification. When mired in messy uncertainty (which is . . . always), we are spoiled children who cannot tolerate frustration. We'd usually rather be cozy and oppressed than empowered and free. Change is haaaaaaaard. Something about patience. Something about the subversion of the personal and collective ego. Something about waiting. Everything is itself *and* a metaphor, or any number of metaphors.

As Jews, to improve upon the all-too-frequently cited Didion line, we tell stories *about* stories in order to live. Yes, this is called overthinking. Shall we take pills to subdue it? Meditation is too hard.

Neediness is unattractive, no way around it. The neediness of posting and the neediness of scrolling: equally unattractive, although the former gets to bask in its own sense of fleeting glory, however small. But here we all are. Tell me who I am! Show me what I want! *Tell* me what to want! Give me new ideas about *what* to want, inspire me to continue on my path! What *is* my path? I'm so lost! Tell me the meaning of life! I'm so freaking lost! Also bored. And lonely. What does it all mean? Looking at people. Thinking about how I want to be looked at. Hideous and . . . like . . . human.

You don't like how we attempt to entertain and enjoy ourselves and each other? You don't like how we pass our stupid fucking time? Distraction changes shape and scale. It evolves. We're all on some weird trip together. But okay: You like rules? You want restrictions? You want limits and boundaries? Okay, rules can be useful. Let's make us some rules.

Just remember: Rules were made to be broken.

I bought a muffin with my coffee recently, in NYC on a brief getaway. Ever the flaneur. Not quite Moses on Mount Sinai for forty days/nights, but same general idea. Blueberry muffin. Not huge on muffins in general, but I needed immediate food because I'd slept late, it was pretty much lunchtime, and if I didn't get caffeine and carbs into my body posthaste, I was most certainly going to die. "Bonking," we call that in our family, which sounds sexual but in fact means you are about to expire from lack of food and/or drink.

The coveted bench in front of the beloved coffee shop was empty, it being long past peak loitering hours, and I made myself at home there, shoved muffin into my muffin-hole, swilled latte like it was the titty-juice of the gods. When the sugar and caffeine hit my blood stream, I was saved! Close call. I was going to live. I was in the prime of my life.

I had with me my HHC, a notebook, a pen, and a novel: *The Lonely Passion of Judith Hearne* by Brian Moore (perfect, depressing, post-WW2 Ireland, tw: "spinster," n-word, alcoholism). I arranged it all beside me, ready to make the most of the sunshine and blood sugar rush and primo bench spot. But what did I *actually* do? Delved directly into the HHC, allowed myself to be dominated by it, checked all the apps (then checked them again). Many, many minutes vanished forever while I ignored the notebook, the pen, the novel, my immediate surroundings, and the remaining half muffin, which I'd carelessly left out on the far end of the bench.

Maybe I answered an email, added something to my calendar. Maybe I checked a list or two. Maybe I texted everyone back. Mostly I scrolled Instagram. There was surely some lust or longing involved, some covetous goods. A dash or two of schadenfreude. More lust and longing, more covetousness. Some envy, but envy can be handily subsumed by a bit of judgment and hatefulness before swinging back around to lust, longing, covetousness.

Cheap drugs.

Eventually I came back into my body and glanced up to see the half-muffin on the other side of the bench get swarmed by birds. First one, then another, then four, then nine. They were going to town on that half muffin. It was a jolly old frenzy, and it reminded me of something. Something about groupthink. Something about simple carbs, cheap drugs. Something about group dynamics. I took a few photos and thought about posting one. But nothing witty enough came to mind, for caption. I couldn't make it mean anything.

15

Upon the Hills with Jephthah's Daughter

ERIKA DREIFUS

> She further said to her father, "Let this be done for me: let me be for
> two months, and I will go with my companions and lament upon the
> hills and there bewail my maidenhood." "Go," he replied. He let her go
> for two months, and she and her companions went and bewailed her
> maidenhood upon the hills. After two months' time, she returned to
> her father, and he did to her as he had vowed. She had never known
> a man. So it became a custom in Israel for the maidens of Israel to go
> every year, for four days in the year, and chant dirges for the daughter
> of Jephthah the Gileadite.
>
> —Judges 11:37–40

During the first of their eight weeks upon the hills, the daughter of Jephthah
the Gileadite and her companions danced. They danced because they were
good girls (most of them, anyway), and they had been conditioned never
to raise their voices, let alone scream.

And all of them, Jephthah's daughter and each and every one of her
companions, needed to do *something* with the screams that were rising from
their hearts and lodging in their throats. None of them could eat, and none
of them could sleep, and none of them could scream. And that is why they

shook their heads and jerked their limbs—but somehow, if you'd watched them, you wouldn't have called their movements contortions. You'd have called them dancing.

Not the sort of dancing with which Jephthah's daughter had greeted her father's return from battle with the Ammonites, virtually bouncing toward him, timbrel in hand—for she had missed him, of course, and worried every day over his safety. It never became any easier, seeing her father off to war. She was an only child, and her mother wasn't in the picture, so the two of them, she and her father, shared an exceptional closeness. No wonder joy had infused her from head to toe as she ran to meet him.

This dancing upon the hills was different. Sad. But still: dancing.

The second week, after all that dancing, even Jephthah's daughter's appetite had returned. Fortunately, her companions had anticipated this possibility. They knew their friend so well, after all, and so they had provisioned her favorites. One companion had prepared sacks full of figs and dates; another had collected baskets brimming with berries; still another, having led a small baking brigade, furnished breads both savory and sweet. That second week, as they continued to dance, they feasted.

The third week upon the hills, Jephthah's daughter and her companions kept dancing and kept feasting. And then, almost without anyone noticing, their silenced screams seemed to transform into sentences. When they paused from dancing, and between meals, they gathered in a circle outside their tents, and they spoke.

Jephthah's daughter herself still said little, but the others' tongues were loosened.

They spoke about their friend's father, Jephthah, which was something they'd never have dared to do back home. He was, after all, and despite the ignominious birth that would also have gone unmentioned back home but could be cited here upon the hills, an important man—a military commander!

They spoke about how this situation had come to pass, about the deal Jephthah had made, and how, even if he'd never intended this dire a result, it was basically all his fault that his only child must be sacrificed as a burnt offering. Was victory against the Ammonites really so important that in exchange for that prize he'd so recklessly promised to offer up to the Holy One whatever came out of the door of his house to greet him upon his triumphal return? Hadn't their friend, smiling and shaking her timbrel, *always* been the first to greet her father at that door when he'd come back from past victories? Wasn't that, moreover, the custom of their people—not even something particular to Jephthah and his daughter? "I do the same," one companion noted, to a wave of vigorous nods.

Even now, wasn't there more that Jephthah could do? Didn't he realize that this was not the sort of sacrifice the Holy One would want, having interceded to stop Abraham from committing the very same act? Couldn't Jephthah at least appeal to the High Priest to annul the vow? (Maybe not, one of the companions pointed out, reminding the group that the High Priest and their friend's father had some not-so-happy history between them.) Still, couldn't *anything* else be done? The fact that Jephthah had acceded to his daughter's request to delay things for two months, to allow all of them to go on this sojourn upon the hills, was something. But frankly, it wasn't much.

Another companion dared to suggest that maybe Jephthah's daughter should simply break her promise to return home at the end of the eight weeks. Maybe they, the companions, could somehow find her a new tribe to join. Or deposit her someplace where she'd essentially live in seclusion—she'd never marry or have children and, in a way, wasn't that in keeping with the spirit of her father's vow? Wasn't it, as one of them phrased it, "another kind of death"?

The companions spoke, and they spoke, but at the end of the week, Jephthah's daughter smiled a small, sad smile, and the look in her eyes told them what they all really knew, at heart—that she would adhere to her father's vow, as he had proclaimed it.

The fourth week, they danced, and they feasted, and they spoke (a few of the companions stubbornly clung to conversations about saving their friend from what seemed to be her fate). And they sang.

As with the dancing, the songs they chose weren't exactly happy ones. But, as people all over the world have known for centuries, if not millennia—sad songs say so much.

The fifth week, one of the companions—having realized that fully half of the allotted time had passed—had the bright idea of asking Jephthah's daughter if there was anything else she might like to do while they lingered upon the hills, apart from bewailing her maidenhood. Did she have any wishes or hopes that they, her companions, might help her fulfill?

At first, Jephthah's daughter refused to disclose any such desires. Then, she confided only in one of the companions, whom she swore to secrecy. But by the middle of that week the secret was out.

Jephthah's daughter didn't want to bewail her maidenhood.

She wanted to put an end to it—before she met that other end.

This required quick planning. Some of the companions couldn't help commenting—not grumbling, exactly, but whispering outside their friend's hearing—that it would have been helpful if Jephthah's daughter had mentioned this sooner. As in, before they'd embarked on this journey upon the hills in the first place. Now, one of them would need to hurry back home, secretly, and put in place the plan they devised. And it was a risky plan that could go dangerously wrong at many turns.

But Jephthah's daughter was their friend, and she was literally about to die. "Put yourselves in my place," she'd said, at last, that fifth week. And of course, even if none of them possessed the boldness to articulate the thoughts—remember, these were *good girls*—it would be a lie to say that they hadn't already reflected, in their own hearts, that as horrible as it would be to die now—and to die as her father's vow mandated, as a burnt offering—it would be that much worse to die without having ever known a man.

The sixth week, while they awaited the possible arrival of the man they'd targeted (in fact, they'd developed a short list of three potential men, because it was by no means certain that their first choice would be willing to risk breaking all kinds of codes and disguising himself and slipping away upon the hills), Jephthah's daughter's companions were determined to keep things light.

So they danced (more happily), and they feasted (so much so that a few of the companions fell briefly ill), and they spoke (laughing heartily whenever anyone uttered anything remotely comedic), and they sang (again, more happily). And they embarked on what one companion dubbed "nature hikes," although, as another commented, what other kind of hikes could these journeys possibly be, considering that they were, in fact, surrounded by trees and grasses upon these hills. And during these hikes they plucked flowers that they made into necklaces, placing the most fragrant and most beautiful ones around Jephthah's daughter's neck. And during the days they turned their faces toward the sun and when night-darkness came they sat quietly around the fire and gazed upon the stars.

The seventh week, they continued to wait. And they began to worry, because, as some of them murmured (again, outside the hearing of Jephthah's daughter), by this point the companion who'd returned home should have rejoined them upon the hills. Maybe something had happened to her along the way. Or maybe their plan had been revealed to someone's parents, or even, G-d forbid, Jephthah himself. The anxiety was enough to drive some of them to sleeplessness.

Finally, one morning, those who were still able to sleep awoke to find that their companion had returned. And she was not alone.

By that week's end, then, the mission was accomplished.

Afterwards, Jephthah's daughter and her companions sent the man home, so that he would be among the crowds awaiting their return soon thereafter.

Jephthah's daughter retreated, largely, into silence—a somewhat more peaceful silence, it seemed—and the companions spoke only to discuss how they would keep what had happened secret. How, in other words, they would sustain the myth that Jephthah's daughter had taken them all upon the hills for these weeks to bewail her maidenhood—and that she was returning to her death still a maiden.

And so, that eighth week upon hills, with the man safely dispatched homeward, Jephthah's daughter and her companions danced, and they feasted, and they sang, and they plucked flowers that they made into necklaces, and they turned their faces toward the sun, and when night-darkness came they sat quietly around a fire and gazed upon the stars. And they spoke. The companions agreed that at this season in the future, they would again travel upon the hills. Not for eight weeks, but for just a few days. Maybe four. They would go upon the hills and mourn for Jephthah's daughter and for the life she had not lived. They would never again speak of the man, not to each other, not to their own future husbands, not to anyone, so that his name would go unrecorded, and his very existence omitted from any chronicle of their friend's life and death.

And then, before they began their slow, steady journey back—they prayed.

16

How David Leaves

Temim Fruchter

Jonathan said to David, "Go in Peace! For we two have sworn to each other in the name of the Lord: 'May the Lord be witness between you and me, and between your offspring and mine, forever.'"

—First Samuel 20:42

1. With curls of smoke and plumes of fire he leaves. With signs and symbols; choreography and embellishment he leaves. The wreckage is the aftermath of an ancient dinner table, toppled mountains of onions, half a loaf of braided bread, the last few figs or leeks or grapes. The wreckage is a chair kicked over or a chair tossed into the flames. Or, is a chair empty, never even pulled from the table to begin with, and that, too, a kind of ruin. With flax and purple wool he leaves. With sky-blue and crimson; with vermillion and turquoise and sapphire he leaves. With a biblical gusto, David leaves, robe behind him funereally dark and bridally long. David leaves and the pillars of smoke that blow from his fiery nostrils hang in the air for days, weeks, months. Like he is a dragon but he is not a dragon. The

beard, perhaps; its own entire act. Not hoary, like Saul's, but deep-sea black. Or no beard at all, if you prefer it. He is, they say, slippery.

2. Like a bandit he leaves. Slinks down the hall just after slipping a note under Jonathan's door, nearly a literal Dear John, but David isn't really worried about the clichés of disappointment. Dear Jonathan, I have to. Dear Jonathan, I didn't want to. Dear Jonathan, it's been fun. More than fun. Dear Jonathan, it was not you, but it was also not me; it was your father. He does not write: *I was afraid.* No *xo* or *I'll miss you* but the kind of ending you could hold to the light and read a thousand times over, willing it into a grand expression of some secret feeling when it was really, truly, only ever an ending. And yes, Jonathan did; the light, and the willing. It was on parchment, on candy wrapper, on loose-leaf paper, on the back of something important. It was naked, envelope-less and unashamed; it was folded so many times it was a small, hard pill of a thing, almost unrecognizable as paper. You could imagine the boy who folded it furrowing his brow, biting his lip, squinting at the crease until it was tight enough. You could imagine the man, leaving by dark of night or gray of morning, unwilling to sign the note, to knock on the door, to say goodbye.

3. Leave them wanting more, he always says, or at least someone must. A slip of a man in a buttery sweater, he is a generous flirt at the art opening before ducking out, shielding his eyes from the sun like a celebrity. A mountain-shouldered man, he charges past the train station like someone late to something important, flint-eyed and focused on the horizon. Be more flash than twinkle; more spark than flame; more hoofbeat than heartbeat; more gone than ever here. He leaves the dinner before dessert and without ceremonial goodbyes; he leaves the opera at intermission; he leaves the movie theater while it is still paint-dark, five minutes before final credits, popcorn unfinished and Jonathan's hand still outstretched across their shared armrest to something

unreturning. Wait, he says. Wait, he was a wait. David, he was a story without an ending. Wait. He was never meant to stay, not like that. Wait, says Jonathan, and David likes the way he says it so much he makes him say it again. Wait. The languid way it arcs and lengthens before its abrupt stop. Wait. How it implies an unquenchable question. Wait. The thin and silky way it follows David singing from the house and still—wait, wait, wait—miles and miles later.

4. With blooms of blood and tight furious veins he leaves. Rope still crudely knotted to a battered headboard, blue-black ripples across skin that could be shoulder or could be thigh; skin that could be his or could be his. Jonathan gasps, a dreadful pleasure. Men given to animal sounds, to their claws and their fur; men outside of the robes that keep them squarely men. The force with which a man's body ripples in the sharp aftermath of another man's teeth. *Fuck*, says everyone, and the sheets, torn and tossed, say it, too. It is not so majestic as anyone thinks. Cock ringed hot, some singed part of Jonathan singing through his center, battered in sweat and salt, damp velvet crinkled at his feet, slick skin long-dried in the stone sun through the windows. A chill sandpapers Jonathan with goosebumps, and not the sweet kind. Waiting for that filthy harpist to come back to bed and wrap him in threat. The perversity of the secret code they share, the one that signals death as much as invitation. Don't come back, says the code. Don't you dare come back, says the code, but the heart says please. *Please.* And maybe this is a kind of majesty after all, the fangs and the fangs and the small soft part in the middle.

5. The first to leave gets a bad rap but David is leaving because David absolutely must. Saul is murderously angry. Saul is jealous of everything David has, including his own son Jonathan. Jonathan, who offered David arms that were only arms. A love, they say, *that did not depend on anything.* David tested this, skeptical. Lie for me, he said, and Jonathan did. Shoot for me, he said. Arch for me,

make your aim perfect, and Jonathan's arrow sliced a thin precision across the clouds. Weep for me, laugh for me, he said, and Jonathan didn't need to try. Be my impeccable alibi, he said, and Jonathan already was. Let me go, David said, and Jonathan's fingers opened in spite of their loyalty to his hungry hands. Be for me, David said, a quiet thing in Jonathan's ear. Only for me. Jonathan says nothing as he slides down David's legs to the floor. *No*, says Saul. Everything depends on *something*, says Saul, and it is then David knows he has to run. He is the one to leave, sure, but David, they say, *wept the longer*. How he wants—rarely, desperately, and against his better judgment—to stay.

6. It is simple, David thinks. Here are the stakes and here are the arrows and here is an open door: All you need to do is walk through it. But the leaving isn't the hard part; it's what a leaving curdles into later.

7. When David leaves, he goes like men go, absent procession or proclamation, and then he runs for his life. It is nothing so romantic. He fights when he must. He is strong and can be brutal when called to the task. He is a man, spear glossy with blood and eyes brimming with God. Jonathan? Someone will ask one day if he remembers. Jonathan? A prince, a warrior, dead in battle. It lives somewhere in the throat, that shimmer never allowed to grow into a feeling. There is no use for a warrior, after all, in kinship. In skin simply for skin's sake, in words between men that go nowhere, wasted as spilled seed. Just some man. Some man who died in war. Jonathan. Does he remember? David thinks of a wide day, a sky that for a very short time seemed unending. He thinks of butter and sandpaper and velvet. He scratches his right shoulder, but through his armor, he can't feel a thing.

8. *I don't run*, he has always joked, *unless someone is trying to kill me*. Well now someone is trying to kill him, so he runs. The details fur at their edges, the way things do

when one is running for one's life. The sharp scent of an impending cold front. The scratch of his sleeve against his sticky brow. The ache that comes from the middle of his back and blossoms outward. He had a sweet thing once. Once, he could make a joke. Now, he is hiding in a cave from a vengeful king and all he can think about is how hungry he is. His tongue pricks thinking of the palace: all that fruit, all that warm bread to dip in tart vinegar. Saul is hungry, too; but his is a stringy, desperate appetite, weak-willed and bottomless. David has always been hungry, running or not. Ravenous, and famously so. He wears his reputation for insatiability like proud armor, a victory song.

9. David is the one to leave, sure, but Jonathan isn't just some ghost or effect or result. Jonathan laid the table. He wants to feed the man he knows to be famous for his hunger. The hungriest man in all the land. Jonathan knows what comes of a proper feeding. And Jonathan, though a prince, knows how to cook. Jonathan, who opened the door and invited him inside. Jonathan, who knew the code. Jonathan, who shot the arrow. Here is Jonathan. He is thick in the thighs, where he holds most of it, and has eyelashes longer than those of any woman he has ever met. In those eyes live all the stars but he is still bashful, more shadow than bright. More second than first. A crooked runner, but a sure shot when he knows he has something to lose. He understands that sometimes a person leaves just when you've started to believe them. His father frightens him, but his father frightens everyone. When David arrives to play music in an effort to make Saul less angry, he brings with him a golden quality of light, like he himself is a thousand candles, and Jonathan the warmer. Jonathan moves closer. He knows what he is doing. He knows what he might lose. He blinks and blinks again. He wants David to see what he sees. Tentative at first but then as sure as a reunion, he moves closer and closer still. Close enough for his fingers to touch the lips of the one-day king.

10. I'm a realist, says David over coffee one morning, the eternal sky shining through the curtains over the hills and valleys of their braided bodies. You're a pessimist, says Jonathan, as he gets up to make pancakes. It's only for now, says David, cruel diviner who can see something fiery past the fields where Jonathan can't. So what? says Jonathan. Isn't everything? He pours the syrup. Jonathan's hunger is feline, reaching upward for something always there. Jonathan is not just the one who gets left. He is the one who protects. Who defends. Who faces Saul when David cannot. Who goes, bereft, and fights. Who, hungry, eats honey from a stranger during war. Who dies. Jonathan is the one who fights and Jonathan is the one who dies. David, though, left standing. David is the one who mourns. Who weeps across time. Who wears a borrowed garment still, just for the faint musk of it. He only leaves like a kind of arrival. He only leaves like a real realist never would. He leaves like an unleashing. He leaves like a pronouncement: *I'm still here.* Can you hear me? I'm still here and I'm still hungry and I've been here all along.

17

Once a Witch

MATTHUE ROTH

Then Saul said to his courtiers, "Find me a woman who consults ghosts, so that I can go to her and inquire through her."

—First Samuel 28:7

Genesis

She was born into blood. As a child, those family stories exchanged about the various members of her family astounded and terrified her—in no small part because it was her family who persisted in telling them.

Big Grandpa took Little Grandpa up a mountain, lashed him to a stone and raised a knife to his breast—

Grandpa traded away his birthright and ran off to the desert to escape his brother's temper—

Uncle Ishmael, least favored, was turned out to the desert as a babe with naught but a skein of water and an angel—

As a girl Serah peered long and hard into the pit where her nine uncles and her father had trapped her tenth uncle, by all accounts an insufferable snob, to sell him into a correctional slavery. The pit was dank and deep, and smelled of putrefaction and human waste. Yet trickling down its sides she saw the crystal shimmer of new water, no small thing in the desert where they lived.

"Your uncle's name was The Extra One," said her aunt. She cast the words downward, like spittle, and Serah wasn't sure whether she was speaking to her or to the pit itself. "Not the last, not the completion, but extra. He was an addition, not needed. Always setting himself apart." Serah's aunt's name was Judgment. Serah tried to be in her presence as little as possible.

"And you," Serah replied, turning her attention from the pit to her aunt's coal-dark eyes. "What were you doing when my uncles were gathered around the pit?"

Judgment scowled.

"Someone had to make dinner that night," she said. "You'll find out one day what it means to be a woman in a man's story."

That Friday night in the dining tent, Serah told her father of his sister's words and he scowled. "She thinks she knows the sum and total of every soul in the land," he said. "And what fortune does my name tell of me?"

"Your name is Which," said Serah. "It doesn't mean anything."

"It means everything," he said, and smiling what was left of his crumbling smile he leaned in to bless her. "For blessings and safeguards, for illumination and pleasantness, and for peace."

She scowled at him. "You forgot 'for long life,'" she admonished.

"For others, long life is a blessing," he said. "For you, my daughter, I am not so sure."

Uncle Extra was not dead but exiled, run off to Egypt. There he had taken political and economic charge of the country. It was no great surprise. Her family was like that.

Her uncles had no food, so they packed up their families and went to join him. Seventy of them crossed the desert, with servants and camels, the brothers swapping barbs the entire journey. The fighting soured as they traveled—day after day the same sand, the same empty sky, the same featureless horizon that never grew closer, and the same faces, growing older, but imperceptibly, because those faces were the only things they looked at every single day, everyone else seemed tortured by the passage of time.

To Serah, it was only moments upon moments, one after the next.

She wasn't sure when she first noticed she felt differently about time than everyone around her. Maybe felt was the wrong word. Maybe it was more like seeing: she saw time the same way you might stare at a bug up close, notice the leaflike veins in its wings and the many tiny hairs, then pull away and see just a flash of shining emerald-black. Time was tiny and enormous. Time could take forever when you let it—walking in the desert, for example, or sitting still on the back of her father Which's camel trying not to slip off its sharp and sticky hair, not to make it sway to the right or to the left, or waiting in the vast marble halls of Extra's palace eating honey dates and grapes while her father and uncles lost what little patience remained to them.

And then her uncle Extra took off his snake-headed helm and revealed himself to his brothers. They hadn't known it was him the whole time? Serah couldn't believe them. They were so feeble, so simple, so . . . living in the story, not paying attention to it as it happens.

"Serah, you have to learn to live a little," said her uncle Jew at the revelry. "You can't just let yourself stop thinking of yourself."

Yes, mused Serah. Her uncle Jew was correct, more correct than he knew. Not just at parties, where she felt herself a staunch and stubborn rock against the tide of the merrymaking, but whenever she found herself in a room full of people, whenever she was with another person, whether roped into conversation or silent on the edge of it, she always felt herself responding with whatever the other expected to hear, following the motions of being alive rather than just plain living. She did not belong here. She was not one of this family, she did not belong among its ranks, and she could barely fake it. She was one of the Children of Israel, and yet all she felt was her lack of Israel, the feeling of being alone among the herd, a sixth finger, a stubby thumb.

The years that followed passed quickly for her, those years of plenty. When all you desire is laid out before you, there is nothing to mark the passage of time—no needs, no wants, no distance between the time one wishes for something and the time one possesses that thing. They were the most wonderful years, she would say to anybody if asked, but—in the aftermath, living another life, if pressed, she would search the dank and twisted corridors of her mind for memories, and though she could recall each lavish meal she ate, the precise design of her palace bedroom—she could not think of a single thing that happened that affected her, that changed her emotionally, that really made her (in the words of her uncle Jew) live.

Once a Witch | 135

They died. All of them—Extra, Jew, Judgment, even her father Which, that relative pronoun, grasping for connection, with all of their ancestors on one side and, on the other, what? Her? Did she count anymore, was she even human? At Which's funeral the members of the family lined up to console her with the ritual words of her people, the words they would learn from a book that wouldn't be written for centuries, *May you be comforted among the mourners of the remnant of Zion*, and she did feel sad—she was good at that part. She always felt sad—yet still there was something missing. They could feel it, too, her family, the way they edged away from her after paying respects, the way she was studiously avoided at the mourning reception, the way she was studiously avoided after that.

After her father's passing, Serah didn't withdraw, not exactly. She just felt the world move away from her, and she didn't move herself any closer. While uncle Extra was still alive, the family lived in his palace, and availed themselves of its many and varied pleasures. But upon his passing, a new ruler came, who had neither the debt nor the inclination to honor the extended Extra family and foreigners in his midst.

How, she wondered, had they not seen this coming? The years of plenty turned, as Serah knew they would. Maybe it was a natural consequence of having outstayed their welcome; maybe, she thought, it was a cycle. You're either the hunter or you're dinner, her uncle Zeb the fishmonger had told her. And as she wandered through the palace (once the ruler's, then Extra's, then the family's) alone, ignoring the upturned noses of her family as she picked up on the murmurs of jealousy and suspicion and discontent from the servants, she could smell the changing of the courses: they were clearing plates, they were preparing for another wave of food. And as far as Serah could see, no one in her family was doing any hunting.

"You're so weird," the boys, her nephews, were fond of telling her. And: "Why don't you act like other girls?" And: "Why don't you act like anyone else?" And: "Why don't you ever get any older?"

That was how she started rubbing mud and sand onto her body, between the lines of her skin. Even if she did not know yet (she would never know, not with certainty) that she was different, the kids around her did. She alone had crossed the desert still intact, neither repulsed nor seduced by the palace in which they now inhabited—swarmed, she thought, like bugs, on a crawling tryst of eternal discovery, constantly shoveling food between mandibles and throat with little regard for how it was served or the dishes it was served on or, indeed, where that food had come from, who had picked it, and who was responsible for its procurement or preparation.

And the old pharaoh died, and the new pharaoh (who, she was not entirely unconvinced, was the same as the old pharaoh—his son, the heir to the dynasty, was far more interested in wrestling the temple alligators than in acts of invasion and diplomacy, while the elder pharaoh, always one to take meticulous care of his health, looked curiously near-identical to this newest manifestation of his ostensible son—his hair shaved closer, his beard at just a different angle—and who would take it upon himself to check the tomb just before its sealing to make sure his mummified remains were on the right side of the sarcophagus?) knew not Extra and his family. Or perhaps he just didn't care to have Extra's grandchildren and their cousins plundering the royal storehouses at all hours of the night. Serah could scarcely blame him.

She found, when the chains had been shackled, when their duties had been assigned, that the slavery in which she found herself reminded her of nothing so much as mortality itself. The repetitive work, day after day, and the repetitive motions within that, your body just a tool, nothing more, an extension of the plow that drank her energy and replaced it with dull gray weariness, the same muscles extended, each of them over and over again, until she could feel the very marrow of her body as cables and pulleys, plumping larger with every stroke, detaching ever just so from the bones they hugged, detaching even more from her brain, leaving it stark and barren.

And so too were her family. The cousins who were older than her got older. She did not. The cousins who were her age got older and stopped wanting to talk to her. She no longer looked like them; or, they no longer looked like her, no longer children, having grown into women and men with new bodies, new muscles; and then into parents; and then into the sad, slow, elderly, and regretful.

And though sometimes they took notice of her, in that nameless slavery that drifted on through the years (and then through hundreds more years) no one thought to take note of Serah, and how she never aged, and how she never changed. She was like those bones, slowly losing touch of her muscles; she was like her brain, reacting on some level to the immediacy and danger behind the threats of the slave drivers, moving to comply, but on another level, to be honest, never really moving at all. She woke up feeling tired; she fell right to sleep, exhausted, and dreamed no dreams.

ONCE A WITCH | 137

When at last the cries of freedom came—had they yelled at all during their slavery? did their bodies even remember how to do it, how to raise their voices, how to say things they were neither commanded nor expected to?—she barely registered them, just lonely shooting stars coasting through the eternal sphere of night.

They thought they were freed. She knew better. They were sheep, and whether they were grazing on Nile grass or at desert oases, they followed their sheepish behaviors: eating, sleeping, being led.

Forty years they stayed in the desert. A different location every night, but the same horizon. They traveled in circles—alone among them she recognized it, the same-shaped glistening pool they passed by thirteen years before, the same burnt bush. Forty years they stayed, an entire generation dead in the sand. She alone remembered; she was the only one left. If others recognized her, or suspected her secret—Savior son of None was too busy scouring political rungs; Calev, his friend, studied her (intently, in the way that men will study a woman; but thoughtfully, in the way that only a man who is on a certain level wholly uninterested in studying women can manage to successfully engage) but, perhaps fearing she might have too much visibility into his own secrets, said nothing.

The land of Israel, once conquered, hung with splendor and richness. Her family (now seventh and eighth cousins, twentieth and thirtieth cousins, an embarrassing richness of cousins, none of whom could quite remember who Serah was or who her father was) numbered in the millions. They swarmed and spread out and infested every corner of the land, planted themselves in its cracks and crevices, and ate off the gold- and bronze-leafed plates they found.

Bodies, crumbs, used dishes scattered all over the desert. It was the house of pharaoh all over again. She watched, first in disgust, then in sadness. She participated in the acquisition, bursting into villages and houses hungry, swiping daggers across the bellies of the unsuspecting and claiming their huts and dinners (they had been slaves, hadn't they? and otherwise, they would die of hunger themselves, wouldn't they?)—but when the frenzy cleared and their stomachs filled and each house was claimed by a different family, and each town by a different tribe, she went unclaimed by them all.

The tribes that bore her uncles' names spread and filled the country, each to their own area. They barely resembled the men whose names were their tribes—their homes, their lives—and remembered them almost not at all.

The tribe of Which grew and thrived. The people drew water from the sea and brought it to the fields and grew crops, and cultivated, and hunted, and tinsmithed and made ceramics and made a civilization. They made families. They made their lives.

And on the edge of that civilization, not far from their lives—still a part of their family, although no one's memory could attest to that any longer—on the edge of a river, filthy, corroded by the dysfunction of nature herself, a swamp really—lived an old woman, older than any old woman that had ever been, a woman rumored by the villagers (her unsuspecting cousins) to be a sorceress, and by the faraway tribunal (more cousins, perhaps a bit less unsuspecting) a heretic, not excommunicated, not opposed to their faith and their G-d and their tradition, but on some sort of unholy detour. A witch.

Apocrypha

The prophet died—his prophet, his friend, the only one worthy any longer of his trust—and the king lost his shit.

The king mourned. He fasted. He rent his garments (the finest Tyre silk of his court robes, spun by the finest domesticated spiders, each a first daughter of their clutch; and his house robes; and his coarse winter robes that turn the frigid air of a harsh desert night to the warmth of a mother's bosom). He stayed up five days without sleeping, and he slept for seven days, rising only to make his water and stare disbelievingly at the rising of the sun.

The sleep he slept was without dreams, and this was the most disappointing of all. The prophet plucked the king from his ancestral land (the land of the Son of Right Hand), brought him to Jerusalem and made him king. For years the prophet told him what to do, made decisions, commanded the king with a divine and utter clarity so that he need not worry about anything but the delivery. He was orator, not author; musician, not composer. He was king.

It was his job, his identity, his title and name, the palace where he lived, his security. And when the prophet took away his crown, delivered it to a boy—a shepherd—he lost not merely kingship, he lost everything.

And then he lost the prophet.

ONCE A WITCH | 139

He roused himself from his bedsheets. He trampled the countryside, stumbling past battalions of the new young king who replaced him. The soldiers, armed to the teeth and on the lookout for a king—stately, rich, handsome, escorted by a coterie of the fiercest warriors in the land—looked through him like a ghost. He wandered the hills, searching each night for many things, but searching in truth for only one thing. In disguise, mottled of face and in the least kingly of his vestment, visiting the most questionable of yeshivos and wine houses, asking the most questionable of characters in each, "Where is your town necromancer?"

And yet the irony consumed him, for by his decree, the necromancers had been driven from the land. As the months plunged into darkness, the wine houses got ever drunker, the king persisted and so did his question.

Until he arrived in the backwoods of the Which lands, to a town called Endor, and then past that town, to the edge of the city, to the dim and dismal swamps, to a thatched hut that seemed only able to stand of its own stubborn will and little else.

He rapped three times upon the door. She took her time, and when she opened the door, she had a placid look on her face. Not bitter, not vengeful, not surprised.

In fact, he was the one surprised. The stories of this woman were plenty, too many to fit inside her young and sticklike body. He expected a crone, wizened with age and plump with the reward of futures told and fortunes made. Instead, she looked almost as destitute as he was.

He was not the witch's first visitor. Mostly, the witch recognized them by their hopelessness. There were several ways they might be more easily identified by the less skilled: The intricately woven tunic in which this man was wound, dirty and ragged, but imported, and of a more finely spun wool than anyone in the village could afford; by the color coding of his cloth cape, a singular combination, a mark, identifiable only by someone who lived in, or dealt with, the capital, of royalty; or by his aura, singularly stomped upon, ground up, spat out. On his way here he towered uneasily over the villagers, twice as tall, not covered with hair—and of course his clothes—large and gangly and awkward. The witch did not understand how adults stood so far from the ground. They missed so much.

One thing about this man that was not like other men: he had not forgotten how to believe. She almost missed it at first. She was not used to people who could still get away with believing. But his eyes burned with a sureness that she wasn't sure how to digest. How had he found her? Did

140 | MATTHUE ROTH

he think he was headed somewhere else? Had he stumbled upon her by mistake? Had he stumbled upon her on purpose?

"You'd better sit down," she said, turning away as soon as she saw him. "This might take a while."

"What might?" His face, disguised, was motionless. He wouldn't give anything away. His identity least of all, but also his purpose.

Seeing as though he wasn't planning to sit—the hut had only one stool, either by virtue of space or decorating budget—she took the seat herself. She perched on its edge, hands between her knees, leaning forward, expectant eyes widening in curiosity.

"Do you know why I've come?" Even with his request, he would not give any more than what was required.

"I know you don't expect me to read your mind," she said.

"I seek a witch who believes in no boundaries. Not possible or impossible, physical or metaphysical. Living," he held his breath, then released, "or dead."

"A necromancer."

"Your kind, in these parts, in these times, are in short supply."

"The supply has fled the country," she said, looking out—there was no window, but he still got the wan and forlorn notion she was gazing at something distinct in the far distance. "The king has made it so. The practice of witchcraft in these lands is no longer tolerated."

"That does not mean it does not exist."

"Here, it does not exist," she said. "I have run as far as I dare. I shall not break the king's law."

He followed her gaze through the knots in the wood. There was no purchase in the outside world, but as he let his vision go—as he unfocused—he thought he could see something, or perhaps it was nothing that he saw.

"To the ends of the earth," he murmured.

"I'm sorry?"

"You have run to the ends of the earth," he said. "So have I. If I swear on my own good name, not a soul shall know of your deed and you shall not be punished, will you perform it? Here, at the ends of the earth."

She looked at him with suspicion, but also, he thought, with understanding.

"Once you get to the end of the earth," she said, "you don't get to return."

And perhaps he came for another reason—perhaps that other reason tonight would still be fulfilled—but this truth, he thought, was what he was brought here to hear.

He nodded, once, solemnly. His nod was famous. It was with this nod that he accomplished as king all that he accomplished.

"You promise, no harm shall come to me?"

Charitably, he bestowed her another nod.

The old woman who was not old returned his nod, and from her feeble body, her waggly chin, he felt his own nod insufficient and childish.

"Then what is it you wish performed?"

"I would like a soul returned," he said. "My dearest friend. My prophet."

"Say his name," she said, and in that dark hut the darkness, impossibly, deepened, enshrouding them both. If she was sitting on a chair, neither its back nor legs were visible. If he was once not alone in that hut, the witch, too, was no longer there.

And the world, he felt, had been turned inside out. As if life and death had no meaning; as if the answers he'd been searching for all his life—answers to questions he didn't even know existed—were right in front of him, growing in the morning dark like moonflowers, ready to be plucked, if only he could bring himself to. He saw the witch—the crone—the old woman—the girl, condemned to live only among her family, turned out from living with her family, spending each day with the dead. She was not a necromancer. She was simply a relic. The people she loved were gone, and she held onto their love instead of living.

What she gave him was infinite. What she gave him was darkness, a darkness without end. What she gave him was what he already had.

A girl who was not a girl.

A king who was no longer king.

A prophet with no will of his own who in his hands held all the power in the world.

And then, there were just eyes. Two, yellow, speckled with truth and light. Seeing his treachery and his lie. Seeing everything.

"You are the king," said the witch.

Judges

In the morning he wakes on a field. On either side of him is an army. There is no hut, but maybe once again, there never was.

The first thing he thinks is, I have fallen back in with my troops. His second thought, less sleep and more sober, is: I no longer have this many troops. Things right themselves in his mind, and he notices the different colors of the banners they have posted. Some are his, some are not. He sits in the center of the battle.

All these boys, he thinks. So many of the soldiers are younger than him, almost as young as he was when the prophet came to him in his fields and anointed him as king. He has lived a life. It's more life than most get.

"I am here!" he calls—to his ranks? to the others? The survivors will guess and counter. "I am king!" To the Creator who gave it to him and took it away? To the witch girl, having seen her prophecy? To whomever she met in that darkness, whoever told her of his secret?

The troops are astonished. The troops are bustling. To all sides there is the sound of metal on metal, breastplates and helms being strapped on, horses baying to run free. He is swarmed on all sides by chargers. "A sword!" he calls, asking, not as a leader, but for mercy, and a sword is slipped to him. He feels a freedom, the need to run. But he holds the sword, and looks for a direction in which to flee, and finds that the only thing in his way is the sword, the wrong side of it facing him, and he throws himself into it, the blade licking through his stained cloak, his stained skin, skewering him straight through. This, he thinks, this is completeness. This is where the prophet would tell him he is meant to be.

18

Isaiah and Power

Aviya Kushner

And they shall beat their swords into plowshares
And their spears into pruning hooks.

—Isaiah 2:4

There was a time in my life when the only book I read was the book of Isaiah.

After my grandfather died, I was shocked and devastated to discover that there was nothing in Jewish tradition for a granddaughter to do. Since I was not obligated to say *kaddish* or even to sit shiva, I created my own mourning ritual. I decided to go to Shabbat services on time each week for a year and read the entire Torah out loud.

Many sections of the Torah were just as I remembered from my yeshiva education, from all my prior years at shul, and from hearing my three brothers practice their bar mitzvah portions at the dining-room table. Other parts astonished me as I read closely. But something happened to me as I read through the cycle of Isaiah *haftarot*, known as *haftarot nechama*, or the *haftarot* of comfort, carefully reading word by word out loud, in the women's section at the Harvard Hillel in Cambridge, Massachusetts. I had just finished a graduate degree in poetry, and as the weeks passed, I stopped thinking of Isaiah as a prophet and started thinking of him as a poet.

145

Shimu shamayim v'haazini aretz—"Hear, O heavens, and give ear, O earth," in H. L. Ginsberg's gorgeous translation.

I shook from Isaiah's grandeur. I knew I could learn all I needed to know about alliteration and assonance from those four words of Isaiah.

I wanted to learn how to do what Isaiah was doing—and I wanted a conversation. So I would riff off one verse in Isaiah, or a snippet of a verse, or a bit of medieval commentary on some of the thornier moments in Isaiah. I did this every morning for about eight years, writing Isaiah poems on yellow legal pads before doing anything else. I sat in coffee shops with the book of Isaiah in Hebrew, with commentaries, and the Ginsberg translation. I often started in Hebrew and eventually moved to English. I also played with an exercise my teacher, the great poet Derek Walcott, used to use in class; Derek would teach "The Fall of Rome" by W. H. Auden, cover the last line, and challenge the class to write a last line for that poem. It turns out it's almost impossible to rewrite the ending of Isaiah 66, just as it's practically impossible to one-up Auden.

Still, I challenged myself to do a variation of Derek's exercise by taking bits and pieces of Isaiah, borrowing a bit of Isaiah as a beginning or as an ending or using an Isaiah rant as the turn of a poem. Writing Isaiah's words each morning, I felt closer and closer to Isaiah, and more comfortable with his power as a poet. Instead of feeling intimidated, I felt like he was nearby, despite the centuries. I started to imagine what he looked like, what he sounded like, and whether he was a night person or a morning person. I regularly imagined Isaiah roaming the hills of Jerusalem.

I also found myself wondering how, exactly, Isaiah began—how he started out as a poet, because that's where I was then. I ignored all the scholarship about Isaiah I and Isaiah II, which some well-meaning people tried to talk with me about, and just focused on the making of a poet, on how Isaiah felt to me. I was interested in how the verses were made.

Then as the year of mourning ended, I was sad again; my grandfather was gone and there was nothing I could do. My year of punctual attendance was over; my ritual had officially ended.

But I kept writing Isaiah poems.

And then I returned to them to edit and shape them. Many years later, I realized those poems were my way of keeping my grandfather alive in my mind.

My grandfather, Shmuel Traum—or Siegmund Traum as it said on his passport—was born into a Chassidic family in Bremen, Germany. He left

Germany in 1935 and arrived in Haifa in 1936, when he was twenty-two. He didn't know when he left that he would never see his parents or his four younger brothers—Yitzchak, Pinchas, Mordechai, and David—again. His father greatly objected to his departure, noting that his youngest brother David's bar mitzvah was just a week away. To the end of his life, my grandfather felt guilty about missing that bar mitzvah.

I was twenty-three when my grandfather died. That year of synagogue earliness, wearing my most elegant clothing and best skirts because my grandfather loved clothing, because he believed in beauty, I vowed to miss nothing as I looked again at the fundamental text of the faith Saba Shmuel was born into, had left, and returned to. As the months went on, I found myself thinking about how rarely my grandfather expressed anger at what had happened to his parents and brothers. The horrible fact of the Holocaust just *was*.

But Isaiah rages at what is and what was, and Isaiah makes anger beautiful. Consider one of the opening lines of Isaiah, in 1:2—*banim gidalti v'romamti v'hem pashu bi*. It's so simple, a whole life story in six words.

I reared children and brought them up—
And they have rebelled against Me!

Notice the "me," which is capitalized in some translations. It captures anger. Anyone who has witnessed estrangement understands Isaiah's furor in all its simplicity. And that idea, that someone has *rebelled against you*. Or perhaps, *sinned against you*.

In Jewish tradition, there are two forms of *mitzvot* and two forms of *aveirot*; there are commandments that have to do with our relationship to God, and commandments involving our relationship with other human beings. But in Isaiah, it's against *me*. It was such a personal, intimate, direct, one-on-one sin, and such an unavoidable anger.

Isaiah is so comfortable expressing anger and making it beautiful. I wanted to learn to write anger.

I realized that as a woman I had been taught—subconsciously or consciously—that I was not allowed to be angry; that women's anger was ugly, unattractive, disgusting, and certainly not beautiful. In time, I began to think that Jewish sadness—Jewish mourning and Jewish pain—is sanctioned in society.

But Jewish anger makes people uncomfortable.

I thought about who had *sinned against* my grandfather, his mother and father, and his family. The list is long. Yes, his neighbors in Germany;

ISAIAH AND POWER | 147

the local police, who removed the family from their home in the middle of the night, doing the Gestapo's dirty work for them; the countries in Europe who did not fight against Hitler or did not fight hard enough; and the many prosperous nations, including the United States, who did not let desperate Jews in so they could save their lives.

There was also the role of the church, which had promoted virulent anti-Semitism for centuries; my grandfather believed anti-Semitism would never leave the earth because people believed Jews had killed God. I remember Saba Shmuel saying hatred of Jews was understandable in that context. And I also remember how he described the 1930s, when his brothers desperately tried to find somewhere to live, because at that time they were too young to emigrate to what was then Palestine and is now Israel: *There was nowhere to go.*

I found myself looking at those six words of Isaiah—*banim gidalti v'romamti v'hem pashu bi*—and wondering if it was broader than what had happened to an individual family, to four teenage brothers and two parents. Of course, the greatest enemy can come from within; Jews can hurt Jews; brothers can hurt brothers; but the more I looked at it the more I thought Isaiah was talking about the entire human family. I was part of a society that raised human beings, he is saying; but they *rebelled against me.*

I kept reading Isaiah through many terrifying moments. Isaiah acknowledges violence and its destructive power over individuals, such as in passages like Isaiah 4:1:

In that day, seven women shall take hold of one man saying,

> "We will eat our own food
> And wear our own clothes;
> Only let us be called by your name—
> Take away our disgrace!"

That was one register—desperation. And I understood that desperation as I waited out the aftermath of a bomb. But in the eight years I intensively read the book of Isaiah and wrote poems back, and in the decade after that when I revised poems engaged with Isaiah, and tried to shape them into a book, I became fascinated by how Isaiah mixes registers. I was moved by something specific—how often Isaiah mixes anger and comfort.

148 | Aviya Kushner

Now, I keep hearing Isaiah rumbling beneath great Jewish poets who also combined anger and comfort, who stared directly at pain. I imagine these poets also had years of immersion in Isaiah. In Paul Celan's personal papers, the words of Isaiah—*kumi ori*—"arise, shine" from Isaiah 60:1—can be seen in Celan's own handwriting, in Hebrew. John Felstiner, in his biography *Paul Celan: Poet, Survivor, Jew*, which I often reread, describes his experience in Celan's library: "While examining Celan's Hebrew Bible in 1984, for instance, I found that someone from a German research team, unable to identify the volume, had placed in it a slip saying *Wichtig?* (Important)?" Yes—it *is* important. Celan's *Tanakh* matters. So does the fact that Celan read Isaiah in Hebrew.

I believe Celan modeled some of his great works on Isaiah. His repetition, his staring at horror, his use of the natural world of animals and plants in his visions, and his attempt to comfort and perhaps self-comfort all feel rooted in the prophets. "Count me among the almonds / Count me" reminds me of *nachamu nachamu ami*—"Comfort oh comfort My people" in Isaiah 40:1. It's that same imperative form, and that same reflexive impulse, repeated.

I hear Isaiah in Celan in the sheer amount of repetition, which is one of the reasons Celan's poetry is so unforgettable and transcendent. Consider the line from Celan's famous poem "Deathfugue"—"Black milk of daybreak we drink you and we drink you," in Felstiner's translation. That repetition and the power it creates always struck me as close to prophetic language. There is something prophetic, too, about a phrase like "black milk of daybreak." Here, Celan also uses Isaiah's present continuous grammatical tense.

I love hearing Isaiah move into Jewish poetry in many languages. I love thinking of Isaiah as present and continuous. Avrom Sutzkever—widely considered the greatest Yiddish poet of the twentieth century, and a member of the Paper Brigade which saved Vilna's Jewish texts and treasures from the Nazis—put himself in conversation with Isaiah in an unforgettable way.

In "Memory of a Meeting with a Wolf," translated from the Yiddish by Maia Evrona, Sutzkever, like Celan, uses "milk" in an unusual way:

His tongue sizzled with the milk of snow. The sparks
of his teeth flickered, with a lift of the head he read my
    ancient thoughts.

And of course, "wolf" evokes Isaiah's famous vision of peace, of the wolf dwelling with the lamb; but Sutzkever's take on Isaiah is complex:

> Human-being, you have forgotten: beast am I, and man are you,
> now is not the time for Isaiah's prophecy to come true.

Writing about *In fayervogn*, the collection Sutzkever wrote in his first five years in Israel, the scholar Ruth Wisse notes: "Addressed in prophetic mode, the poet is charred by the Holocaust but intact 'with a wolf in one eye and in the other—your mother.' The wolf in his eye is the raw animal knowledge he was forced to acquire to offset Vilna's tender legacy."

That "animal knowledge" of the survivor marked and separated Sutkzever, who had been part of Vilna's vibrant Yiddish literary scene and who was already recognized as a major poetic voice by the time Vilna's Jews were forced into a ghetto. Writing in 1948, Sutzkever knows that there is a gulf between Jews who had survived the Holocaust and then fought in Israel's War of Independence, and Jews like his own brother Moshe, who, like my grandfather, had arrived in the 1930s—who had never lived in a ghetto or survived a concentration camp.

Wisse paraphrases Sutzkever: "Even had you been greeted by Isaiah, he would have offered his prophecies with lowered leaden eyelids and shamed lips. Don't look for consolation from even your own brother. Between the two of you there lies a Warsaw Ghetto Uprising." Sutzkever, according to Wisse, does not accept Isaiah's promise of comfort in *Shabbat Nachamu*, the Sabbath of Consolation, which had so comforted me in my year of mourning; it happened to be the bar mitzvah *haftarah* of one of my brothers. I kept rereading her take: "It might seem only natural to turn to such passages in what appears to be the fulfillment of the biblical prophecy," she writes, "but the poet expects no such consolation, for how can that prophet look this survivor in the eye?"

Perhaps looking a survivor in the eye and looking Isaiah in the eye was part of what I was doing in my year of punctual shul attendance, in that time of trying to become a poet while imagining how Isaiah would respond to the twentieth century in Jewish history. I paid close attention to the encounter with evil in how Isaiah describes the authoritarians of antiquity, as he details the cruelty of Sennacherib. And then there is Isaiah 37, which promises that a "remnant shall come forth from Jerusalem" and takes aim at the King of Assyria, in verse 38:

150 | AVIYA KUSHNER

Assuredly, thus said the Lord concerning the king of Assyria:

> He shall not enter this city;
> He shall not shoot an arrow at it,
> Or advance upon it with a shield,
> Or pile up a siege mound against it.
> He shall go back
> By the way he came
> He shall not enter this city
> > declares the Lord.

In other places, Isaiah's vision for the future is greater than a surviving remnant and a retreating enemy of a king. The vision is a peace that is huge and expansive and includes the animal kingdom as well as human beings—as in Isaiah's iconic 11:6. What I love about this passage is how everything is Isaiah's:

> The wolf shall dwell with the lamb,
> The leopard shall lie down with the kid;
> The calf, the beast of prey, and the fatling together,
> With a little boy to herd them.

I wanted to learn to do that, to feel that every iota of the world is in my terrain as a writer. As I riffed off Isaiah and lived with his words, I felt that this soaring vision of the future is not just prophecy and poetry but power. It is confidence in naming the future and in knowing these words will be a part of it.

It is the power of asserting that a poem will last. Of writing verses so good that there is no doubt.

Though Isaiah was probably my most important teacher of poetry, I have tremendous gratitude for the incredible poets I was lucky enough to study with face to face. I remember Derek Walcott telling us that we did not need to understand the language to understand a good poem. From the music we should be able to guess the subject, and from the change in music we should be able to understand that the poem is moving from one subject to another. I would add that there is something about encountering real, actual poetry that is so powerful that it does not matter if we understand every word.

I think it's impossible to understand every word of Isaiah, because of the great distance between the ancient era and our own. But maybe it doesn't matter. Hebrew may have changed, but humanity has not. I thought of what understanding really meant—Isaiah's challenging Hebrew, word by word, or his essence, his anger, his comfort—as I read my teacher, the wonderful poet Robert Pinsky's description, in his memoir, of his encounter with his bar mitzvah *haftarah*, Isaiah 66, which I happen to have used as the ultimate challenge in my years of riffing off Isaiah: "The beauty of chanting words with their meaning mostly inaccessible, with every flame-shaped character on the scroll related to breath—somewhere in that maimed ceremony was my avenue toward giving my life to poetry."

My grandfather never described his own bar mitzvah. He had to give his breath to construction; deprived of the chance to complete high school, he spent five decades pouring concrete. He was not given the opportunity to choose to give his life to poetry, but the fact that he was able to run away with just his life—barely, on what turned out to be the last legal boat—is what gave me my life.

I realize now that there are all kinds of questions I should have asked, all kinds of inquiries I should have made about what made his life his life. When my grandfather left Germany, in a train that took him to a ship, he had no civil rights. I didn't really absorb that until this past summer, when I returned to the train station in Bremen from which he left Germany. The Nuremberg Laws had taken his right to property, including the few possessions he had with him like the *tefillin* bag his mother had sewn and embroidered for him. It amazes me now that this *tefillin* bag made it out of Germany.

Late in my grandfather's life he described being stopped at every station on the way and ordered to present his papers for the SS. And to my great sadness, because my *yekke* grandfather valued beauty and punctuality and pristineness in everything, he threw out the threadbare *tefillin* bag before he died, so as not to leave his descendants with anything in poor condition.

My grandfather, who saw so much human ugliness, was right to insist that beauty matters, because it adds joy to life—but Isaiah was right to combine beauty and power, to use the imperative for all it had. I believe this combination, this intense comfort with using poetic power, is what drew Celan and Sutzkever and Pinsky, who all gave their lives to poetry, to return to Isaiah again and again. On hot nights, when I still read Isaiah out loud, spellbound by the image of heavens as throne and earth as footstool, by that intimate vision of God, I feel in my body that Isaiah is all about beginning again. I feel myself standing up, listening to Isaiah's commands, condensed at their utmost moment into just two words that Celan felt compelled to copy out in all their light:

Kumi ori

Arise, shine.

Reading Isaiah as My Grandfather's Granddaughter

God will have mercy on Jacob, despite it all—
so there's hope for us humans,
something soothing in the offing.
After all, Isaiah says Babylon's destruction
will mean salvation for Jacob. Tell me, Isaiah,
does redemption always mean destruction
of another? Is that what you mean, just hope
as hard as you can that you are Jacob,
or maybe it just seems that way to me,
the grandchild who should not have been,
whose great-grandparents died so fast,
in the snow, on the border between lands
and destinies, the girl whose grandfather escaped
on the last boat, at the last minute, in the last breaths
before the Mediterranean became red,
before shame forever polluted the blue water.

19

The Job Book

STEVE ALMOND

He will be misled by falsehood, and falsehood will be his recompense.
He will wither before his time, his boughs never having flourished.
He will drop his unripe grapes like a vine; he will shed his blossoms
like an olive tree.

—Job 15:31–33

I first met Dina Falcon during the fall rush of 2007. That was me, preening among the nervous frosh gathered in the living room of Sigma Mu. I wore a pink Lilly Pulitzer knock-off with a real Kate Spade clutch that had cost me an entire summer slinging Beef 'n Cheddars at the Arby's on Route 119.

Dina was the social chair. She looked, to me, impossibly chic: an electric blue blouse and shimmering, velvet hip-huggers, wedges that showed off the crimson wink of her pedicure. She glanced at me, then the clutch, then gathered me into a hug. "Look at this little Yinzer," she whispered into my ear. "I could just eat you."

Yinzer was the word we used to describe someone from the Pittsburgh area. I didn't understand how she could know that about me; I hadn't spoken a word. Later, I would discover that Dina had researched every girl who might walk into the house. She stored this intel in a thick notebook she carried at all times, her Job Book, which she studied at night, while the rest of the Sig Mus slept.

Dina stepped back from our embrace and looked me squarely in the eyes. She had the wide lazy smile of a lioness. I could feel her holding my palms ever so lightly. She grinned around her eyetooth, as if we'd just shared a wonderful secret the others didn't know.

Two weeks later, the embossed envelope appeared in my mailbox. Beneath the formal invitation, Dina had inscribed three words in her small, impeccable script: *We're sisters now.*

Dina had it all back then. She was ambitious, kind, popular, a business major with a fashion sense that was safely daring and a battered Chevy Impala she called the Crapmobile. She had a boyfriend, a tender, muscled lacrosse player named Kirby, who escorted her to class beneath his umbrella. She had a best friend, Vivian, who had survived a car wreck and gone on to place nationally in the hurdles. By junior year, she was president of Sigma Mu.

We all envied Dina but it was impossible to resent her. She would loan out her clothes to any sister who asked. She was generous with advice, too, the kind of person who had an instinct for how you were hurting and what to say and when to say nothing at all. She exhorted us to set healthy boundaries and urged us to build a support network safe from what she called "energy suckers" and promoted the power of prayer without embarrassment. She also knew how to cut loose on Saturday nights, always the first one onto the dance floor, careening gracefully and hollering Ashanti lyrics as the party swirled around her.

Later, she would be on her knees, scrubbing jungle juice off the baseboards, making sure they gleamed before she went to bed. I could see the ropy little muscles of her forearms as she thrust the industrial sponge. She knew how to deep clean, having worked summers at the Rayne Drop Inn to pay for her college apps. It was during these sessions that Dina would lean close and unleash a flat burst of Yinzer syllables, the ones she had carefully excised from her college accent. *Wanna gah dahntahn fera Pitsy sala?* To which I would respond, instantly, tenderly, *Wifries and dat? Yah curse.*

At the Sadie Hawkins dance sophomore year, my date, Scott Chase, wound up going down on my friend, whose name was (no lie) Katie Licht. I did not witness this carnal event, thankfully, though it was disclosed to me no fewer than seven times. Dina banished both participants and later slipped into my room, stroking my back while I blubbered.

"You just dodged a bullet," she said finally. "Walk with your head in the light, yinz. Grace always arrives with a serpent."

Dina's faith struck me as strange and miraculous. Because I knew Dina had a shit childhood, worse than mine, in a Dollar General town called Clymer, with a dad who lurched into view every few months and a mom who brought home bar flies then disappeared into her Vicodin. Her older brother was in the can. Her younger sisters had dropped out of high school. That left Dina to get her mom into rehab, take on debt, scrape her way to college. She had done this on her own, with no bitterness, wielding her belief like a scythe.

Everyone knew Dina would eventually lead the kind of exalted life we recognized from the magazines we studied on the toilet. She knew how to gather people to her, how to inspire devotion. I loved her furiously, achingly. We all did.

Dina graduated two years ahead of me, but thanks to social media I knew that she had moved out west, to Santa Barbara, and joined a clothing company called Hot Minute then moved on to a second, Beaux Vêtements. Every week, she streamed a new video of her friends—Vivian among them—wearing the latest Exclusive Releases, patterned skirts and wool wraps, scoop collars and peasant blouses. They would vamp like models then turn to the camera and crack up. Often they were outside, on a deck with the sun setting in the background. A continuous scroll ran beneath, thick with urgent exhortations (*Limited Edition! Only Two Left! Sold Out: Order Now to Lock in Your New Ship Date!*).

The idea was that you could order these items on the computer itself. This was back in the aughts, before Amazon had turned us all into porch zombies. The tech was still clunky, but the clips were prancing and playful, like hanging out with Dina in the hours before a party, when she would throw open her closet and let us run our hands across the goods.

We ordered what we could afford. The garments were never quite as fetching as they had looked on-screen, but we did our best with lighting and posted photos of ourselves on the socials, tagging Dina, waiting for her to pin the photo, add a comment or an emoji, some sign that she was still watching over us.

Dina had started as an Independent Retailer and been promoted to something called a Brand Ambassador. We had no idea what these titles meant but we could see from her posts that she was climbing the ladder.

THE JOB BOOK | 157

She had a whole team of sales reps who raved about making thousands every week, selling clothes from their basements. There were the pics from corporate retreats in Vegas, mimosas in Block Island, snorkeling in Belize.

The summer after we graduated, Dina launched her own company, Quality Thread. She reached out to her sorority sisters, offering us a chance to sign on before she started hiring outside. *She who withholds kindness from a friend forsakes the Lord*, she wrote, and most of us leaped at the chance. Who wouldn't? The clothes were adorable, the hours were flex, the profit potential astounding.

QT Girls made 25 percent on their own sales, plus a nifty commission on every sale their recruits made, and a smaller commission on every sale one of *their* recruits made. We had no idea what multi-level marketing was. The arrangement just struck us as smart business.

So why didn't I sign up? That was the question my Sig Mu sisters kept texting me. I was Dina's protégé in college, after all, the one who inherited her room and later her role as president.

I had my reasons. For one thing, I'd been accepted into the graduate program in Speech Pathology at the University of Pittsburgh. That didn't mean I couldn't join the team and earn from home. But there was something in the manic zeal of the operation that reminded me of my mom, the way she would head off to one of her Mary Kay parties, too carefully made up, only to return home deflated, with a faux Naugahyde valise full of unsold product. If the party was at the home of a friend with younger children, she would take me with her as a designated babysitter, and I would sit in some playroom, pretending to sip tea and listening to my mother's cheery voice, tinged with imploration.

I also knew a bit more about Dina's history than the other girls, because one night, just before she graduated, we got to drinking peach schnapps and she told me that she'd done certain things at the Rayne Drop Inn, to make ends meet during a particularly lean time.

"Things?" I'd said.

"There was this unspoken system among certain members of the cleaning staff and certain regular guests. Like, traveling salesmen."

She was quick to note that she had served mostly as a "coordinator," participating only once or twice, when unavoidable, in the performance of a function that was, as she described it, purely mechanical. "No need to make the big eyes, Yinzie. Everyone's selling something. Youth, beauty, innocence. All commodities exist to be corrupted."

We were tucked away in a little nook of the basement called the Dry Out, so named because it was where we took girls to sober up if they got too fucked up at parties. "People love to get high and mighty about sex work. It makes them feel like their jobs are honorable. Like slaughtering chickens is honorable."

"Or prying roast beef scraps from grease traps," I said.

"Or scrubbing the shit stains off the bowl where some 400-pound trucker dropped his first load after five days on the road." Dina laughed, then turned away and vomited quietly, almost elegantly, into her Nalgene bottle. This was something she did from time to time, so casually that it struck us as perfectly normal.

"Weren't you scared?" I asked. "Dealing with these creepers?"

"Are you kidding? Those guys were kittens compared to my mom's boyfriends."

I looked at Dina, plying her for an elaboration, but she closed her eyes. She wasn't going to go there. I understood, or thought I did anyway. My mom had dated a guy my junior year in high school, a real estate agent named Chuck who hugged me too close, who hovered outside the bathroom when he knew I was in the shower, who made certain comments about my body when my mom wasn't around. I hated it, but I never said a thing.

"When you know someone's weakness," Dina told me, "you're the one with power. Come on, Yinzie. Think. These sad married dudes putting it all on the line for a hand job." Dina smiled her lioness smile. "What if someone kept a record? What if someone took a photo?"

"You *didn't*."

Of course she did. That was how Dina operated. It all went down in the Job Book.

"You blackmailed them?"

"I offered them a choice. They could have the truth hanging out there, or a little bonfire could make it all go away." Dina pantomimed making a little bonfire, setting it alight. "Men are born for trouble," she said. "Even as the sparks fly upward."

I've thought about this moment a lot over the ensuing years. Why would Dina confess all this? I think she must have needed someone to

THE JOB BOOK | 159

know, to understand how far she would go in pursuit of her destiny. More recently, I've come to suspect that she was trying to warn me, to keep me safe from her ambition.

I should tell you at this point that I did get a peek inside her Job Book, just once. Dina had taken off for a long weekend, forgetting that she'd promised to loan a particular skirt to this girl, Melissa Owens, whose boyfriend was maybe going to *propose*. Dina called to ask that I retrieve the garment from her closet. Engorged with pride, I dutifully took down the combination to the keypad she'd installed on her door and delivered the item to Melissa. That should have been that, had the urge to snoop not caught hold of me.

I waited till everyone else was asleep before returning to her room. I wasn't hunting for the Job Book. She'd undoubtedly taken that with her. But when I reached under her pillow and felt its contours my heart went spastic. I knew Dina would be furious at this violation, and for a moment I suffered a vision of her hovering in the night outside her window, staring at me through the gauzy golden curtains she'd hung.

It was really just a thick, three-ruled notebook, the cover of which read *Job Book 2007*. Inside was page after page of data: a detailed breakdown of the sorority's financials, proposed party dates, themes, budgets, the name of every girl who had rushed that year, with detailed biographical notes, hometowns, birthdays, majors, boyfriends, best friends, behavioral tendencies, lists of what they liked to wear, sketches of particular patterns. There were similar entries devoted to her professors and mentors. At the bottom of every profile Dina had written a series of characters that began with V2.

V2: MA, PD, DI

V2: ED, SA

V2: CD, SP

I was so perplexed by these that I took photos of several profiles with my phone, hoping to break her code, I guess. Later, stricken by guilt, I erased them. It was stunning to see how thoroughly Dina was casing out the world around her, laying the groundwork for her ascent. It made me even more thrilled to know her, and a little scared.

You probably know some version of what happened next. Quality Threads went bonkers. Within a year, Dina and her team had recruited 7,000 QT Girls. They were getting so many orders at one point that they had to quietly absorb the manufacturing capacity of three other companies to keep up with demand. An antitrust case came out of that eventually, along with claims about the use of child labor.

For the years in question, though, Dina was flying. Her face was on the cover of the very magazines we'd studied in college. Then she launched a magazine herself, expanding her reach into the fertile valleys of the Lifestyle Industrial Complex. Sportswear begat footwear, hydration begat energy drinks which begat energy bars, which opened the portal to diet and wellness, kitchenware, accessories, makeup, emollients.

She married sweet, dim Kirby, had a son, then twin girls, the account of both pregnancies tastefully arrayed across the pages of *People* and *Us*, the preeclampsia scare, the brave decision to break the silence about the pain of episiotomy scarring, the babies themselves, pink and gorgeous in QT Pie onesies.

She bought all the stuff that comes with an abrupt entry into wealth, stuff that can seem absurd until you find yourself in possession of a billion actual dollars, at which point properties become necessary business write-offs, so why not make sure they're in desirable locations: Taos, Sun Valley, Martha's Vineyard, Paradise Cove? And because you now have to be in so many places, you need a private jet, which isn't as lavish as it sounds, because the government offers a zillion incentives. You need the capacity to reach your audience, too, the means of production, studios and server farms, the human infrastructure: security, legal, finance, media relations.

It all sounds pretty decadent, and I guess it was. But mostly, cheering from afar, I was happy for Dina, happy and amazed and vindicated and maybe a little tempted, sitting in my shitty grad housing, then my shitty postgrad housing, doing my internships in aural rehab and audiology, amassing envelopes that brought word of my debt, dating the same bleary boys, languishing in the blue profile of their gamer faces. Birthdays and holidays I could count on a package from Dina, crammed with goodies, always with a handwritten note: *He performs wonders that cannot be fathomed, Yinzie, miracles that cannot be counted.*

That was part of what made Dina such a juicy target. She was loud about her faith. It wasn't just the Biblical soundbites. She publicly tithed ten percent of her income to the church, and paid for a whole new building to house Calvary Baptist, where she'd worshiped as a kid. One entire branch of her clothing empire was dedicated to faith-based garments, cardigans and camis stenciled with *Lean in to Jesus, Make Heaven Crowded, Yet in My Flesh Shall I See God.*

THE JOB BOOK | 161

The fall came swift and savage. It began with revelations about QT Girls who felt they had been misled, driven into penury by the start-up costs. There were tearful videos of young women displaying their defective stock, blouses with torn hems, leggings with crooked seams. Then came the copyright suits, filed by companies who claimed Quality Thread and its subsidiaries had swiped designs. This led to further scrutiny of the company's manufacturing process and the overseas factories, where the grisly nature of globalism becomes visible to the fragile American consumer.

It was only a matter of time until reporters began digging into Dina's personal history. A fifteen-year-old police report for solicitation of prostitution emerged, in which Dinah Falcone, then an employee of the Rayne Drop Inn, was named as a person of interest. (Much was made of the dropped *e.*) I was contacted by a dozen reporters, and twice as many tabloid television shows. My social media channels were overrun with messages from kind strangers with a few easy questions.

The clickbait kill shot came a few weeks later, posted by a feminist aggregator called Hagar's Revenge: *Did Dina Falcon Traffic Underage Girls?* It was taken down a few hours later, by court order, as if that could possibly matter. Dina was officially symbolic now, a cautionary tale. "Whatever the truth of these allegations," Maureen Dowd wrote, "it's hard to miss the more disturbing pattern here: a sanctimonious girl boss preaching female empowerment and delivering female exploitation." Those of us who knew Dina tried to do our part. But Instagram testimonials couldn't compete with think pieces in the *Times.*

Dina issued a statement of the predictable sort, then sat for an interview with *60 Minutes*, deflecting Lesley Stahl's insinuations with an air of weary patience. "I worked a minimum wage job cleaning motel rooms in high school, like millions of women in this country. I don't know if you've ever done work like that, Leslie." Dina paused, quite skillfully. The crucifix at her throat glinted. "It's not a lot of fun but it helped me get to college, which helped me start a business that helps women achieve financial independence. I made some mistakes along the way, and I'll take my lumps for them. But it's not against the law to be poor in this country, or to work to stop being poor."

"So you're denying there's any truth to these reports?"

"As long as my breath is in me," Dina said, "and the spirit of God is in my nostrils, my lips will not speak falsehood, and my tongue will not utter deceit." Her tunic was the color of ash, so that she appeared, in that moment, to be a kind of singed nun.

The businesses collapsed, of course, the profits siphoned off by law firms and creditors. But that hardly mattered, given what happened next, the part of the story that everyone knows about, how Kirby and the children boarded the company's private jet, along with Vivian and three associates, bound for Pittsburgh, how Dina stayed behind to sit for depositions, how the plane hit bad weather over the Great Lakes, how the pilot lost her bearings, how there were no survivors.

Dina's life, which had long struck us as operatic, had gone Biblical; the scale of her loss beyond our reckoning. A photo surfaced—taken by a paparazzo at considerable distance—showing a haggard, skeletal figure, hunched over a chaise longue at a "recovery facility" in Sedona. The image was widely condemned and even more widely circulated. Those who had gloried in Dina's disgrace assumed a guilt-stricken silence. The rest of us sent condolences, heartfelt and puny.

I reached out for months, with no response. I hadn't thought about Dina for nearly a year, in fact, when I received a call at the clinic where I worked. A female voice, already impatient, said, "Please hold for Ms. Falcon."

A click, the hum of static, then: "Yinzie?"

"Dina. Omigod. It's you." I started crying, something I did a lot back in college. "Where are you? Are you okay? Can I see you?"

"That's why I called you, dingus. Get out your calendar." The old Dina flashed before me, the lioness, though I could hear the slur and wobble on her words, the lead tongue of sedation, which made me cry harder.

"Knock it off, Yinzie."

"I'm sorry. I'm just so—"

"Julia will handle the details."

"It's good to hear your voice again, Dina."

"Sure." The rust of her laughter hung between us. "Sure."

The events of that strange week began with a flight into Telluride and proceeded south by Hummer. The vehicle tunneled through profound darkness, then turned off the highway and came to a coded gate, then a second gate, further down the gravel road. I was ushered to a bungalow, relieved of my phone, told to get some rest. It was after midnight, but I lay awake for a long time, pondering why I had been summoned, what Dina wanted from me, what I was supposed to say to her.

THE JOB BOOK | 163

I woke to the smell of coffee. A buffet had been set out. A woman in business attire stood nearby, smiling in a wincing way that suggested I was already behind schedule. "Welcome," she said. "Ms. Falcon sends greetings and regrets. She has a few obligations this morning that she can't wriggle out of but hopes to see you for a late lunch."

"Could I just say, like, a quick hello?"

"She's off site."

"And you're Julia?"

"Oh no. Julia is in legal."

I certainly hadn't arrived expecting a slumber party. But I wasn't quite prepared for the protocols of Dina's fame, the way her staff made you feel handled.

"What should I do?"

"Eat something. Take a shower. Have a look around."

The compound consisted of a dozen bungalows clustered around a large chalet. Sunbeams lit up the cliffs beyond, rounded layers of orange rock, as if lava had been poured out like cake batter. The severity of the landscape made me feel small and foolish. I found myself panting, each breath a cold needle to the lungs. Lunch came and went, then twilight, dinner, a glass of wine. A second day spent in restless ambling. I began to lose time.

Finally, on the third morning, a familiar voice: "Wake up, little Yinzie."

Dina wore giant sunglasses and a hoodie that fell to her knees. Her breath carried the rot of someone not eating regularly. There wasn't much to hug.

"Sorry it took me so long to get free. Lotta knots to untangle."

"I get it," I said, stupidly. "I'm just glad to be here. You look great."

"I look like a scarecrow." Dina flung her arms crosswise. "Please—no BS. Promise? Good. Let's go."

"Where?" I said.

"You'll need a sweater."

Out we went, into the lavender dawn. We staggered down a rocky path below the deck of her chalet, which I now recognized from her videos. Dina walked at a blistering pace, as if she might zoom into the horizon. I kept remembering how she always would be up before anyone else, a highlighter in her fist, a stack of spreadsheets at her mercy. I never knew whether to interrupt her.

"Can we go a little slower?" I called out.

"Just a few more minutes, Yinzie."

She stopped dead at the crest of a small rise and gestured to a range of mountains in the distance. "That's my man. The Sleeping Ute. We caught him right at dawn."

"The sleeping what?"

"Ute. The native indigenous people. He's lying on his back. See the feathered headdress? And that crag—that's his chin." She went on pointing out body parts, till, at last, the image resolved.

"He was a warrior God who did battle with the forces of evil. Conked out while he was recovering from his wounds and never woke up. That's the story." Dina stared at the Sleeping Ute, bathed in the pink dawn. I wondered, for a moment, if she envied him; if she felt that he'd found an easy way out.

"Maybe one day he'll shock us all by getting up and wandering off to some other desert." She winked at me from behind her giant glasses. "Wouldn't that be a hoot?"

It turned out that Dina did want to talk, though only about the past we'd shared. The grand drama of hitting a Pittsy bar as a high schooler, hustling drinks from men who touched our necks in reverence and breathed in the fruity vapors of our youth. The boyfriends who bought us mall jewelry then drove us out to empty parking lots, the magic of our pale skin pouring out across the night. Even the peculiar, comforting reek of the Sig Mu bathroom: face cream and body wash and epic, post-coffee craps.

She had access to any grief counselor on earth, after all: Brené Brown, Gabor Maté, the Oprah-approved gurus. But Dina needed me. I was the person with whom she could travel back in time and feel again the exquisite burden of hope.

The night before my departure, I was summoned to a private dinner in her chalet. "I sent my staffers away," she told me. "I know they make you nervous, Yinzie."

"Nonsense," I said, though of course it was true. Every time they looked at me, I got the feeling they were about to blindfold me.

Dina had set out a Cabernet with a label that even I recognized. "Should you be drinking?" I asked carefully.

"Meaning what, Yinz? You think I have a problem?"

"I don't know," I said. "Do you?"

Dina smirked. "Don't believe everything you read, sister."

THE JOB BOOK | 165

The wine rippled out, into a decanter shaped like a swan. It went down so smooth we hit the bottom of the bottle before we were done with our salads. I hadn't been drunk in a while; I suspect the same was true of Dina. She wobbled into the kitchen and emerged with a clay vessel the size of a toddler. "Chicken tagine!" The dish thudded onto the table. "Braised thighs. Garlic. Green olives. What's the other thing? Preserved lemons."

The smell: dizzying. We moved from individual portions to direct assault, our forks flung like harpoons. "Oh my fucking God," I said. "Why can't I stop eating this?"

"That's the heroin."

I laughed and burped at the same time, an unfortunate quirk of mine. "She's lurping, folks," Dina said.

"Lurp lurp."

"Maybe I should get more wine?"

"Correct," I said.

Dina returned with another bottle. She was dressed elegantly, modestly, in a patterned wrap, her black hair unbound so that it fell around her shoulders. "It's good to see you ditch the ponytail. I always loved your hair."

She swigged from the bottle. "Smoke and mirrors, Yinzie. I'd be bald as that Star Trek dude without extensions." She took hold of one just above her temple and yanked it from her scalp with an eerie and astonishing calm.

"Jesus."

"This is nothing," Dina said. "Get me looped enough and I'll show you my boils." She twirled the extension like a lasso, while I tried not to stare at the white patch of scalp, circled in pricks of red.

"Do you want to talk?" I said. "Like, *really* talk."

Dina eyed me, then the bottle, as if we'd conspired to soften her defenses. "That *really* worries me, Yinzie. I think you mean you want me to talk about the family. That's something I handle through prayer."

"Understood. I know you loved them."

"I loved the kids," Dina murmured. "I just didn't see them enough." She stood abruptly and turned away. A muted sob rose from her throat.

So now we were into it, I thought. I got up to comfort my old friend. But Dina slipped away from me. "Just give me a minute, please," she snarled. Then, more softly, she added, "I forgot the dessert."

Dina returned five minutes later, with fresh mascara and a giant tiramisu cake dusted in gold foil, which she set down in front of me.

"Is there a knife?"

"No sharp objects for me," Dina said. "That was a joke. Now help me make this monstrosity go away, you little Yinzer whore." She plunged her fingers into the top of the cake.

She was behaving erratically. But I got the point. She wanted me to back off, to stop intruding upon what she wished to remain private. I plunged my fingers into the cake and began shoveling it in, too.

"You're such an oinker," she said.

I can't remember how the subject of Kirby came up. It must have had to do with how we were eating, some comment about how he would have been disgusted. "He could get pretty nasty," Dina said. "Especially after QT took off. He didn't like playing second fiddle."

"Nasty how?"

"He started sleeping with Vivian. That was certainly a red flag." Dina sighed. "We weren't headed anywhere good. That's my point. But it's terrible what I did to them."

"What *you* did?"

"I bought the jet. I hired the pilot. I assumed a female pilot would be more cautious. But who the heck knows? I'm a woman and obviously I wasn't cautious."

"You were doing what men do all the time."

"That's not as strong an argument as you think it is." Dina gave me a little cake slap. "You're missing the point, Yinzie."

"Which is what?"

"I thought God was showering me with his blessings. I got caught up in the plenitude. I mean, look at you: you managed to build a nice life for yourself."

I thought about that life: the garden-level apartment with leaky radiators, the erstwhile boyfriend (Derek), who was going to finish his dissertation any month now, my two cats, Knit and Purl, both afflicted with urinary tract infections.

"You're hailing me for being timid."

"You played it smart, Yinzie. You stayed clear of the blast zone."

"I don't like hearing you talk about your life that way. Like you're some kind of bomb that detonated."

"Who said bomb? I was the target."

It was the first time I'd heard Dina cite her misfortune. She had been so steadfast in the face of each new tribulation. The Lord giveth and He taketh away. That was her mantra.

But for those of us who loved Dina, we couldn't fathom why God would behave like such a sadist. The answer in the Book of Job, for those of us who went looking (and I did) was that God had created a universe booby-trapped with suffering. The human role in this arrangement was not to question why, for instance, He might murder your whole family. You were just supposed to accept His infinite wisdom and keep praying, even though the real reason He did it was because Satan gaslit him, a ploy instantly familiar to any sorority sister. It seemed to me, as I read the verses, completely obvious for the millionth time that the Bible was written by a bunch of insecure penised lunatics.

I reached for the wine, staring at Dina, who was staring at the remains of the tiramisu, the gold shavings slowly sinking into ladyfinger goo. She was one whose life had become a torture chamber. Stupidly, perversely, I wanted to know what it meant. Such was the human curse: not that we suffered, but that we kept yearning for it to mean something.

"Why would you pray to a God who treats you like that?" I said finally.

Dina sighed. "None of this happened by accident. You know how I grew up, Yinzie. You been to Clymer. When you got reckless people around you, grown men and women, you learn to make yourself tough. That's what girls like us have to do if we want out. Tell me I'm wrong." She had slipped into her Pittsy accent, that soft mutter I knew from bruised dawns and diner binges. "Maybe God wanted a tough nut to crack."

"Yeah but—"

"Yeah, but nothing. I shot my shot. I'm not going to spend the rest of my life bawling for dollars in therapy or playing Buddha at some five-star ashram. *For sighing has become my daily food; my groans pour out like water.* I can't live like that. Walking around so *vulnerable* to everything." The word was bitter on her tongue.

Dina began to utter strange abbreviations. "CD. SA. DI."

"What are you talking about?"

"Shorthand, Yinzie. Chronic Depression. Social Anxiety. Daddy Issues. Just something I devised for my Job Books."

She pronounced *Job* with a long *o*, as in the Bible, so that for a minute I couldn't figure out what she was saying. Then my mind flashed to the notebook that had been her constant companion in college, all those years ago. I could see her room again, the gossamer sheen of her curtains, and there I was, skulking around with my awful bangs, reaching under her pillow, staring down at Dina's impeccable lettering. For months afterwards, I'd puzzled over her code. What did V2 mean? Version 2? Volume 2? At last it dawned on me: *Vulnerable to.*

Dina had studied all of us, had discerned and catalogued our weaknesses, the particular ways in which we were susceptible to suffering. She did this in an effort to understand us, to comfort us, to hold power over us maybe, but mostly, I think now, to master her own fears.

When I returned to the present, Dina was staring at me. "It was a long time ago," she said quietly. "Don't sweat it." She took off her sunglasses and her eyes, ringed in fatigue, still flickered with the old magic. *It's our secret,* that look said. *Just you and me.*

My gut went queasy. Dina knew I'd looked at her Job Book, had known from the jump. Maybe I'd failed to return it to the exact right spot under her pillow. Or she'd had it dusted for fingerprints. Probably she just recognized my weakness in the face of such a temptation.

I began to apologize but before I could even get through that I was weeping, thinking about how I was leaving tomorrow and Dina would be all alone in this beautiful prison, surrounded by sad mountains and eternal loss. I was projecting, of course. The wine had made *me* want to wind back the clock, to see in Dina all the grace and power she'd once held. I stumbled over to my old friend and wrapped her in a hug. I could feel her bones twisting against me, but I wouldn't let her go.

"I can't believe this happened to you. It's all so fucked up," I whispered. "I love you. You know that, right? Will you let me come visit again? Or I could extend my ticket."

"You're sweet," Dina said. Even then she was turning to stone. "I'm going to hit the showers. I've got mascarpone all over my face."

I released Dina and she stepped back. Through the window behind her, the sky was a black veil pierced by stars. "Just because we can't find a design doesn't mean there isn't one. Nobody knows what lies on the other side."

A month later, Dina failed to appear for her daily briefing. The assumption was that she had taken a hike, perhaps gotten lost. When she hadn't turned up by dusk, her staff contacted the local sheriff. No vehicles had gone missing. Her phone and credit cards had been left behind. There were no suspicious calls or intruders. Deputies conducted a search of the immediate area, which eventually became a federal effort, with drones and helicopters and what all.

The media, of course, assumed suicide. It made for a neat arc. I figured that was probably right. Dina had finally collapsed under the weight of her grief, and decided, as a Christian, to discover what lay on the other side.

The more I've thought about Dina, the less certain I am. She despised the idea of martyrdom, surrender, public anguish. She took the darkness she was born into and crushed it into diamonds. The glitter seduced the world. But it was the hardness she was after. Death wouldn't give her that.

I certainly don't know where she is. I suspect she walked away, like the Sleeping Ute, and found another desert. I do know that Dina destroyed her Job Books, because a year after her disappearance, a message appeared in my in-box, with the subject line: FYO. There was no text, just a link to a grainy video of someone casting a stack of notebooks into a roaring fire pit, one by one. The setting is outdoors, but it's impossible to say where because it's nighttime. The footage is also super bouncy, because the person is filming with one hand and feeding the fire with the other. At one point, the camera swings around, for just a second, and Dina winks. You can see that she's taking a lot of pleasure in watching the sparks fly up.

20

Root

Ilana Masad

But Ruth replied, "Do not urge me to leave you, to turn back and not follow you. For wherever you go, I will go; wherever you lodge, I will lodge; your people shall be my people, and your God my God. Where you die, I will die, and there I will be buried.

—Ruth 1:16–17

And there was, in the Days of Judges, a great hunger across the land. And a man went from Bethlehem in Judea to live in the fields of Moab—he, his wife, and his two sons. And the man's name was My God is King, and his wife's was Pleasantly, and his two sons' Illness and Annihilation, and he from the Fertile lineage, from Bethlehem, and they all came to the fields of Moab and dwelled there. And Pleasantly's man, My God is King, died, and she stayed, she and her two sons. And they married Moabite women, one named Nape and the other Root, and they stayed there some ten years. And their men died too, Illness and Annihilation, and Pleasantly stayed, widowed and grieving her sons.

Root awoke, a sunray wriggling snakelike on the packed dirt floor in front of her, the light's motion caused by the breeze disturbing the flaps of her tent. For a delirious moment, she thought she was full, but it was only her bladder pressing against her hunger, dulling it. Rising from her pallet, she reached for the scarf flung across a stool and used it to gather up her tangled curls and lift them off her neck. The day had barely started but there was a wetness in the air that signaled sweat would come soon.

She didn't bother changing out of her light shift. She, Nape, and Pleasantly were alone, finally, after what seemed like an endless mourning period. First her own husband, then Nape's, each man's death prompting family visits, community members sharing their fire and scant food, the inevitable swindling peddlers hocking cures for loneliness and grief and even—Root almost admired that particularly brazen young one, his beard patchy but his voice as deep and authoritative as a man thrice his age—promises of miraculous childbearing.

Stepping out of her tent, Root wasn't surprised to find the banked fire still unattended, and she went about the business of bringing it to life and placing a pot of water on it to boil clean for the morning ablutions. She shook the large leather skein and began to consider the long walk down to the river. She and Nape needed more water, and plenty of it; Nape's blood had come yesterday, so hers would arrive soon too, and they would need to wash out their rags.

It was thinking of the river's rushing green water that urged her to finally make her way to the still untouched latrine she'd dug last night. Root was the earliest riser among them, though Pleasantly usually awoke very soon after her. It hadn't always been so. One of the stories Pleasantly told of My God is King, whom Root had never had the chance to meet, was of his allowing her to sleep late. Their life together had never been easy—Root could barely remember, herself, a time without famine—but My God is King was a good husband, and amorous, too, Pleasantly told Root and Nape one evening not long ago, the three of them tipsy on wine and the end of another long day of well-wishing company.

"He would make love to me in the mornings, and oh—such love, such knowing!—that I had to bite my fist to keep from waking the boys," Pleasantly had said, giggling, her too-thin fingers hovering in front of her mouth, as if part of her wanted to cage these effusive words. This image of Pleasantly, equally proud and ashamed of her former pleasure, had stuck in Root's mind, and as she pissed now, she grew warm, the powerful sensation of much-needed bodily relief hinting at the kind she'd grown near to experiencing with her husband. Near, but not quite, nothing like what Pleasantly described.

"Root?" The voice, as if conjured by her imaginings, called again, drawing closer. Root hastily shook herself and rose from her squat, flushing, and flustered because there was no reason to. She'd lived with Pleasantly and Nape for ten years now, and such daily functions weren't secrets between them. Still, it seemed wrong to have her bare haunches seen by the very woman whom she'd been imagining in the throes of tremendous passion. "There you are," Pleasantly said, rounding the small copse of trees that hid the latrine. "Good day, Daughter."

"Good day," Root responded. Pleasantly's hair was yet loose, messy from sleep, and Root had the unreasonable urge to mimic her and release her own from its binding scarf.

"Come." Pleasantly held forth a hand for Root to clasp and began to lead her back towards the fire. "You and Nape and I must talk, now that we are once again all alone."

And she heard in the fields of Moab that Adonai remembered his people to give them bread. And Pleasantly said to her daughters-in-law, Go, return, each woman to her mother's household; Adonai will grace you, as you have graced the dead and myself. Adonai will give to you, and you will find rest, each in your own woman's household; and she kissed them, and they raised their voices and wept. And they told her: But we will return with you, to your people. And Pleasantly said, Return my daughters, why would you go with me: if I had sons still within me, they would have been men for you. Return, my daughters, go, for I am too old for men: and even if I had hope, and had a man tonight and birthed sons—for them you would wait, for them to grow up, to them you would anchor yourselves, unable to marry? And they raised their voices, and wept on; and Nape kissed her mother-in-law and left, and Root clung to her. And Pleasantly said, See, your sister-in-law returns to her people, to her gods; return, follow your sister-in-law. And Root said, Don't beseech me to leave you and turn back: for wherever you go I will go, and wherever you sleep I shall (but did she really? Was she brave enough?); *your people are my people, your god is my god. Where you die I shall, and there I will be buried; so Adonai has blessed me and will continue to—only death will divorce me from you. And Pleasantly saw that Root insisted on accompanying her, and she ceased her talk. And the two of them went, until they came to Bethlehem, and when they arrived in Bethlehem the whole city roared towards them and asked, Is this Pleasantly? And she told them, Do not call me Pleasantly, call me Misery, for I have been miseried by Adonai, very. I left full and emptied I am returned by*

Adonai. Why do you call me Pleasantly? Adonai has tortured me and Adonai has harmed me. And Pleasantly returned, Root the Moabite with her coming from the fields of Moab, and they came to Bethlehem at the start of harvest.

No one called her Misery.

Why had Pleasantly said what she had said to the people of Bethlehem, her family and her friends, people who long ago made their peace with never seeing her again? Root wanted to ask but dared not. She was raised well, in the shadow of Chemosh's brilliance, and under her father's roof was taught the value of patience coupled with silence. During the ten years of her marriage, her husband—kind, molded by Pleasantly to resemble the man she had married and so loved—learned to coax her into speech, when best to evoke her confidences, and sharing a bed with him and living quarters with his mother and brother and sister-in-law had loosened her tongue somewhat.

But the first time she was laughed at by a Judean man on the road for not understanding his clipped, harsh syllables, she felt it harden once more. Her own language was not so very different; even their written characters, her husband had once told her, were similar. Still, Pleasantly began urging her to practice when they next made camp, and showed Root the way she held her mouth to make her ריש come out quick rather than keeping it in her throat, how to keep the חית similarly grounded on her tongue and away from the gullet.   •

"Again," Root had said, a demand more than a request, a plea more than a demand, and the only word she'd spoken since her mother-in-law told the laughing man off for making fun of a foreigner. And Pleasantly obliged, and Root watched those lips and mouth move around words she barely paid attention to and tried to make her own do the same, and failed.

And now they were living in Bethlehem, a city bigger than any Root had dwelled in for longer than a day's market trip, and yet, somehow, everyone knew what Pleasantly had said, how she had blamed her god for her unhappiness. Root had never before thought Pleasantly was so; melancholy, occasionally, for her husband, and certainly heartbroken over her sons, but not, in disposition, at the core, unhappy.

And suspicion was cast upon herself, Root, for being the cause of Pleasantly's pronouncement, though the older woman did not appear to hear those whispers that reasoned that Root was a Moabite, and so must have influenced their once-pious Pleasantly, swayed her. Root had never much discussed religion with anyone after leaving her father's home; she followed her husband's and his family's traditions and learned to care for them in the way that habit, especially when it is commonsensical and useful, can become beloved. Once a year only she had traveled back to her father's household for the Sunfeast, although it wasn't true what the Judean people said about human sacrifices; those only occurred very rarely, usually at grand occasions for the Moabite king, and always performed with willing men and women whose lives had already been dedicated to Chemosh's worship. But Root did not try to explain this to the gossipers. She hoped that if they believed her capable of eating another human, they would not openly molest her.

There came a time when Root knew she would have to overcome her shyness, for she and Pleasantly had worn out their welcome at two relatives' households. Pleasantly did not seem very concerned as they placed their few parcels in the small room allotted them in the third relative's home, but Root knew, too, that her mother-in-law was adept at keeping her worries at bay. She had waited the full mourning period for each of her sons before broaching the topic of returning to her homeland, after all. Root often meditated on how difficult it must have been for Pleasantly to grieve in the absence of anyone who had known her sons when they were seedlings swelling her belly, babies suckling her breasts, toddlers waving around sticks and lisping their prayers. Perhaps, having been a woman so alone for so long, Pleasantly had learned to trust that everything would come to rights, whether through her god's will or the goodwill of people.

And perhaps, Root thought as they lay beside one another once the stars came out, Pleasantly humming faintly as she did when especially sleepy, perhaps her mother-in-law did not want to appear as if she were boasting, and that is why she cursed her fortune upon arriving. Few people, and fewer women, traveled to an enemy nation and returned to tell the tale.

And Pleasantly had a relative, a dauntless man from My God is King's family: and his name In Him Courage. And Root the Moabite said to Pleasantly, I will go to the field and glean, and be favorable to him; and she told her, Go my daughter. And she went and she came and gleaned after the reapers, and it happened that she reached the plot of In Him Courage, from My God is King's family.

Reaching his field was no accident. For weeks, Root had been listening, dutifully following Pleasantly on her visits to women whose faces were round with sustenance, and whose arms, when they kneaded dough

ROOT | 175

together in the kitchen, bore the stretch marks of recently gained flesh. Her own and Pleasantly's bodies were slowly beginning to lose the signs of their long famine—her mother-in-law's nipples no longer drooped downwards as her breasts remembered they were more than emptied sacks, and her own thighs faintly touched for the first time in many years.

And in listening, Root learned. She learned of the custom that held that her husband's family members could and even should wed, or at the very least impregnate, her. She knew now why Pleasantly had so strongly urged her daughters-in-law to return to their mothers' households, to their own customs. Now that she was here, Root understood, she was an asset that Pleasantly had not planned on having. As a widow and grieving mother of childless sons, she would have been welcomed and cared for all her days, her family duty-bound to their god to do so. But as a woman with a childless eligible daughter-in-law, Pleasantly was expected to foist Root on a willing relative of My God is King and dwell with them.

That Pleasantly had not yet done so—nor even, when alone, made noises as if she would—made Root respect and love her mother-in-law ever more. She wept that night they moved to the third relative, and steeled her resolve, and made her proposal the morning after, and set off to do what she believed now that she must in order to keep Pleasantly safe and sound and by her side.

And In Him Courage came from Bethlehem, and he told the reapers, Adonai is with you, and they responded, Bless you, Adonai. And In Him Courage said to his young man in charge, To whom, this young woman? And the young man in charge answered and said, A Moabite, she, returning with Pleasantly from the fields of Moab, and she said she'd glean and collect the grain into sheaves, and she did so from morning until now, resting only but little. And In Him Courage told Root, Hear me, Girl, do not go and glean in any other field and do not stray from here, and you will become acquainted with the young women. Keep your eyes on the fields they reap and follow them—I have ordered the young men not to touch you; and if you are thirsty, go drink from the vessels they have filled. And she fell forth to bow upon the earth, and said to him, Why have you taken a liking to me, and I a foreigner? And In Him Courage responded and said, I was told and told all you did with your mother-in-law after your husband's death (Root dared not look up, but she began to tremble, for what could he mean) *and you left your father and mother and country of birth* (she had, it was true, but it was a small price to pay to remain with Pleasantly) *and you went to a people you'd not known before* (and, she thought but dared not say, a people who did not know her). *Adonai will reward your deeds, and richly will you be paid by Adonai the gods of Israel under whose wings you have come to shelter. And she said, Do you like me, sir? For you have comforted and spoken to me as to one of your handmaidens, and I will not be as one of them* (had she said so, really, or had she said she wasn't worthy of being even one of them? She could not, later, quite recall, her heart beating so hard with the long morning's work, arms and back aching, her bow as much about seeking relief in this tall man's shadow as about respect). *And In Him Courage said, At mealtime, come here, and eat of the bread and dip your share in the vinegar. And she sat beside the reapers, and he gave her a dish, and she ate some and was sated. And she rose to glean, and In Him Courage ordered his workers and said, Even if she gleans near your bundles, do not suspect her; and even drop some of your own sheaves for her to glean, and do not scold her. And she gleaned in the field until evening, and she husked her gleanings, and had ten days' worth of grain.*

And she carried and brought it to the city, and showed her mother-in-law what she'd gleaned and shared the leftovers of her meal. And her mother-in-law asked, Where did you glean today, and what did you do, for the field owner did well by you. And she told her mother-in-law whom she gleaned from and told her, The name of the man I was with is In Him Courage. And Pleasantly told her daughter-in-law, Blessed is Adonai, who has never ceased doing good by us, the living, and by our dead. (Then why, Root's rebellious curiosity wondered, had she said otherwise? Had she intended to cast suspicion upon Root? Surely she had not.) *And Pleasantly said, The man is our kin, of our saviors he is. And Root the Moabite said, And more, he told me to stick with his workers until all his harvest is reaped. And Pleasantly said to Root her daughter-in-law, Good, my daughter, go out with his young women who reap and you will not be harmed in another field. And she stuck with In Him Courage's young women, and gleaned until the end of the barley harvest and the wheat harvest, and returned to her mother-in-law.*

And she was tired. Bone-tired, like she had been the week of her husband's death, or the day that Pleasantly had tried to convince her and Nape to return to their homes. She had stayed in the fields with the reaper women for the duration of the harvest, and while she was well used to sleeping upon the earth, even relished it, she was not, she realized, used to the company of young people. She herself was not yet old, but she had been married and widowed, and had left her home not once but thrice—the shelter of her father's house, the shadow of Chemosh's brilliance, the warmth and welcome of her people—for a life amongst those who would consider her a stranger. The youthful reapers were still unmarried, and often spent their nights sneaking gifts or letters to one another, flirting under the cover of darkness, occasionally transgressing loudly, as if for show, in the patches of as-yet-uncut wheat.

But she was not bitter. Arriving back at the third relative's home with a cart full of wheat—the cart and asses lent by In Him Courage's overseer—Root had not only food but stories to share with Pleasantly, and for that she was grateful. The relative was overjoyed as well, for Root and Pleasantly shared a large portion of the gleaning with the household as thanks for their care and assurance for a continued stay.

Alone, finally, in their room, Pleasantly said, "I have a treat for you. Wait."

Root did so, leaning against a wall and thinking of how comforting it would be to sleep by Pleasantly's side once again, sharing in the familiar rhythmic breath. She picked at one of the many calluses on her feet, her fingers recalling suddenly a sensation from childhood—picking olives from the trees as a small child riding on her mother's back.

"Here, Daughter." Pleasantly held the door open, a small stool in one hand and a brush in the other. The relative's maidservants carefully carried in the family's large bathing basin, steam still rising up from its contents. "Come, undress."

"O, Pleasantly!" Root did not yet rise but her back straightened and her cheeks felt tight and dry as she smiled, a steady joy pulsing within her. She had not bathed in warm water for some years—before the death of her husband, certainly.

"Quick now, before it cools," Pleasantly urged, clapping and waving the maidservants out of the room. She helped Root up and out of her shift and undergarments and held her at arm's length for a moment, examining her nude form. "You are still young," she said, almost awed. "You will bear children just fine one day soon, I know it."

Root blushed, her flesh tingling as if chilled even though the breeze coming through the window was warm and the steam rising from the bath hotter still. Pleasantly stopped assessing her body and looked at her face. Root met her gaze, feeling very bold. She let Pleasantly stroke her cheek, clenched her thighs around the small hammer knocking between her legs, and suppressed the desire to take her mother-in-law's hips in her hands and draw them toward her. Instead, she allowed Pleasantly to place her in the bath, succumbed to the gentle washing that was nothing like the rough scrubbing her own mother practiced. Pleasantly seemed to linger in places that made Root murmur with pleasure, and she took her time with the sweaty mess of hair Root had kept covered for the duration of her time in the fields. By the time the water had cooled, Root was half asleep, so thoroughly and well touched that she felt as if she were made of wax, and melting.

And Pleasantly her mother-in-law said, Daughter, I wish for your comfort, for your own good. And now, In Him Courage our relative, lo, he is separating the wheat from the chaff tonight. And you, washed, anoint yourself, and wear your dress upon you, and go down to the threshing floor, and do not show yourself until he has finished eating and drinking. And when he is abed, go to his place of slumber, and uncover his feet (or did she tell Root to uncover herself at his feet?) *and lay beside him and he will tell you what to do. And Root said to her, All you tell me to, I shall do.*

And she went down to the threshing floor, and did as her mother-in-law commanded. And In Him Courage ate and drank, his heart full, and went to sleep at the edge of a haybale, and she came quietly and uncovered his feet and lay there. And in the middle of the night, seized by anxiety he awoke and drew back, for a woman lay at his feet. And he said, Who are you? And she said, I am Root, here with you, asking you to spread further your wings and be my savior. And he said, You are welcome to Adonai, Daughter—this grace is better than your last, for you do not go after the young men, whether poor or rich. (Her first, surely, was accompanying Pleasantly to Judea, but this? Was this grace? Or desperation?) *And now, Daughter, do not fear, all you ask I shall do, for every person who enters the city gates knows you are a dauntless woman. And while I may be your savior, there is one closer than I. Sleep tonight, and in the morning, if the good man will wed you, he shall, and if he does not wish to, I shall myself, by the name of Adonai, only sleep until morn. And she lay at his feet until morn, and arose before man may recognize his brother, so that no one would know a woman came to the threshing floor. And In Him Courage said, Bring your kerchief and hold it, and she held it, and he measured out grain and placed it there, and went to town.*

And she returned to her mother-in-law who said, Who is there, and Root said it was she and told all that the man had said to her. And she said,

ROOT | 179

This grain he gave me, for he told me Do not return empty-handed to your mother-in-law. And Pleasantly said, Sit, my daughter, until you know what will happen, for the man will not idle but will have the matter done today.

And just as Pleasantly spoke, so it came to be. Later, Root would hear of what occurred, how In Him Courage went to the city gates and gathered witnesses and spoke to the man who was closer kin than he to My God is King and thus to Root herself. She would hear of how In Him Courage made certain to shame the man who would not marry her because she was a Moabite and he feared his seed and lineage would be tainted. She would, one day, be proud to be the wife of In Him Courage, a Judean who did his duty, who made sure even a foreigner remained unmolested by his men in his fields.

But while she and Pleasantly awaited the verdict which was to shape the course of their lives, Root considered the long journey she had taken for this woman, her mother-in-law. She thought of the dusty roads they had walked, recalled how they prayed for safety before crossing the rushing Jordan and in thanks when they arrived safely on the Judean bank. She could not count the number of nights they had spent side by side, clutching each other for warmth on cool desert nights.

And now, no matter which man married her, she would be able to provide a comfortable home for Pleasantly. Root regretted none of it. She had meant what she had told her mother-in-law, this woman she could not quite understand, but whose strength and care she admired so. Only death would divorce them.

And In Him Courage took Root for his wife, and came to her; and Adonai gave her a pregnancy, and she birthed a son. And the women said to Pleasantly, Blessed be Adonai who did not undo your savior, and who will call the babe's name across Israel. And he will be a balm to you, and ease your return, for your daughter-in-law whom you love birthed him, and she better than seven sons. And Pleasantly took the babe and kept him near her and fostered him. And the neighbor women said it was like Pleasantly had birthed a child, and he was called Worker, and he fathered God's Gift who fathered David.

21

Bauhaus City

OMER FRIEDLANDER

What real value is there for a man in all the gains he makes beneath the sun? One generation goes, another comes, but the earth remains the same forever.

—Ecclesiastes 1:3–4

The new garden city, Tel Aviv, was built in the first decade of the twentieth century on three low ridges of sandstone hills parallel to the coastline of Jaffa. One of its founders was my grandfather, Ze'ev, an architect of the Bauhaus movement, who fled Nazi Germany to Mandatory Palestine to build in the International Style. The architecture was functional, made of inexpensive reinforced concrete, and painted white. Ze'ev lived with his family in one of these new homes, on the ground floor. The apartment had long and narrow balconies, from which to enjoy the breeze from the sea to the west. It was raised on pillars, for children to play below among the bougainvillea and jacaranda bushes. One of the children playing hide and seek between the dilapidated white pillars was my father, Yigal.

Luckily, I did not grow up with my father, who was not a perfect man. I was raised by my mother in the northern suburbs of the city. I am an architect, just like my father, and his father before him. I work for the municipality, where I give the authorization for the demolition of old buildings, which will be replaced by high-rises and shopping malls. When my father heard that I gave the green light for the demolition of my grandfather's building, his childhood home, he felt betrayed.

A month before the demolition order was scheduled to take place, I started receiving letters from my father, all addressed to Kohelet. That was the nickname my father gave me: Kohelet, the existential complainer. Nothing was ever good enough. Anyway, I received a letter from my father every other day. Some were long and rambling tirades, others were very short, only a line or two. I was not used to hearing from my father so often. We hardly spoke in those days. Sometimes, I wanted to postpone the demolition order so I could keep hearing from him, even though these were letters meant to sabotage my work.

My father's letters were written in his careful handwriting, as structurally sound as the buildings he designed. There was a letter dedicated to each part of the building. The white walls, the stairwell, the pillars, the balcony, the rooftop. Sometimes, the letters were dry descriptions: the corners of the dusty stairwell, the four dilapidated pillars. Other times, there were memories, like the time my father and all the neighborhood children dipped their hands in wet cement to leave a part of themselves in the foundation. One moment my father attacked me, calling me vain and weak, spiteful, and the next he pleaded for me to preserve the building. These were love letters. But they were not ordinary love letters addressed to a person. They were love letters to a building.

The Walls

Kohelet, on these walls you wish to tear down I marked your height every year until you were twelve and moved out with your mother. The markings were written on the doorframe of your old room. On the blue and green kitchen tiles, there was a stain. Do you remember it? A bright red stain. After a wet dishcloth went over it a few times, it was the color of dried blood. I was teaching you to make my famous spaghetti sauce. You got overexcited, with the fire and the tomatoes and it all bubbled up and splattered over the wall. Do you cook in your own home? You have never cooked a meal for me in your entire life.

There are traces of our life, still, in those walls, even if they have been painted over. You may call me sentimental, but I ask you: Are your projects

182 | Omer Friedlander

simply ways to make more money or to increase your vanity? Do you not care about what you build and what will be left after you are dead? I care about legacy. I care about my father's legacy. I care about my own legacy. I don't care so much about your legacy, my son, because I see that it is empty, a hollow house. Inside, do you feel anything? Are you nostalgic about your childhood? Do you remember the good times, too, or are you only bitter about the bad? Tear down those walls, my son, tear them all down. I dare you.

Ever since I got the paperwork for the demolition of my grandfather's building, I have been imagining my father's response. I know that this will hurt my father the most. He sends letters and I don't respond. He is melodramatic, nostalgic for a past that never existed. I enjoy reading his letters. I imagine going to the construction site, taking the rubble in my hand, and running my fingers in the dust. I do not care about the building which will be constructed in its place.

My mother hated the house. She hated it because every time she passed it in the street, she thought of all the misery she endured there because of my father. She thought of the leftovers she would find in the bedroom, in the yard, in the kitchen. Remnants of other women scattered like dandelion seeds in the air. A pink hair clip, a steel-toothed comb, lip balm, even a pair of soiled underwear. Once, she told me she would take down the entire house if she could, bury the soiled underwear and my father in the rubble.

The Stairwell

Kohelet, I used to play a spitting game in the stairwell. I would go up to the top floor and lean out over the stairwell, which circled like the shell of a snail, and spit all the way down. From the fifth floor, I could hear the splat as my spit hit the ground. One day, I spat straight on the shining dome of a bald man. It belonged to my neighbor, Mr. Klachkin. You know the rest of the story, how my father intervened at the very last moment, so I will spare you the details. My son, you have never done anything wrong in your life. You have never broken the rules. Only now, you go against your own father. You are following all of the correct procedures, of course. You will approve the demolition order on high in your municipality seat and have all the neighbors sign an agreement and pay them handsomely. You don't need my approval, as I no longer live there, so congratulations—you have not broken any formal rules! But you have broken an even greater rule. This is the rule of loyalty. You have broken the trust between us. You are cannibalizing yourself, and you don't even realize it. One day, you will wake up and realize that you have eaten everything up. There will be nothing left. You can stand at the top of the stairs and try to spit down on my head, my son, but your mouth will be dry.

My father constantly cheated on my mother. I could hear them arguing all the time. When we lived in the Bauhaus, with its thin walls, I heard them shouting at each other and bickering, and I promised myself that I would build a house with walls so thick that you would not even hear a bomb go off in the other room. My father was a military man and fought in several wars. He performed calisthenics every morning and forced me to do the same. He woke me up at six to run until I puked. Even now, at the age of seventy-three, he is stronger than I am. He kept his head shaved smooth, just like when he was a soldier. He had remarried after my mother died, to a woman who was not much older than I am.

My father was a handsome older man. Whenever my girlfriends stumbled upon a picture of him, they would gasp. They pretended to fawn over him. He had a kind of angular jawline with none of the smooth circularity of the Bauhaus style. His hair was short, efficient, practical, speckled with silver from the time he was thirty. His eyes were the color of parched cacti, always hungry. On the lookout for a woman on the horizon. He wore tight-fitting shirts and dusty work pants, the kind laborers wore, even though he never did the manual labor himself.

I inherited none of his looks. I resembled my mother. My hair was dark and thinning, weak. I was never strong, despite the exercises my father forced upon me. I took up running long distance at one point, because it was the only thing that made my mind go blank, and my frame became slim and supple. I wore expensive clothes, fancy brands. My father called me vain. Even as a teenager, I resembled those new high-rise buildings which were cropping up everywhere. Sleek, shiny, soulless, my father called them. I never pretended to be anything other than what I am. I never got my boots dirty with the workers. They had their job and I had mine.

The Pillars

Kohelet, you know the story of the hero Samson. The source of his superhuman strength—which allowed him to kill a lion with his bare hands and slay an entire army of Philistines with only the aid of a donkey's jawbone as a weapon—was his long hair. If his hair was cut, his strength would fade. Think of this house as the source of my strength, just like Samson's hair. You tear it down and I will die.

The harlot, Delilah from the valley of Sorek, seduces Samson so that he may reveal the source of his strength. After much persuasion, you and I both know what kind of persuasion I'm talking about, he reveals to her that the source of his strength is his hair. A razor has never touched it. It has never been cut. Samson falls asleep in Delilah's lap, and she cuts his hair while he rests. When he loses his strength, his eyes are gouged out and he is put to work grinding grain in a millstone. Samson is brought to the temple of his enemies, the Philistines, to perform for the rulers and kings. The temple is crowded with onlookers. Everyone wants to see the disgraced hero. Samson asks his captors to allow him to rest against the pillars of the temple, to lean on them for a moment. Samson prays to God to give him strength. He summons all of his might and breaks the pillars, causing the temple to tumble down and collapse, killing everyone inside. I know you want to destroy me, to bring down the house on my head. You are blank, transparent like a pane of glass. I can see through you.

Tonight, I go over the plans of the new high-rise which I will build to replace my grandfather's Bauhaus. The Bauhaus was painted in a pale color, to blend in with the desert, to be one with the landscape, but the high-rise will stand out. It won't hide away, like my grandfather's generation, like those meek Jews from the old country. My building will make room for itself and proudly proclaim: I am here! My grandfather passed away when I was seven years old, but in my mind he was a figure of legend. Visiting him was like seeing a count or a duke. He always wore a white suit, white pants, white socks, and white shoes. He had majestic, startlingly pale silver hair, and I remember he smelled of tobacco pipe smoke.

My grandmother was worlds apart. She was a miniaturist by profession. She constructed models and dollhouses. She was quite talented, but demand for such luxuries in the new Israel was not high, so she worked in a camouflage-net factory in a kibbutz, I forget which one. This was around the time of the founding of the country. The new military needed camouflage nets, so the factory was set up. The entire factory, built on a downward slope, was itself camouflaged. The roof of the building was covered in netting and soil, and small trees and shrubs were planted across it, so that from an aerial point of view that camouflage factory did not exist. The nets were hand-painted to reflect various natural environments, mostly in tones of beige and brown, the color of the desert sand, and the occasional dull green. The goal of the camouflage net was to disguise an armored vehicle or a hiding sniper. It was used as a tarp to cover a lone soldier out in the field, or it was draped around a tank patrol.

During the war, my grandmother hid in the Black Forest. She remembered the vivid green of the trees in the Black Forest. How lush and bright they were compared to the dull, dusty, and dead trees of Israel. In the forest, she lived on berries she foraged and the occasional rat she managed to catch. At times, she caught sight of her reflection in a pool of water and could hardly recognize herself. She grew lean. Her jaw jutted out and her eyes bulged. The skin hung on her brittle bones. Her stomach caved in, and her ribs became prominent, spread like a xylophone. She slept in the trees, always listening for the thud of soldiers' boots, the whisper of voices. She was coated in a layer of crushed earth, damp and brown, fitted with dry leaves and twigs. She was a human tree, the perfect camouflage for the Black Forest.

The Balcony

Kohelet, I remember one day your mother tossed all of my things from the balcony. She threw away all of my father's sketches, his plans for the White City. The old, yellowing paper came fluttering down and it was carried away by the sea breeze, scattering everywhere. I found a few of the sketches, years later, in a flea market. I bought them all back, at an exorbitant, outrageous price. I paid for my own father's sketches! Must I now buy my own house from my son? What will it take for you to back down? Even at my age, I could still knock your teeth out. Those pearly white teeth, scattered all over, would make for finer architecture than whatever monstrosity you're planning to build.

My grandfather was scared of heights. My father liked repeating this fact, often. It amused him. My grandfather, the architect, was so terrified of heights that he always lived on the ground floor. He never went up the stairs to the rooftop of his own building, nor the rooftops of all the buildings in the city which he designed. Perhaps, he had never been on a rooftop in his life. Rooftops in Tel-Aviv were all alike, with their silhouette of water boiler tanks and pigeons on electrical wires. You've seen one, you've seen them all. There was only one time he went up to the roof and it had to

186 | OMER FRIEDLANDER

do with my father and the neighbor, Mr. Klachkin. After my father spat on Mr. Klachkin's bald head, he fled up to the roof and the neighbor followed. My grandfather heard them arguing all the way from the first floor. He grasped the railing and made his way up, his head spinning. He was dizzy from vertigo by the time he reached the fifth floor. When he swung open the roof door, he saw Mr. Klachkin, who was slightly insane, dangling my father in the air by the collar of his shirt. He was not holding him off the edge, nothing as dramatic as that, but still my grandfather was so furious that he forgot his fear for a moment. Or perhaps he overcame it? He rushed over to Klachkin and punched him in the jaw.

My father never protected me. Once, a kid in school made fun of my fancy clothes and I came home crying. My father was red in the face he was so angry. He wasn't angry with the kid, he was angry with me. He had not raised me to be so weak. He told me that the next day I had to go up to the kid and punch him in the jaw. If I didn't my father would punch me in the jaw. What choice did I have but to punch the kid? I punched the kid and then to punish myself I told my father that I hadn't had the courage to, so he punched me. I felt terrible. It wasn't the pain, although my jaw throbbed for weeks afterwards. It was the humiliation.

The Rooftop

Kohelet, the rooftop was where I loved my father the most. He had overcome his fear of heights. He had protected me against Klachkin. My father, in my eyes, was a giant. I worshiped him. I was so small in his shadow. Anyway, you would not understand. You don't see the difference between the two-hundred-ton giant blue whale, weighing about as much as thirty-three elephants, and the millions of microscopic plankton that feed him daily.

Do you remember we read a book once about whales? It had a very sad ending, the whale beached on the shore and slowly died. At first you cried, because the ending was so sad. Then you had an idea! What if they carve up the whale and remove all the blubber and use its skeleton as the structure of a new building? People could visit inside the whale. It would be put to good use! It would be functional. You thought your father the architect would like that idea. And I told you: Do you think you're very clever? It may seem like a new idea, but it has been done before. Then I told you the story about a young blue whale beached on the rocks somewhere in Sweden hundreds of years ago. Half a dozen coal-barges and steamships and fishermen's vessels were needed to haul the whale to shore. Watching the vultures peck at the carcass, an amateur set-builder without a theater decided he must save the creature's giant body. He enlisted the help of his theater troupe, a ragtag assortment of jugglers, performers, and disgraced opera singers, to help. The whale's heart and its other organs were preserved in barrels. The bones were boiled clean white. The skin of the whale was stretched tight over its skeletal frame, held together by a thousand nails. The hinged jaw was made to open, so visitors could descend into the belly of the beast. The inside of the whale was outfitted with upholstered carpeting and plush royal-blue wall hangings, fitted with silver stars like the midnight sky. So you see it has all been done before.

The last time I met my father, a few years later, we went for lunch. The new Conservation Law was passed and the various Bauhaus buildings in the city were protected under UNESCO. My grandfather's building, the one my father grew up in, had already been demolished. My father and I met on neutral ground, to the north of the port of Jaffa, where our city of Tel Aviv began, nothing but a few lines traced in the sand dunes, dividing up the plots of land to sixty-six Jewish families in a lottery using seashells. My father ordered a whole blue sea bass and joked with the waiter. I ordered a citrus ceviche with chili and coriander and looked out at the sea. We each ate our fish, without speaking. My father was methodical with his knife, just like in every other aspect of his life. He cut along the spine, removed the eyes, sliced off the shining skin. At the end of the meal, we both reached for the check. We held it between us, like a game of tug-a-rope, for what seemed to me like hours. It was probably a few seconds. I looked into my father's eyes, and he looked into mine, and it was as if the battle for the check would settle all the unaccounted-for balance between us.

22

Haman

Max Gross

But when Haman saw Mordecai in the palace gate, and Mordecai did not rise or even stir to his account, Haman was filled with rage at him.

—Esther 5:9

Among the very worst students who attended the Morris and Elaina Levy Hebrew School in Paramus, New Jersey, was Alexander Igorevich Gornick—whom Rabbi Samuels hated much more than he deserved.

There were legitimate reasons to dislike Alex. For one thing, he was stupid.

Unquestionably so. Listening to him trying to read Hebrew was a profound exercise in learning to control one's rage; Alex spent agonizing minutes sounding out each Hebrew letter and vowel, like he was a first grader and not a middle schooler. Even the other students looked ready to hand their feckless compeer his ass if he didn't hurry the hell up.

Alex's Torah studies work was, if anything, worse. It was mystifyingly bad. On one worksheet he actually wrote that *Joseph* brought down the Ten Commandments from Sinai—not Moses. "Moses was the greatest prophet in history," a stricken Rabbi Samuels said to Alex after he handed in this abomination. "The story of him bringing down the tablets is . . . I mean, it's not like you even have to have read the bible to know it. All you have to do is watch TV. You watch TV don't you?"

"Yeah."

That was probably all the kid ever did. And apparently he didn't even do that especially well.

However, Rabbi Samuels had more picayune reasons for scorning the young scholar: He smelled.

A musty spoor emanated from Alex that sent Rabbi Samuels back in time to when he was, himself, a young boy and forced to spend afternoons in the care of his grandmother whose apartment in Bensonhurst reeked of cabbage and fish and other revolting aromas. It didn't matter whether it was first thing in the morning (after Alex had presumably showered) or at the end of a long day, Alex stunk just the same. Rabbi Samuels fully expected to receive Alex in tears from the other kids one of these days taunting him with a name like "smelly" or "stinky" or "pigpen" or some denigrating variant thereof. (He never did.)

Plus, Alex was chubby—and aggressively interested in keeping himself so. He was always asking about snack time. Always. It was his first and last question of the day. It was as if snacks were the only reason his parents sent him to Hebrew school.

"It's not snack time, Alex," Rabbi Samuels would growl the second or third time Alex petitioned for goldfish or pretzels. "I don't want to hear about it again." For goodness sake, the kid was eleven years old, not five. (Actually, the five-year-olds asked less frequently.) Alex could learn some self-control. But the rabbi's sharp response didn't have the least effect; half an hour later when Rabbi Samuels closed the Tanakh, Alex was asking again.

When snacks were finally served he crammed Hydrox cookies in his mouth like they would be confiscated if he didn't dispose of them quickly. He sucked down his juice boxes with the vigor of a drunk handed a flask of whiskey. There was very little doubt in the rabbi's mind that Alex was creeping into the kitchen on his way to and from the bathroom and helping himself to the macaroons or fruit salad or whatever else was left out. The little sneak.

Most of all, Rabbi Samuels hated just how little Alex cared about his failings. Rabbi Samuels marched him into his office one day in the middle of the semester and told him he needed to shape up or he would not receive a Bar Mitzvah.

Most children looked terrified to be given the business all alone in the rabbi's office. They would sob and beg for mercy—and there would almost always be some change in behavior. For a few weeks homework would be turned in on time. Mistakes would become less frequent. (Although there was typically a reversion.) Not Alex. The next day his Torah homework included the double whopper that King *Nathan* had slain the Philistine giant Goliath using a *bush axe*. (Where did he get *that*? What the heck *is* a bush axe? Charitably, Rabbi Samuels wondered if this was some Russian mistranslation of a tool that could be mistaken for a slingshot.)

Rabbi Samuels decided to tell Mrs. Gornick that her son was not taking his Jewish education seriously.

"Alex never does any of the Hebrew language worksheets," Rabbi Samuels said. "When he does do them there's a mistake on every line."

Nadia Gornick, who had come to New Jersey by way of Moscow and spoke English in a heavy Eastern European accent, looked very unlike her son. She was slender and pretty, with lustrous black hair and she dressed fashionably. The only time she resembled Alex was when she seemed to shuck off the rabbi's warnings.

"I'll talk to him."

Not that Alex's work or behavior improved one whit.

However, despite his completely uncoerced, unaffected disdain for Alex Gornick, Rabbi Samuels still knew it was wrong to hate a child—no matter how gross and unappealing he was. He should do his very best to treat Alex no differently than the other students. He subsequently tried to reach Alex with kindness. He asked the boy his opinion on Teenage Mutant Ninja Turtles, which were a big thing at the time, and whether Alex thought it was possible that David Cone on the New York Mets was Jewish. "It sounds like a Jewish name," the rabbi said donning a forced smile. "Both first name and last. Could be."

Alex looked perplexed, like he had never heard the name before.

"I don't know."

Another disinterested, bored, infuriating response. Typical. So damn typical. And through his frozen grin a single thought pulsed through Rabbi Samuels's mind over and over: *I hate this kid, I hate this kid, I hate this kid . . .*

Nevertheless, it was incumbent upon him to get the boy ready for his Bar Mitzvah. (The threat of Alex not receiving one if his work didn't pick up was, admittedly, all bluff.) And so he sat with Alex in his office once a week and explained the ancient history of the Jewish people; their exceptional status before the Lord; the importance of the written law; the differences between the written and oral traditions and their historical evolution; and so forth.

He described slavery in Egypt and wanderings in Sinai; he explicated the destruction of Solomon's Temple and the Babylonian exile; he spent two weeks in the run up to Purim teaching Alex about the scroll of Esther (Rabbi Samuels's favorite book of the Tanakh) and another two weeks expounding on the Roman destruction of the Second Temple.

Alex asked no questions. Occasionally Rabbi Samuels felt it necessary to see if the lesson was penetrating Alex's curl-topped, blubber-insulated skull.

"Do you understand?" he asked.

The boy just nodded wordlessly. The rabbi might as well have been talking to himself.

As for Alex's parshah Rabbi Samuels gave him the prayers in English transliteration, which he only did with the idiots. After twelve months Alex would presumably memorize what he had to say.

But that proved too much to hope for. "Can I bring this up to the Torah with me?" Alex asked a week before the assigned day holding the folded, weathered sheet of paper with the transliteration.

What was the point of fighting it?

"I suppose."

On the morning of the Bar Mitzvah, Rabbi Samuels's homily from the bima was strictly boilerplate.

"Alex, today, you are responsible for your actions before the law," Rabbi Samuels said. "This sounds grave, but it is a privilege. You are one of the chosen. Your parents knew the pressure to forsake the old ways under the Iron Curtain, but they fought for their heritage, and for the right to give you a fuller life here in America. It's up to you to pass this gift and responsibility along to the next generation." But that was as personal as Rabbi Samuels's address would get.

Rabbi Samuels felt obliged to put in an appearance at the party, which took place at a wedding hall in Hackensack. Only four kids from Alex's Hebrew school class showed up—Simon Gillison, Douglas Klein, Mara Golden and Jason Sanders. With the exception of Sanders, they were all losers.

Perfectly nice kids, of course. Douglas was, far and away, the smartest kid in Hebrew school, and had already been skipped ahead to high school.

192 | MAX GROSS

(His mother let it be known that even high school was having trouble keeping up with young master Klein and he would probably wind up taking advanced calculus at Seton Hall in between his high school classes.)

But Rabbi Samuels suspected Douglas might have a touch of Asperger's syndrome. He couldn't navigate a conventional conversation without saying something spectacularly weird. Simon and Mara were normal enough, but they were both short and odd looking, and in Mara's case stocky. Rabbi Samuels wondered what Jason was doing there, being that he was reasonably personable and popular with his fellow students, but this question was answered when he spotted Jason's father laughing it up in Russian with Alex's father.

The spread the Gornicks put out looked like it was meant to impress their Russian friends, not their son's American ones. It was all Russian salads, gloopy with mayonnaise, and meat jellies and other things that no child could possibly find palatable. There was—to the rabbi's fleeting delight—a caviar station, but it went so quickly that Rabbi Samuels didn't get a single bite.

Midway through the afternoon a Russian-speaking deejay with a shaved head and yellow-tinted aviator glasses appeared and blasted techno music, which he occasionally interrupted with Madonna and Prince and a klezmer song. A mazurka broke out midway through the festivities, and several drunken relatives stood up to offer toasts to the parents of young Alex.

The rabbi sat in his assigned seat silently and came to the conclusion that he, too, might have been awkward and smelly if he had grown up in such environs. Not that this decreased his dislike of the Bar Mitzvah boy. Thankfully, the Bar Mitzvah—and, with it, Hebrew school—was over and Rabbi Samuels would likely never see Alex Gornick again.

The majority of Rabbi Charles H. Samuels's students faded in his memory after two or three years. Not that he didn't love and care for them at the time, but for the most part Rabbi Samuels was more concerned with present students than the foggy memory of their antecedents—at least that's what he told himself.

One would think that Alex Gornick would have been one of the students whom the Rabbi could easily forget about, but the opposite was true.

This is not to say that Rabbi Samuels, at first, concentrated on Alex the way some people thought about a disloyal ex-wife, or a childhood bully, or a prison guard who tormented them in solitary confinement. Alex would go days or sometimes weeks before making an appearance in Rabbi Samuels's conscious or unconscious mind. But unlike the Douglas Kleins or Jason Sanderses, Alex consistently returned. Sometimes it would be in a dream where Alex's dumb, witless face would be peeking out of a window; other times Rabbi Samuels would be on a jog through Dunkerhook Park and suddenly find himself thinking about the boy in such panicky, anxious detail he had to stop and catch his breath.

You see, about six months after the Bar Mitzvah Rabbi Samuels was sitting with his daughter, Nellie, as she was watching an afternoon rerun of *The Facts of Life*, and at a commercial break he heard an announcer exclaim, "Hey, kids! Do you like fun?"

"I like fun!" cried a small, smiling girl with fine blond hair, standing in front of a white background.

"I like fun!" shouted a Black twelve-year-old boy with a burgundy sweater and slacks whom the camera cut to.

"I like fun!" yawped a pudgy child with curly dark hair, in a blue-and-white checkered button-down shirt and khakis. This child was Alex.

"We all like fun," the announcer continued, "so come on down to Orange County Fun Park!" and the mise-en-scène shifted to the three children laughingly crashing into each other driving bumper cars, and then screaming wildly as a roller coaster twisted around in a loop and took a treacherous dive downwards.

There was no mistaking that this third child was Alex, and yet Rabbi Samuels stared in stupefaction at the screen, quietly insisting to himself that it could only be a lookalike.

"Hey!" said Nellie turning to her father. "Was that Alex Gornick?"

Rabbi Samuels was speechless.

"I don't know," the rabbi finally croaked. "I don't think it could have been him."

Nellie was a year and a half younger than him, but she knew Alex. Not just from Hebrew school but from Joseph Scheuerle Junior High School, where she was in seventh grade and Alex was in eighth.

"It sure looked like him," she said.

"It *couldn't* have been him," Rabbi Samuels declared.

"Why not?"

However, Rabbi Samuels failed to summon an answer that wouldn't betray years of pent-up resentment and dislike.

"I don't know," Rabbi Samuels finally said. "I just can't see Alex Gornick as an actor."

"Did you see the commercial?" Mrs. Irene Shiloni, the secretary of the synagogue, asked Rabbi Samuels the moment he walked through the door for Shabbat services.

As he got dressed for shul on Saturday morning Rabbi Samuels had briefly wondered if anyone in the congregation would mention the commercial, and quickly shooed the question away as highly far-fetched, given that Alex's family almost never appeared in synagogue.

As far as Rabbi Samuels could tell the Gornicks were Jewish in a very Soviet way; back in Russia they were both bashful and fearful of the fifth line of the internal papers citizens had to carry on their person at all times that included ethnicity. (Not that the Slavs needed secondary confirmation.) It had been a cloud hovering over the family for generations, until it turned out to be their salvation when they were suddenly permitted to leave the Union of Soviet Socialist Republics under glasnost.

And, as with almost every Soviet family Rabbi Samuels had met, the years of official censorship and rebuke had left them knowing nothing about the actual rigors of the faith.

Shortly after the family had moved to Paramus the boy's father, Igor, had shown up to services and unobtrusively taken a seat in the back—obediently standing when the rest of the congregation stood, swaying when the rest swayed, and turning to the relevant page in the siddur when advised by the rabbi. But it was obvious he had no idea what was going on. He never sang a prayer on his own, and his eyes never went down to the open prayer book in his lap.

But in those days, Rabbi Samuels admired and pitied Igor Gornick—along with the rest of the Soviet Jews. They had been spiritually starved. The fact that Mr. Gornick had wanted to relearn what his ancestors knew was extremely laudable.

Plus, the story that the rabbi had been told about Mr. Gornick only increased his esteem. Up until very recently the family had been living in two rooms in Brighton Beach, with Mr. Gornick patiently standing on line at the Hebrew Immigrant Aid Society for care packages and driving a cab all hours to make ends meet. But when HIAS had discovered that this dark-haired, laconic newcomer with scarcely a penny to his name had a PhD in physics from Moscow State University, introductions were made and interviews were arranged. By the end of the year he was working as a nuclear engineer for the US government. It was an astonishing success

HAMAN | 195

story. And Rabbi Samuels was eager to hear about such tribulations directly from the source.

But on the few occasions Rabbi Samuels tried to engage Mr. Gornick he was guarded and succinct, in a uniquely Russian way. A courteous question like, "How did you like the service?" was acknowledged with an indecipherable grunt. "So, I understand you're originally from Moscow?" was likewise answered in the tersest possible terms that left little room for elaboration. The man was as boring as his son, despite what anyone would agree were enormously interesting life circumstances.

Unlike Alex, however, Igor Gornick had the option of abandoning synagogue when it grew tedious, and that's precisely what he did. One week he didn't show up, and that was the last he was seen at Mount Solomon until the high holidays. And he wasn't particularly missed; nobody aside from the rabbi had bothered to talk to him or anyone else in the family. Except, of course, Mrs. Shiloni, who was now aching to celebrate the fortunes of the Gornick family scion.

"What commercial?" Rabbi Samuels asked.

"You know, the one for the theme park?"

"I don't think I saw it," Rabbi Samuels murmured.

"Oh," said Mrs. Shiloni, who in her excitement did not detect any subterfuge or deception in the rabbi. "There's this commercial for an amusement park in Orange, and guess who's in it?"

Rabbi Samuels winced, slightly.

"I give up."

"Alex Gornick!"

Rabbi Samuels feigned surprise.

"Really?"

"Uh-huh."

"Well," Rabbi Samuels said. "That's something."

"He was great in it!" Mrs. Shiloni exclaimed. "He had lines and everything."

That was ridiculous. The kid was on screen for five seconds. He shouted "I like fun!" and that was the end of his speaking role. A parakeet could be trained just as easily.

"No kidding," said Rabbi Samuels. "I'll have to keep an eye out for it."

Alex's freshman foray into acting would lead to much bigger things in a short amount of time.

He appeared in a couple of other local New Jersey commercials; he sat with a family of actors at Monty's Steakhouse in Hoboken where he helped devour a massive porterhouse; and he played the child in an unfortunate family whose tires had blown out on the interstate but thankfully took their Chevy to Paramus Auto Repairs, where the service was prompt and the bill was reasonable.

However, two months after his debut he booked a national spot for Apple Jacks cereal.

The commercial featured Alex sitting listlessly at his kitchen table, looking as bored and stiff as Rabbi Samuels remembered him back in Hebrew school. The disembodied hand of a parent pours a bowl of Apple Jacks. Suddenly, the moment he puts a spoonful in his mouth the screen lights up and Alex is sent into shining ecstasy. His kitchen turns into a party with a four-piece horn set blasting salsa music. (Not that there was any conceivable connection between salsa and Apple Jacks, Rabbi Samuels tartly noted.) Other kids appeared and danced around Alex. In the midst of this jamboree Alex stands up and begins dancing, too, before swallowing the cereal. Abruptly, the party vanishes and Alex is cast back to his dreary kitchen table.

Alex then impishly lifts a second spoonful of cereal up to the light before popping it into his mouth and the screen cuts to a closeup of the cereal box with the horns blaring in the background. "Every bite is a party," an announcer said provocatively.

Apple Jacks was a real coup for Alex's career. Soon thereafter Alex booked a spot for Dial Soap and children's cough medicine, but he also began appearing in TV shows and movies. He was a friend of D. J.'s on an episode of *Roseanne* and was Tom Hanks's precocious middle son in a notably second-rate comedy that had Hanks playing a mad scientist. (It went straight to video.)

And Alex—who had once been siloed in Rabbi Samuels thoughts strictly on the three days per week that they saw each other in Hebrew school—now became someone who could jump out at him any time he switched on the television. (Those readers who would advise Rabbi Samuels to simply keep the TV turned off must understand that he had small children and a television's utility as a piece of familial bargaining power, a source of household tranquility, and as uncompensated babysitter can only be left fallow for so long.)

Even if Rabbi Samuels had been willing to forgo television, Alex would have nonetheless been an important topic of conversation in the Samuels household because nearly every child at Joseph Scheuerle Junior High carefully tracked the life and career changes of the single celebrity in their midst.

"Alex Gornick had to leave early this week," a breathless Nellie Samuels told the rest of the family over the dinner table one night. "He had to fly out to Hollywood to shoot an episode of *L.A. Law!*"

L.A. Law was Francesca Samuels's favorite show and she was duly impressed.

"Alex got Jimmy Smits's autograph," Nellie told the family a week later. "And Corbin Bernsen's. But that's not as good."

On the set of the Tom Hanks picture Alex and the other kid actors shared a trailer where they had use of a pinball machine, a gumball machine, and a full-sized video arcade Ms. Pacman which Mr. Hanks graciously played against the junior cast one rainy afternoon. "Tom Hanks is a real gentleman with the kids," Nellie informed everyone.

"How's Alex keeping up with his grades?" Mrs. Samuels asked.

"Oh, it's hard," Nellie said, "but I think he's keeping up."

This proved ill-informed on Nellie's part, because it soon came to light that Igor and Nadia Gornick had to meet with Principal Farkas about Alex's academic performance—and the commute back and forth from California was deemed the most likely culprit in its lack of quality. The Gornicks briefly entertained the notion of picking up and leaving New Jersey for California, but eventually discarded the idea.

"Besides," Nellie explained—like she was a little mogul elucidating the ways of the studio world to her ignorant, benighted parents—"Alex is an *East* Coast actor. Those are the agents that know him. It would be like losing nine months to go back and start again with the *West* Coast casting agents."

Mrs. Samuels laughed, while the younger children at the dining table—Ethan and Ariel—listened raptly to their elder sister in between mouthfuls of spaghetti and meatball. Rabbi Samuels just gritted his teeth.

"There's no way that idiot should advance to high school," Rabbi Samuels finally spat. And it was such a sharp, barbed judgement that everybody at the table sat up a little straighter.

"What do you mean by that?" asked Mrs. Samuels, with an expression on her face that bordered on reproach.

"Nothing," Rabbi Samuels said, "I'm just saying it's wrong for a kid to get special treatment. It undermines the work of all the other kids in his class. They put in the effort. Meanwhile, Alex is playing Pacman with Jimmy Smits."

Silence.

"Tom Hanks," Nellie inserted.

Nobody spoke for a few moments.

"I can't imagine the other children care," Mrs. Samuels opined.

"It's true, they probably don't," Rabbi Samuels conceded. "Maybe they should. Nellie? Alex is going to go ahead to ninth grade next year. But it doesn't sound like he knows the material . . ."

"OK . . ."

"*You* know the material."

"I'm in seventh grade."

Rabbi Samuels smiled at his daughter.

"You know what I mean. Let's say he was in seventh, not eighth. Maybe you would have had more fun goofing off and not doing all the work and flying off to Hollywood. Would that have been fun?"

"Yeah . . ."

"Is it fair that he got to do that stuff and you didn't?"

Nellie was mildly baffled by this line of questioning. She had little idea why her father was getting so riled up but sensed that he needed to be placated if the dinner table conversation was going to move in a different direction.

"I guess not."

"Let me tell you something about Alex," Rabbi Samuels continued, unwilling to let the topic rest. "He was a *bad* Hebrew school student."

The children—and even Mrs. Samuels—listened to this revelation attentively.

"Why?" asked Ethan.

"He didn't do any work," Rabbi Samuels said. "When he did, it was terrible. He didn't put in any effort."

Nobody spoke.

"And this was *before* he became a child actor," Rabbi Samuels continued. "He doesn't even have the excuse that he was flying back and forth from California."

The children considered this with the sense of betrayal one is apt to feel upon reading *Mommie Dearest* or *I, Tina* and discovering the howling flaws of previously venerated figures like Joan Crawford and Ike Turner.

"He shouldn't have even received his Bar Mitzvah," Rabbi Samuels said. "I regret the part I played in giving him one."

It was later that evening, when Mrs. Samuels was putting the younger children to bed, and Rabbi Samuels and his eldest daughter were left alone to do the dishes, that the rabbi would commit his sole criminal act against the unfortunate Alex Gornick.

"You don't know the half of Alex's dumbness," Rabbi Samuels said as he scrubbed the pasta pot. "The kid pro'lly cheated on the only tests he did well on."

It would be difficult to look at this statement—brief and seemingly speculative as it was—as anything other than a searing example of premeditation and malice aforethought on the rabbi's part.

First, Rabbi Samuels had waited until his wife was safely out of earshot before he spoke, which suggests he didn't want any witnesses around to question the statement and insist on further verification and scrutiny.

Second, the speculation was paradoxical and easily debunked. Should Nellie have asked her father which exams Alex cheated on there could be no plausible example . . . because he failed them all.

Finally, the question of whom Rabbi Samuels had decided to pose this hypothesis to was most incriminating.

Nellie—as her father knew better than anyone—had a big mouth.

Arnold and Arlene Berlowitz no longer spoke to the Samuelses anymore because one night after an impromptu dinner invitation Francesca Samuels remarked to her husband on the car ride home that the stew served was "absolutely revolting. It honestly reminded me of dog food."

Several other criticisms of the Berlowitz décor (their new rug in the living room "looked like somebody had vomited on it") and Mrs. Berlowitz's fashion decisions (her outfit "made Arlene look like she weighed five hundred pounds") somehow escaped the confines of the Samuels family station wagon and flew into the ears of Michelle Berlowitz, Nellie's hitherto best friend.

Not only were the Samuels never again invited to dinner, the Berlowitzes switched synagogues a few months later.

Nellie was reprimanded, but both Rabbi and Mrs. Samuels blamed themselves for the incident. They should have known that talking to Nellie was like talking to a reporter for the *Daily News*. Everything you said was being recorded and filed away. The most scandalized interpretation of your words would later be offered to whoever would listen. Nellie had no sense of loyalty to her sources, only to her audience. Everything from lost wallets to family fights to cases of diarrhea was meticulously repeated to classmates, or teachers, or babysitters, or Terry, the muscular Trinidadian security guard at Joseph Scheuerle who somehow knew to ask Rabbi Samuels how his stomach was feeling a day after an extremely unpleasant bout of the runs.

Nellie seemingly kept this anodyne musing of her father's to herself as she dried the forks, serving spoons, and wooden salad bowls and returned them to their assigned spots. But these ruminations would be cast out into the world in the coming days. It got around—first among the students, but slowly to the faculty—that Alex was a cheater. He was snowing anyone sucker enough to show him any leniency. Just as he had snowed his Hebrew School teachers.

It is one thing for a child of good faith—who simply undertook too many responsibilities—to receive extra consideration by his teachers. It is quite another if the child in question is making a fool out of the teacher.

Previously, Alex's teachers had permitted him to retake the exams he had failed and given extensions to the papers he had due—but in the swirl of rumor that followed, the school's posture hardened. There would be no makeup exams. Term papers would be expected *before* he left to shoot a commercial in California, not after. And the charitable C-minuses he received in the course of handing in his normal half-assed work were now judged more harshly. He was suddenly getting Fs in Biology, English and Spanish.

And then one afternoon when Rabbi Samuels was alone in his office he received a phone call from Joyce Farkas, the principal at Joseph Scheuerle Junior High School, asking if he had a few minutes to speak about Alex Gornick.

"Of course."

"This is a sensitive matter," Principal Farkas said. "I'm hoping I can count on your discretion."

"Of course."

Rabbi Samuels had interacted privately with Principal Farkas once before; she had called him, Father Owen O'Dowd of St. Stephen's, the Reverend Larry Carter of the Lutheran church, and Imam Aadam Noor of the Islamic Center of Paramus, into her office to discuss ways to teach

HAMAN | 201

the children about their respective religions. "I'd like them to learn about some of the more obscure holidays and traditions," she said. "You know, beyond the Thanksgiving pageant and nativity play." She had responded enthusiastically to Rabbi Samuels's suggestion of adding a Purim spiel in March before the spring break—and that was the last they had spoken.

"There's been a rumor going around that got back to me," the principal started, but then stopped abruptly—hoping, perhaps, that Rabbi Samuels would feel compelled to fill in the words she knew she should not say.

"Yes?"

"The rumor is that Alex cheated in Hebrew school."

Rabbi Samuels didn't say anything.

"Look," Principal Farkas said, "if he did or didn't, I'm not sure that's my business. I just want to be clear about that. When you get down to it, what he did in Hebrew school is a separate matter. Not to say it wouldn't be absolutely dreadful. But I'm just trying to gauge how good or bad a kid he is. Like, does he deserve a little leeway—or has he already gotten too much?"

"I see."

Neither party spoke as the rabbi formulated his response.

"Let me put it this way," Rabbi Samuels said with a barbarous twist of the knife. "I never *caught* Alex doing anything."

About a month after this, Nellie announced to the dinner table: "Alex Gornick is being held back next year!"

This was the first time Nellie had spoken Alex's name in some time. Weeks earlier Alex began cracking down on his studies—which meant taking a temporary hiatus from acting—and Nellie had a lot more to say about Ashley Turtel whose mother let her get her ears pierced, and the outbreak of headlice in the sixth grade which was widely attributed (fairly or unfairly) to Michael Kellogg, and Amanda Brodsky who won the gymnastics competition against Weehawken. However, this newest development about Alex was scurrilous enough to rate a mention.

"Oh, no kidding," said Francesca Samuels. "I guess that's what happens."

"Yeah," Nellie continued, eager to get the details out as quickly as possible. "Gonna have to repeat the *whole* year. The entire eighth grade. Nobody can believe it. They're not even going to put him in summer school."

"Why not?"

"Well, they offered it to him," Nellie said, shoveling a forkful of mashed potatoes into her still moving mouth, "but his parents figure that'll be too hard on his acting career. Better to repeat a whole nother year than lose the summer."

But—as Rabbi Samuels heard in dribs and drabs in the ensuing months—Alex's summer didn't go very well.

Alex was suddenly too old for kids parts any more. He could fake his age at thirteen—as Nellie doggedly reported back—but Alex experienced a growth spurt and he was currently stranded in the mysterious phase between childhood and adolescence when changes are at their most glaring and unsettling. He could not get ketchup commercials, or shampoo commercials, or even Stridex commercials. (Alex's agent sent him on an audition for one of those and, given the fact that zits had ruthlessly colonized Alex's forehead and chin, all but assumed Alex would be a shoo-in. Alas, no. The casting agent typically hired actors with good skin and faked their pimples.)

But life went on, and that fall and winter Alex would become much more integrated into the fabric of Joseph Scheuerle—as everyone agreed he should be.

Rabbi Samuels was relatively pleased with this. Now that the boy was safely defanged, Rabbi Samuels freely muttered "nudnik" or "dummkopf" or "farshtunkener" when Alex's name was invoked. Nellie listened to these putdowns without comment, never completely sure why her father disliked her classmate, but decided it was prudent not to press the matter.

Nellie wasn't even sure she should tell her father that Alex had been cast as Mordechai in the Purim pageant with Nellie as Esther—but she knew she would eventually have to, and sensed he would have more to say on the matter than normal.

A few years earlier, when she was only seven, she was sitting with her parents as they watched Ronald Reagan on the nightly news standing before the Brandenburg Gate say, "Mr. Gorbachev, tear down this wall!"

"Straight out of Esther," Rabbi Samuels said, which prompted her mother to roll her eyes.

"Whaddya mean?" Nellie asked.

"That's essentially what Mordechai did in the scroll of Esther," her father answered.

"When confronted with tyranny he didn't shut up and keep his head down—he ripped his clothes, draped himself in sackcloth and ash, and made a big stink about it. He didn't just let himself get slaughtered."

It was a peculiar connection, certainly—doubly peculiar because her parents were reluctant to praise the President of the United States—but, then, her father always looked for ways to talk about the scroll of Esther and its heroes.

"It's the greatest book in the canon," Rabbi Samuels declared on more than one occasion, "because it's the most subtle." And he would proceed to tell Nellie for the nth time that he had written his thesis about Jewish and gentile interaction in the ancient world (both in Eretz Israel and the Diaspora) when he was a student at Jewish Theological Seminary—with a focus on Mordechai's maneuverings in the Persian court of Ahasuerus to oust his anti-Semitic viceroy of Haman.

This was often accompanied by a long explication of the sybaritic ways of King Ahasuerus; the unfortunate fate of his first wife Vashti who refused to perform a striptease before the court ("Where does the Bible say 'striptease'?" a dubious Nellie asked; "It's all under the surface," her father answered); the sex factory Ahasuerus subsequently created out of kidnapped Persian virgins (something Nellie and her classmates in Hebrew school were taught was a "beauty contest"); and, finally, the noble, selfless Esther (aka Hadassah), the wily Mordechai, and the unbendingly evil Haman.

Nellie shuddered to herself when she presented her father with the cast list, expecting a long discussion to follow—and, indeed, one did, but she simply listened patiently for three-quarters-of-an-hour before she found a lull in this monologue.

"Dad?"

"Yes?"

"Would it be OK if I invited some of the kids who are in the play over to rehearse in the basement?"

Rabbi Samuels froze.

This would doubtless include Alex and there was not a snowball's chance in hell that Rabbi Samuels would allow Alex Gornick in his house.

"This house isn't a theater, Nellie. I don't want a bunch of kids making a ruckus."

"We won't make a ruckus," Nellie protested. "Not at all—we'll be good!"

"No Nellie. Your mom and I are too busy to entertain your friends."

"But you wouldn't have to entertain anybody—it's a *rehearsal*. We'd be doing everything ourselves."

"I said no."

The back-and-forth carried on a few minutes longer, with Nellie growing more unhinged. Two nights earlier Amber Glickstein had slept over—she whined—why was this any different?

Nellie flew into a full-blown tantrum and accused her father of every tyranny under the sun; she was summarily sent to her room and told she could not come out until she apologized and vowed to speak more respectfully to her elders.

Nevertheless, Nellie's mother couldn't help but ask her husband what was behind the ruling later that night as they were each preparing for bed.

"What's the big deal?" Mrs. Samuels asked. "Why can't she have her friends over?"

"I don't like Alex Gornick," Rabbi Samuels said. "I think he's a bad influence."

Mrs. Samuels smirked.

"What?"

"Nothing," she said squirting a blob of Dove moisturizer into the palm of her hand. "But you might have to get used to him."

"What does that mean?"

Mrs. Samuels looked up at her husband with her mouth cracked open in a half-smile.

"I think it's pretty obvious."

"What is?"

"Nellie likes him."

Rabbi Samuels broke into laughter, but it was apparent that his wife was not joking, and the smile on his face melted.

"That's not funny."

Mrs. Samuels shrugged.

"I'm not being funny," Mrs. Samuels said. "Come on, Charlie. You can't tell me this is the first time it's occurred to you."

However, the shock on her husband's face suggested the opposite was true. No, he had never suspected any such thing. If Mrs. Samuels had announced that she was cuckolding him with his best friend he wouldn't have looked half as surprised, or half as hurt. Wordlessly, he got out of bed and went to the hallway bathroom where he clasped his face in his hands, filled with emotion he could not justify and didn't quite understand.

Rabbi Samuels could not even be bothered to wonder if this was a piece of speculative fantasy on his wife's part or if she had any solid evidence to back it up. She was obviously right. He thought of all the belittling names he had called Alex in recent months and Nellie's careful lack of response.

He wondered if he was in some way the one at fault. If, in telling Nellie that Alex was no good and a cheat, he hadn't redrawn her perception of him as someone cooler and more risk-tolerant than he really was. Someone who thumbed his nose at authority and instilled the kind of thrill that, say, a Marlon Brando did when he strode atop his motorcycle in *The Wild One*. Growing up in Brooklyn Rabbi Samuels remembered the screech of girlish delight from the audience that rose up to the rafters when Peggy Maley asked Brando, "Hey, Johnny, what are you rebelling against?" and Brando answered with flawless indifference, "What do ya got?"

Rabbi Samuels was retrieved from this torrid reverie by a knock on the bathroom door.

"What's going on in there?"

He had no idea how long he had spent huddled on the toilet near tears, but it must have been a while. He was no more composed than when he entered the lavatory.

"Nothing," Rabbi Samuels gasped in a voice that was raspy with disuse. "I'll be out in a minute."

The day of the Purim pageant Rabbi Samuels fantasized about all sorts of things that could prevent him from attending the show. The false deaths of long-lost relatives. Fake bomb threats at the Hebrew school. Phantom dogs that he hit with his car that he needed to rush to the animal hospital. And he tried to gauge just what kind of fallout he could expect from Mrs. Samuels if he claimed to have suffered such a disaster.

But he nevertheless despairingly loaded the two youngest into the car, and sat next to his wife in abject silence as they drove to Joseph Scheuerle Junior High School, like he was headed to an execution rather than a school play.

Even though Purim wasn't until tomorrow many of the kids had apparently gotten the idea to show up in costume and they flitted around the auditorium in fairy wings and Dracula capes, swilling pink lemonade and eating prune hamantaschen that was being sold at the door—all of which only accentuated how miserable Rabbi Samuels was.

Eventually, the lights went down and the show started.

An unfamiliar boy took the stage, apparently acting as the chorus for the production.

"Cast your minds back, O spectators," the young man said in a boyish tenor with a single spotlight on him. "Back. Back. To the time of exile of the Hebrews. To when King Ahasuerus ruled 127 provinces from India in the east to Nubia in the south. To when the king's royal throne sat in Shushan, and from there all the affairs of Persia and Media were settled. . . ."

206 | Max Gross

The lights suddenly came up on a scene of gaudy Babylonian excess; a banquet table was set with goblets of wine, great roasted birds, grapes, and cornucopia of fruit. (Some of the fruit was ahistorically chosen; there were bananas and pineapples sharing space with the figs and pomegranates.) The eighth graders were decked out in gold lamé fabrics and costume rubies and sapphires if they were playing the satraps or their wives—humble white loincloths and turbans if they were slaves. The slaves fanned the aristocrats with giant palm leaves. One eighth-grade boy beat a tom-tom drum and an eighth-grade girl danced, as if she were the evening's entertainment.

On to the stage bounded Jacob Silverberg, the only kid in the school who was fatter than Alex. By his blue robes and golden crown Jacob appeared to be cast in the role of King Ahasuerus.

"Come, my subjects!" Jacob called out. "Feast! Drink! Be merry! Because my kingdom is the most resplendent in the entire world, and I call on you, my subjects, to respect it by enjoying it!"

The children on stage whooped and hollered for their king.

And as he sat with the sweating Dixie Cup of pink lemonade in his hands, Rabbi Samuels momentarily forgot all about Alex Gornick, and was taken aback by the elaborateness of the set design and costumes. Great effort and ingenuity had gone into the production; far more than the rabbi had expected.

And slowly the story began unfolding—in the midst of the gaiety an inebriated Jacob Silverberg told the girl dancing to the tom-tom to summon Queen Vashti to the revels.

Amber Glickstein slowly and deliberately marched onto the stage a moment later with a handmaiden over each shoulder. In an inspired piece of stylization Amber was made up to look like a kabuki princess—she wore a long sea-green kimono and her face was painted white with only her lower lip sporting a rectangular dab of red.

"Dance for the nobles and governors, my queen," Jacob said. "Show the world your talents. Show them your allure. Prove that you are the greatest jewel in my kingdom!"

But Amber only stared back at Jacob contemptuously. Every child on the stage remained fixed on her. Amber's eyes went from her sovereign to the courtiers around her before she spoke.

"Never."

The play was only a few minutes old, and yet the audience felt the drama of the moment. Eventually Jacob stood up.

HAMAN | 207

"How dare you," he snarled. "How dare you! Get out of my sight this instant! Never return! I never want to see you again!"

Amber unhurriedly turned around with her entourage and vanished, not to be seen on stage again. But the audience—including Rabbi Samuels—was engrossed in the whole spectacle. And as he watched Jacob Silverberg huff and puff with anger and outrage Rabbi Samuels had to wonder if the production would have been better served if Alex had been cast as King Ahasuerus instead.

Alex was sort of perfect for the role—dim, epicurean, doltish, lazy, and lucky. All the elements that the ancient king had in such abundance. But Rabbi Samuels filed this critical note away for another time. He was simply pleased this production took the book of Esther seriously; it wasn't the boring and sanitized Purim spiel he had expected.

The play continued—a plan to replace the queen was put into action. A train of goofy young girls drove in front of the king to try to lure him into marriage. One attempted a ridiculous dance. Another triumphantly pulled a live rabbit out from under his throne and a coin out of his ear. Another cartwheeled around the stage like she was the ancient precursor of Mary Lou Retton. (This prospective bride was played by the famously limber Amanda Brodsky.)

Then, in a darkened corner of the stage away from the "beauty contest," came Nellie and Alex as her uncle Mordechai.

"Is this something I should do, uncle?" Nellie asked. "Should I try to woo the king?"

"I'm not sure you have much choice in the matter," Alex replied.

"But how should I do it?" Nellie asked. "I wouldn't measure up to the other girls who came before me. They knew acrobatics. And dancing. And magic tricks. What do I have to offer?"

Alex smiled tenderly.

Rabbi Samuels had been surprised when Alex first strode onto the stage; the growth spurt which had momentarily hobbled Alex's acting career had slimmed him out. And while he was powdered and coiffed to look his best, one could see the faint glimmerings of a more attractive future than his homely past.

"You, Hadassah, don't need a thing," Alex said. "All the king will need to do is lay eyes on you to know that you are the only possible choice."

She smiled tenderly, and brushed her hand along Alex's cheek, as an affectionate daughter might do.

Not that Nellie had ever done such a thing to Rabbi Samuels. She wasn't into the "mushy stuff" as hugs and kisses were referred to around the Samuels house, and neither were her parents. Rabbi Samuels said the priestly blessing from the book of Numbers over his children every Friday night imploring God to give his brood the attributes of the great biblical figures, but that was the extent of his affections.

"Go in, just as yourself," Alex advised, "and we will see what will happen. Just one thing: Hide the fact that you are a Hebrew."

At that point, Rabbi Samuels couldn't take any more. He brusquely stood up, loudly enough that a number of eyes went from the stage to him, and marched out of the auditorium. As he opened the door he threw his head over his shoulder to observe the action on the stage, and he saw Alex staring at him. He closed the auditorium doors and meandered around in the fluorescent lit hallway, figuring that he would go back to his seat near the end of the production.

This was a long time before the invention of the smartphone, reader, so there was little for the rabbi to do as he waited. (He figured there was at least another hour.) He still had a cup of lemonade in his hands that he quickly finished and wandered up and down the halls examining trophy cases and the framed photos of the various wrestling teams, track teams and fencing teams that Joseph Scheuerle had fielded over the years.

After about twenty minutes the auditorium door opened again and Mrs. Samuels came out, a frown on her face.

"Where the hell did you go?"

Rabbi Samuels was somewhat taken aback by his wife's obvious annoyance.

"Bathroom."

Mrs. Samuels looked skeptical.

"Well, why haven't you come back to your seat yet?"

Rabbi Samuels looked down, as if he were a little boy caught in a lie searching for a plausible excuse.

"I didn't want to create a disturbance."

Mrs. Samuels snorted.

"You *already* created a disturbance the way you left."

Rabbi Samuels cheeks went red.

"I did?"

"Are you kidding me? Yes, you did. You left in the middle of a dramatic scene. You were very loud Charlie. I don't know if Nellie saw you, but if she did I'm sure she's extremely hurt. Joel Baumgarten certainly saw you. You should have seen the look on his face."

"Sorry."

Mrs. Samuels simply shook her head in disbelief.

"All right," she said as if he were her child and not her husband, "you used the john. Now let's go back."

Rabbi Samuels slowly, rigidly followed his wife back to his seat. The play continued, but the rabbi could no longer follow. He felt a sweaty, sinking feeling settle over him, like he was in deep trouble—but he couldn't say why. All he knew for certain was that Alex Gornick was to blame.

"I don't know what I did," Alex said from the stage, loud enough to snap the rabbi out of his bilious trance.

The palace set had been cleared away at least a scene or two earlier, and Alex was alone on the stage with one of his putative confidants. This had apparently come after an encounter with Haman, the viceroy of the kingdom, in which Haman had been driven to murderous rage by Mordechai's refusal to bow to him.

"Perhaps it's the way I talk," Alex said. "I came from a distant land. And I suppose it's difficult to fully trust the stranger."

As he said this, Rabbi Samuels smirked. It was true of both actor and role. He had never thought of Alex as an immigrant, because one thing he had apparently done reasonably well was lose his Russian accent. But he was speaking from the heart.

"Maybe it's because I don't know the proper etiquette of Shushan. Maybe I don't know the rituals and customs that Haman follows."

That was certainly Alex. He didn't know squat about the toys that the other kids talked about, or the movies they saw, or the sports they played. It was one of the reasons it was so peculiar that Alex should have gone into the most populist of all artistic mediums. And while it felt a little silly to hold it against him, Rabbi Samuels couldn't help it.

"Maybe he doesn't like the way I look," Alex said.

Alex's gaze suddenly fell on Rabbi Samuels and it stayed there for a few moments. The theater was quiet.

210 | MAX GROSS

"I admit," Alex finally continued, "I'm not the most handsome man in the world. We all look funny to some people. It is in the bill of indictment against my brethren, wherever we are exiled. We look different. And this is something that we will never be able to escape."

Rabbi Samuels held his breath. Alex's first two statements in this monologue were an interesting confluence of the play and the actor, but for the first time something deeper about Alex Gornick dawned on Rabbi Samuels. He was scorned and ridiculed. And Alex's prime tormentor was himself. He felt a shiver down his spine.

"And maybe it has nothing to do with me," Alex continued sedately, not allowing the many lights and the many eyeballs of parents and teachers to ruffle him. "Maybe it has to do with Haman. Maybe there are demons within him. Maybe he hates me because he hates something in himself that I remind him of."

One could hear a pin drop as Alex allowed the silence to continue and the audience to contemplate his words.

"Maybe I don't respect him the way he thinks I should," Alex finally said, his eyes not moving off of Rabbi Samuels. "Maybe by making me bow down to him he believed it was a way for all Jews to bow to him—and that was one compromise I was unwilling to make. That is something I could not betray. I would rather die than experience a world in which Haman is god."

Wait a second . . .

As if he were in a dream and not sitting in a crowded theater it occurred to Rabbi Samuels that this young actor was not reciting the lines that had been written in the script, but words that were directed towards him—his nemesis.

It seemed impossible. Rabbi Samuels could not fathom that *he* was Haman, and *Alex* was Mordechai. Haman, the usurper. Haman, the Amalekite and sworn enemy. Haman, the evil exterminator of the Jewish people. Haman, whose name was to be blotted out. *He* was Haman?

Moreover, the little fool was the hero? Alex was Mordechai? Alex was the master manipulator who through his cunning and foresight saved the Jews? Alex Gornick? The kid who didn't know how to bathe?

Rabbi Samuels rose again. But this time he didn't leave the auditorium. He simply stood in the audience and stared at his adversary.

"Sit down!" Mrs. Samuels said a little louder than she intended.

But it was no use. His wife's opprobrium was not enough; Rabbi Samuels was no longer in control his actions. His loathing consumed him. He hated Alex Gornick more than anyone he had ever met. More than a Nazi. More than anything.

Mrs. Samuels grabbed his sleeve but Rabbi Samuels ripped it away. He ignored the eyes on him. He lunged towards the stage with abandon, only to be tackled before he made it past the thirteenth row.

23

Scroll of Stars

MICHAEL DAVID LUKAS

They burned the House of God and tore down the wall of Jerusalem, burned down all its mansions, and consigned all its precious objects to destruction.

—Second Chronicles 36:19

1

You came into this world, my dear, with the first light of a new day, under the protection of the harvest star, in the eighth year of the thirteenth generation after the Fall. When you broke through the veil, after a long night of labor, when you crossed over the border between this world and that, I remember glancing out the window, and there, in the purple light of dawn, was the brightest morning star I had ever seen.

I was the first person to hold you, you know, the first person in the world to take you into their arms. I'm sure I've told you this before, but it bears repeating. I caught you, slapped your feet, cut your cord, and before raising you to your mother's breast, I cradled your head in my palm. Even then I could see that you were extraordinary, full of beauty and grace. I'm biased, of course. What kind of grandmother would I be if I didn't think you were perfect? But this was something else, something larger than any of us. Even before I drew your chart, I could sense it. In the glow of your skin, in the shape of your head, in the quiet of the animals all around us. You too were silent, for a long while, taking it all in. Then you began to fuss, you were an infant after all, so I gave you to your mother.

Because the official midwife was otherwise disposed—caught up in a long and difficult birth that would end eventually in the death of both mother and child—the business of your chart fell to me. It wasn't the first time I had drawn a star chart, but I was out of practice. When I saw what yours revealed, my first reaction was to doubt myself. Assuming I was tired, that I had mixed up one of the figures or forgotten to carry the remainder, some silly mistake, I made myself a strong glass of tea and sat down at the kitchen table.

Again, I came to the same result, the same lunar mansion, the same constellations in ascendance, the same three planets joined together in celebration of your arrival. It was the chart of a great king or priest, not the daughter of an insignificant Hudi fabric merchant. And yet, there it was, plain as the morning star. You had, you have, the stars of someone whose story will be told for generations.

Glancing out the kitchen window, I drew the chart once more, checking my work at every step. When I arrived at the same results a third time, I did the only thing I could do. I tore up your charts, fed them to the fire. Then I invented a new set of stars, the modest chart of a child born a few moments after you were. On your third birthday, when we took you to have your star mark inscribed, this was the chart we gave to the priests.

I knew it wasn't right to tamper with your stars like that. People have gone to the Tower for much less. But given the situation, what else could I do? I didn't want to attract undue attention, as I knew your true stars would. At the same time, I knew that none of it really mattered. Not in the way you might think.

As powerful as they may be, our stars don't bind us. They can guide us, of course. If we read them correctly, they can help us understand the shapes of our stories. Like a cloud or a birdsong, the lines on a person's face. They can help us see where things might be going. As you know, anything can tell a story. You just need to know how to look.

2

You had a fever once, when you were younger. It may have been River Fever. It may have been something else. It can be difficult to tell sometimes, particularly during the wet season. Whatever it was, it hit you hard. I remember looking at you in your sleeping basket—you couldn't have been older than three—stretched out and limp, your skin gray, beads of sweat pooling at the edge of your upper lip. Even then you were beautiful, your eyes closed and searching beneath their lids.

On the third day of the sickness, when your fever spiked, I told your mother to get some rest and I sat with you through the night. I told you stories to keep myself awake and although your eyes were shut, I could see that you heard me, that you wanted me to keep speaking. So I did, telling you the stories that my grandmother told me, the old Hudi stories that sustained us through the darkness of the first generations—and long before that—stories of Abraham and Moses, Adam and Eve, the Sacrifice, the Exodus, the Flood.

I must have fallen asleep at some point because when I woke the room felt different. The rains had stopped, and you were sitting up, looking out into the night. I couldn't see what you were staring at, but I smelled its musky scent and instinctively, I must have known. I took a few careful steps toward the window and when I saw it, I stopped cold. Pacing back and forth in the small garden below your room was a full-grown tiger. It didn't seem to notice me at first, but after some time, it raised its majestic head, looked me straight in the eye and loped off into the night.

Soon after the tiger left you went back to sleep, and when you woke the next morning the fever had broken. You didn't say anything about what happened. I don't know if you even remembered. But I could tell that it had affected you, that something in you had changed. There was a deepness to your gaze that hadn't been there before. And that morning, while you were eating your porridge, you started asking questions about the Old World.

"Grandma," you said, looking up at me, your cheeks still flush from the fever, "tell me what it was like before the Fall."

You asked me this as if I had been there myself, which of course I hadn't. But I didn't have the heart to correct you. Besides, I knew the stories well enough. My grandmother had told them to me alongside the old Hudi stories, just as her grandmother told them to her. Thus, the tales had been passed, hand to hand, on back through the generations.

That morning, instead of David and Devorah, I told you everything I knew about the Old World, about the flying machines and the mechanical carriages, the automated restaurants, the magic picture boxes, and the invisible web of information that made it all possible. But, as much as you asked, I wouldn't tell you how it ended. I didn't say anything about the wars or the destruction, the endless storms and fires. I didn't even mention the Fall, because you were too young and because I knew that it would bring up questions I wasn't prepared to answer. I didn't tell you any of this, but I could see in the lines of your face that you already knew. Maybe not the specific details, for how could you? But you knew that something terrible had happened, that it must have been something horrible, to wipe all that from the surface of the planet.

3

In every generation there is a Moses. In every generation there is a Moses and there is also a pharaoh. There is good and there is evil. The trouble, my dear, lies in knowing the difference between the two. It might seem like the simplest thing imaginable, to separate good from evil, to know right from wrong. But nothing, in fact, could be more difficult.

For who among us sees pharaoh in the mirror? Who actively seeks to do wrong, to be evil? There are some, to be sure. But in large part, the world is filled with people who regard themselves as basically good, essentially honest, recalling the harms perpetrated against them, but blind to the damage they inflict on others. And then, of course, there are all the unintended consequences. Good and evil may seem simple in isolation, but they don't exist in isolation. Our choices are always relative, cumulative, and multiplied by power.

You remember that old tale about the farmer and the shopkeeper, don't you? The farmer's crop fails and, when a rapacious shopkeeper refuses to give him a loan, he is forced to wander from town to town seeking charity. Eventually, the farmer comes into an unexpected inheritance, returns home, and buys a shop of his own. The story ends with the farmer, now a shopkeeper himself, refusing to give a loan to his neighbor. And so, the story asks, what is evil? Where does it reside? Is evil—or good, for that matter—in the intention or the act? Is it in the person or the role? The balance of power itself?

Such questions can never truly be answered. Still, we must try. We must continually ask ourselves where we stand and how, what it is that brought us to this moment and why, who we hold power over and when. We must ask what we are hiding and what we are revealing, what we have wrought, alone but also with others, whether it is our time or if there might be someone else waiting in the wings.

This may be the moment for which you were created. Or perhaps it is the time for another. That, my dear, is up to you.

4

We say "before the Fall" and "after the Fall." But it wasn't one thing that destroyed the Old World. It was the flooding, and it was the war. It was the fires and the storms, the heat, the cold, the disease. It was the mistrust and the hatred, the indifference, and those last frantic attempts to put things right. It was all this and more, more than we'll ever know. It was, my dear, quite simply, the end of the world. And it continued on for years, well into the period that we call the first generations.

Can you imagine what it would have been like? To live through that? To watch an entire world collapse? Each year was worse than the last, until the unimaginable was just another day. And in the midst of all that, telling stories? Singing songs? Teaching your daughters to write for the sole purpose of copying a few old books that may or may not be useful to future generations? Can you imagine, sitting at the lip of a cave, high up in the mountains, the sun red and sky raining ash, risking your life to protect the stories of a world that had unleashed such violence?

They're called the Hudi storytellers because, in later generations, they would often travel from town to town, singing old Hudi stories for a meal or a bed. But they weren't all Hudi. And, in addition to the stories they sang, they were also—more importantly, perhaps—archivists, copyists, librarians. While the rest of the world was busy foraging and fighting, these brave women collected the books and artifacts others wanted only for fuel. In so doing, they kept the spark of the Old World alive. Without them, we

SCROLL OF STARS | 217

would have no arches, no domes, no iron, no cotton, no spinning wheels or paper. Bronze would be little more than a vague recollection, a curious glint you might come across while digging a well. And the canals that keep us cool, that water our fields and connect our neighborhoods, they would be nothing more than muddy ditches.

They kept this knowledge alive through the darkness of those first generations. Still, there are some ideas, they knew, that are better left forgotten, certain books better uncopied. People accused the storytellers—and, later, the Hudis in general—of keeping those uncopied ideas to themselves. But really they were protecting us. They understood that the stories of one world don't necessarily feed the next, that there's a place for old stories and a place for new ones. They understood that sometimes we need to bend the stories we've been given if we want to keep ourselves from repeating the same mistakes.

5

Your mother never wanted me to tell you the old stories. She said all that was dead and gone. They were relics of another world, one that was probably best forgotten. I can't say I disagree. But I told them to you anyway. In part because they were the only stories I knew. When you were going to sleep, I would whisper them into the darkness of your bedroom. Even though you were drifting off, I could tell that you heard me, that you understood.

I told you all the stories I could remember, but always in pieces, always the beginnings and middles, never the ends. You never heard what happened after Moses demanded his people's freedom, after Joseph recognized his brothers, after Abigail urged the king to consider the effect of his actions. Of course, you're probably wondering why I did this. Why tell you the stories at all if I was going to stop halfway through? Well, my dear, I may not know much, but I know how these stories work. I've seen how they break off and multiply, how they repeat and refract through the generations.

In every generation there is a Moses. Yes, true. But what if Moses would rather be a David or a Judith? Telling you the stories as I did, I wanted to give you a sense of possibility. I wanted you to know the shape of the story you're in, but also to know that you can break free. Every story has an exit, you just need to be able to see your way out.

218 | MICHAEL DAVID LUKAS

I can't say what will happen after you unlock the door, when you step out of one story and into another. Because I don't know. I've never been there, that place beyond the stars. Though I hope very much that one day you can tell me what it's like. Is it empty and cool? Is it dim or is it bright? Can you feel a breeze? Is there weather at all? I like to think it's something like floating, like drifting, like falling off the edge of the page. But maybe it's not like that at all. Perhaps there are no words to describe it.

The pull of story is strong, my dear. I know that as well as anyone. You want to feel solid ground beneath your feet. But give yourself a moment there, in the uncertainty. Let yourself seep into it. You'll find a new story soon enough, and it will be unlike anything you could have imagined.

Contributors

Elisa Albert is the author of the novels *Human Blues, After Birth, The Book of Dahlia*, the short story collection *How This Night Is Different*, and the essay collection, *The Snarling Girl*. Her work has been published in *n+1, Tin House, Bennington Review*, the *New York Times, Michigan Quarterly Review*, the *Literary Review, Philip Roth Studies, Paris Review, Los Angeles Review of Books, Longreads*, the *Cut, Time, Post Road, Gulf Coast, Commentary, Salon, Tablet, Washington Square*, the *Rumpus*, the *Believer*, and many anthologies. She has taught creative writing at Columbia University's School of the Arts, the College of Saint Rose, Bennington College, Texas State University, University of Maine, and the Fine Arts Work Center in Provincetown, Massachusetts. A Pushcart Prize nominee, finalist for the Sami Rohr Prize and Paterson Fiction Prize, winner of the Moment magazine debut fiction prize, and Literary Death Match champion, Albert has served as Writer-in-Residence at the Netherlands Institute for Advanced Study in Holland and at the Hanse-Wissenschaftkolleg in Germany.

Steve Almond is the author of twelve books of fiction and nonfiction, including the *New York Times* bestsellers *Candyfreak* and *Against Football*. His first novel, *Which Brings Me to You* (cowritten with Julianna Baggott) is a major motion picture starring Lucy Hale and Nat Wolff. His last novel, *All the Secrets of the World*, is in development for television by 20th Century Fox. His work has appeared in the *Best American Short Stories*, the *Pushcart Prize, Best American Mysteries*, and the *NYT Magazine*. His most recent book, *Truth Is the Arrow, Mercy Is the Bow*, is about craft, inspiration, and how to keep going at the keyboard. Almond teaches at the Nieman Foundation for Journalism and lives outside Boston with his family.

Shalom Auslander was raised in Monsey, New York. Nominated for the Koret Award for writers under thirty-five, he has published articles in *Esquire*, the *New York Times Magazine*, *Tablet*, and the *New Yorker*, and has had stories aired on NPR's *This American Life*. Auslander is the author of the short story collection *Beware of God*, the memoir *Foreskin's Lament*, and the novels *Hope: A Tragedy* and *Mother for Dinner*. He is the creator of Showtime's "Happyish." His most recent book is *Feh: A Memoir*.

Rosebud Ben-Oni was born to a Mexican mother and Jewish father. She is the author of several collections of poetry, including *If This Is the Age We End Discovery* (2021), which won the Alice James Award and was a finalist for the National Jewish Book Award. Paramount commissioned her video essay "My Judaism Is a Wild Unplace" for a national media campaign for Jewish Heritage Month, and her poem "Poet Wrestling with Angels in the Dark" was commissioned by the National September 11th Memorial. She performed at Carnegie Hall on International Holocaust Memorial Day, as part of "We Are Here: Songs from the Holocaust." Most recently, her poem "When You Are the Arrow of Time" was commissioned and filmed by the Museum of Jewish Heritage—A Living Memorial to the Holocaust. In 2023, she received a Café Royal Cultural Foundation grant to write *The Atomic Sonnets*, a full-length collection based on her chapbook *20 Atomic Sonnets* (2020), which she began in honor of the Periodic Table's 150th Birthday in 2019. She has received grants from the New York Foundation for the Arts, Queens Arts Fund, Queens Council for the Arts, and CantoMundo. Her work appears in *POETRY*, the *American Poetry Review*, *Academy of American Poets' Poem-a-Day*, *Poetry Society of America (PSA)*, the *Poetry Review (UK)*, *Poetry Wales*, *Poetry Daily*, and *Tin House*, among others.

Sarah Blake is the author of the novels *Naamah*, a queer radical reimagining the story of Noah's ark, and *Clean Air*, and the poetry collections *In Springtime*, *Mr. West*, and *Let's Not Live on Earth*. She received a Literature Fellowship from the National Endowment for the Arts. Her work has appeared in the *Los Angeles Review of Books*, the *American Poetry Review*, and the *Kenyon Review*. She lives outside of London, UK.

Zeeva Bukai is a fiction writer, born in Israel and raised in New York City. Her stories have appeared in *OfTheBook Press*, *Carve*, *Pithead Chapel*, the *Master's Review*, *Jewish Fiction*, *Mcsweeney's Quarterly Concern*, *Image*

Journal, *December*, the *Jewish Quarterly*, and elsewhere. Her honors include a fellowship at the New York Center for Fiction, residencies at Hedgebrook Writer's Colony, and Byrdcliff AIR program in Woodstock, New York. She received the Master's Review fiction prize, the Curt Johnson Prose Award, and the Lilith Fiction Award. Her work has been anthologized in *Frankly Feminist: Short Stories by Jewish Women*, and *Out of Many: Multiplicity and Divisions in America Today*. Her debut novel is *The Anatomy of Exile*. She lives in Brooklyn with her family.

Madeline Cash is the founder and coeditor of *Forever Magazine*. Her work has appeared in the *Drift*, the *Baffler*, *Carve*, *Hobart*, and the *Literary Review*, among other publications. She is the author of the story collection *Earth Angel*. Her debut novel, *Lost Lambs*, is forthcoming in 2026.

Erika Dreifus is the author of *Birthright: Poems* and *Quiet Americans: Stories*, which was named an American Library Association Sophie Brody Medal Honor Title for outstanding achievement in Jewish literature. A fellow in the Sami Rohr Jewish Literary Institute and adjunct associate professor at Baruch College of the City University of New York, she writes and lectures widely. Erika is also the publisher-editor of the *Practicing Writer*, a free (and popular) e-newsletter for writers of poetry, fiction, and creative nonfiction. She lives in New York City.

Omer Friedlander was born in Jerusalem in 1994 and grew up in Tel Aviv. His debut story collection, *The Man Who Sold Air in the Holy Land*, won the Association of Jewish Libraries Fiction Award and was a finalist for the Wingate Prize. The book was longlisted for the Story Prize and chosen as a Sophie Brody Medal Honor Book. Omer earned a BA in English literature from the University of Cambridge, England, and an MFA from Boston University, where he was supported by the Saul Bellow Fellowship. His short stories won numerous awards, and have been published in the United States, Canada, France, and Israel. A Starworks Fellow in Fiction at New York University, he has earned fellowships from Bread Loaf and the Vermont Studio Center. He currently lives in New York City.

Temim Fruchter is a queer nonbinary anti-Zionist Jewish writer who lives in Brooklyn, New York. She holds an MFA in fiction from the University of Maryland and is the recipient of fellowships from the DC Commission on the Arts and Humanities, Vermont Studio Center, and a 2020 Rona Jaffe Foundation Writer's Award. She is cohost of Pete's Reading Series in Brooklyn. Her debut novel, *City of Laughter*, is a *New York Times* Editors' Pick.

Max Gross was born in New York City in 1978 and is the son of two writers. He attended Saint Ann's School and Dartmouth College. He worked for ten years at the *New York Post* before becoming Editor in Chief of *Commercial Observer*. He previously wrote a book about dating called *From Schlub to Stud* but has since been rescued from the single man's fate by his beloved wife and son. *The Lost Shtetl*, his first novel, won the 2020 National Jewish Book Award for Fiction.

Aaron Hamburger is the author of a story collection titled *The View from Stalin's Head* which was awarded the Rome Prize by the American Academy of Arts and Letters and nominated for a Violet Quill Award. He has also written three novels: *Faith for Beginners*, nominated for a Lambda Literary Award; *Nirvana is Here*, winner of a Bronze Medal from the 2019 Foreword Reviews Indies Book Awards; and *Hotel Cuba*. In 2023, he was awarded by Lambda Literary with the Jim Duggins Outstanding Mid-Career Novelist Prize. His writing has appeared in the *New York Times*, the *Washington Post*, the *Chicago Tribune*, the *Village Voice*, *Tin House*, *Michigan Quarterly Review*, *Subtropics*, *Crazyhorse*, *Boulevard*, *Poets & Writers*, *Tablet*, *O, the Oprah Magazine*, *Out*, the *Massachusetts Review*, the *Bennington Review*, *Nerve*, *Time Out*, *Details*, and *The Forward*. He has also won fellowships from Yaddo, Djerassi, the Civitella Ranieri Foundation, the DC Commission on the Arts and Humanities, and the Edward F. Albee Foundation, as well as first prize in the Dornstein Contest for Young Jewish Writers, and his short fiction and creative nonfiction have received special mentions in the Pushcart Prizes. He has taught creative writing at Columbia University, the George Washington University, New York University, Brooklyn College, and the Stonecoast MFA Program.

Aviya Kushner grew up in a Hebrew-speaking home in New York. Her debut poetry collection *Wolf Lamb Bomb* (2021) won the Chicago Review of Books Award in Poetry, and was named a *New York Times* New and Noteworthy selection, and Foreword INDIES Finalist. Her nonfiction book *The Grammar of God: A Journey into the Words and Worlds of the Bible* (2015) was named a

National Jewish Book Award Finalist, Sami Rohr Prize Finalist, and one of *Publishers' Weekly*'s Top Religion Stories of the Year. She is a 2022 National Endowment for the Arts fellow in translation. She is the *Forward*'s language columnist, and her essays have appeared in *Longreads*, the *Los Angeles Review of Books*, the *Wall Street Journal*, and the *Wilson Quarterly*. Her work has been supported by the Howard Foundation, the Illinois Arts Council, and the Memorial Foundation of Jewish Culture. She serves on the executive committee in nonfiction at the Modern Languages Association, the board of the American Literary Translators Association, the advisory board of the Jewish Languages Project, and the advisory board for Bloomsbury's series in creative writing. She is an associate professor at Columbia College Chicago, where she directs the MFA Program in Creative Writing.

Sara Lippmann is the author of the novel *Lech* and the story collections *Doll Palace* and *Jerks*. Her fiction has won the *Lilith* Prize and been honored by the New York Foundation for the Arts, and her essays have appeared in the *Millions*, the *Washington Post*, *Catapult*, the *Lit Hub*, and elsewhere. She is the cofounder of Writing Co-lab, an online teaching cooperative.

Michael David Lukas has been a Fulbright Scholar in Turkey, a night-shift proofreader in Tel Aviv, a student at the American University of Cairo, and a waiter at the Bread Loaf Writers' Conference in Vermont. Translated into more than a dozen languages, his first novel, *The Oracle of Stamboul*, was a finalist for the California Book Award, the NCIBA Book of the Year Award, and the Harold U. Ribalow Prize. His second novel, *The Last Watchman of Old Cairo*, won the Sami Rohr Prize, the National Jewish Book Award, the Prix Interallié for Foreign Fiction, and the American Library Association's Sophie Brody Medal. A graduate of Brown University and the University of Maryland, he is a recipient of scholarships from the National Endowment for the Arts, Montalvo Arts Center, New York State Summer Writers' Institute, Squaw Valley Community of Writers, and Elizabeth George Foundation. His writing has appeared in the *New York Times*, the *Wall Street Journal*, *Slate*, *National Geographic Traveler*, and *Georgia Review*. He lives in Oakland and teaches at San Francisco State University.

Ilana Masad is a queer Israeli-American writer of fiction, nonfiction, and criticism. Her work has appeared in the *New Yorker*, the *New York Times*, the *LA Times*, the *Washington Post*, *NPR*, *StoryQuarterly*, *Tin House*'s Open Bar, *7x7*, *Catapult*, *Buzzfeed*, and many more. A graduate of Sarah Lawrence College, she has received her master's in English from the University of Nebraska–Lincoln where she is currently a doctoral student. She is the author of the novel *All My Mother's Lovers*.

Ariana Reines is a poet, playwright, performing artist, and translator. Her book *A Sand Book* (2019) was winner of the 2020 Kingsley Tufts Prize and longlisted for the National Book Award. Other books include *The Cow* (Alberta Prize, 2006), *Coeur De Lion* (2007), *Mercury* (2011), and *The Origin of the World* (2014). Her Obie-winning play *Telephone* (2009) was commissioned by the Foundry Theatre and has been performed in Norwegian translation (2017) and at KW Berlin (2018), among others. Current commissions include *Possession* (2023), a sculpture and performance collaboration with Liz Magic Laser, at Pioneer Works in Brooklyn, New York, and *Divine Justice* (2022), a 24-hour theatrical environment at Performance Space New York. She has taught at Columbia University, the European Graduate School, NYU, Tufts, Naropa, the New School, Yale, and many others. In March 2020, while a divinity student at Harvard, she created Invisible College, a hub for poetry, art, sacred study online. She lives in Upstate New York.

erica riddick (she/they) is a passionate ambi-brained educator/ritualist, founding director of Jews of Color Sanctuary, and creator of the Bilhah Zilpah Project and Parasha Play. erica is the Jewish Women's Archive 2022–2024 Twersky Education Fellow and Mandel Foundation 2024–2026 Teacher Educator Institute Fellow. erica facilitates the Jewish Studio Process, Dismantling Racism from the Inside Out, and Changemakers (a peer-supported social entrepreneurial incubator of Realize Change). These projects balance the work of Design Theanthropic, a residential design and renovation initiative, and community action research on projects within beloved communities. erica adores a good story through reading, watching films, live-action role playing gaming, and performing improv.

Seth Rogoff is the author of six books, most recently *The Castle*, a fictional return to the unsettling world of Franz Kafka's iconic unfinished novel. He is the chair of the Journalism and Media Studies program at Anglo-American University in Prague, Czech Republic.

Matthue Roth is the author of the Jewish punk-rock road-trip novel *Never Mind the Goldbergs* (named a Best Book for the Teen Age by the New York Public Library and a Popular Paperback in Religion by the American Library Association), the memoir *Yom Kippur a Go-Go*, the picture book *My First Kafka*, and others. Beginning his career as a slam poet in San Francisco, Roth gained attention for his unusual blend of religious themes with frank sexual material, and appeared in the 2002 live Broadway production of *Def Poetry Jam*. He has written for *The Forward*, *Tablet*, and *Jewcy*. By day, he's a creative writer at Google, and helped create the Google Assistant. He was also a writer at Sesame Street, and he cocreated the animated series BimBam and the creative community Hevria.com. In 2014, Roth and his wife, restaurateur Itta Werdiger-Roth, were included in the *Jewish Week*'s "36 under 36." He often lectures about being a Hasidic Jew, a punk, and a parent, and lives with his family in Brooklyn.

Moriel Rothman-Zecher Moriel Rothman-Zecher is the author of the novels *Before All the World*, which was named an NPR Book of 2022, and *Sadness Is a White Bird*, for which he received the National Book Foundation's "5 under 35" Honor, and which was a finalist for the Dayton Literary Peace Prize, the winner of the Ohioana Book Award, a finalist for a National Jewish Book Award, and longlisted for the Center for Fiction's First Novel Prize. His poems and essays have been published or are forthcoming in the *American Poetry Review*, *Barrelhouse*, *Colorado Review*, *The Common*, *Nashville Review*, the *New York Times*, yhe *Paris Review's Daily*, ZYZZYVA, and elsewhere. Moriel is the recipient of two MacDowell Fellowships for Literature (2017 and 2020) and a Wallis Annenberg Helix Fellowship for Yiddish Cultural Studies (2018–2019), and he holds an MFA in Poetry from the Bennington Writing Seminars, where he was the recipient of a Donald Hall Scholarship for Poets (2021–2023). Moriel has taught creative writing at University of the Arts in Philadelphia, the University of Dayton in Dayton, online through the Catapult Writing Program, and as guest faculty at the Miami Writers Institute. Moriel is currently a Visiting Instructor of Creative Writing at Swarthmore College.

Anna Solomon is the author of three novels—*The Book of V.*, *Leaving Lucy Pear*, and *The Little Bride*—and a two-time winner of the Pushcart Prize. Previously, she worked as an award-winning journalist for National

Public Radio's *Living on Earth*. Anna's short fiction, essays, and reviews have appeared in the *New York Times Magazine*, the *Washington Post*, *Ploughshares*, *One Story*, *Vogue*, the *New York Times Book Review*, *Tablet*, and elsewhere. She is the recipient of awards from MacDowell, Yaddo, Bread Loaf, the Rhode Island State Council for the Arts, and the *Missouri Review*, among others, and her short story "The Lobster Mafia Story" was chosen as Boston's One City One Story read. She is also coeditor with Eleanor Henderson of *Labor Day: True Birth Stories by Today's Best Women Writers*. A graduate of Brown University and the Iowa Writers' Workshop, Anna teaches writing at Barnard College, Warren Wilson's MFA Program in Creative Writing, and the 92Y Unterberg Poetry Center. She was born and raised in Gloucester, Massachusetts, and lives in Brooklyn, New York, with her two children.

Daniel Torday is the author of *The 12th Commandment*, *The Last Flight of Poxl West*, and *Boomer1*. A two-time winner of the National Jewish Book Award for fiction and the Sami Rohr Choice Prize, Torday's stories and essays have appeared in *Tin House*, the *Paris Review*, the *Kenyon Review*, and *n+1*, and have been honored by the *Best American Short Stories* and *Best American Essays* series. Torday is a professor of Creative Writing at Bryn Mawr College.

Michael Zapata is a founding editor of *MAKE Literary Magazine* and the author of the novel *The Lost Book of Adana Moreau*, winner of the 2020 Chicago Review of Books Award for Fiction, finalist for the 2020 Heartland Booksellers Award in Fiction, and a Best Book of the Year for NPR, the AV Club, Los Angeles Public Library, and BookPage, among others. He is the recipient of an Illinois Arts Council Award for Fiction and the City of Chicago DCASE Individual Artist Program Award. He is on the faculty of StoryStudio Chicago and the MFA faculty of Northwestern University. As a public-school educator, he taught literature and writing in high schools servicing dropout students. He currently lives in Chicago with his family.